616.8527 Norden, Michael J.,
N   1954-

        Beyond prozac.

$23.00

BEYOND PROZAC

BEYOND PROZAC

Brain-Toxic Lifestyles,
Natural Antidotes &
New Generation
Antidepressants

MICHAEL J. NORDEN, M.D.

ReganBooks
An Imprint of HarperCollinsPublishers

The photographs on pages 41 and 42 are used by permission of The Sun Box Company.

The photograph on page 44 is used by permission of Pi Square, Inc.

HarperCollins books may be purchased for educational, business, or sales promotional use. For information please write: Special Markets Department, HarperCollins Publishers, Inc., 10 East 53rd Street, New York, NY 10022.

FIRST EDITION

Designed by Nancy Singer

Library of Congress Cataloging-in-Publication Data

Norden, Michael J., 1954–
    Beyond prozac : brain-toxic lifestyles, natural antidotes & new generation antidepressants / by Michael J. Norden.
        p.   cm.
    Includes bibliographical references and index.
    ISBN 0-06-039151-0
    1. Depression, Mental—Alternative treatment. 2. Depression, Mental—Treatment. 3. Fluoxetine. 4. Stress management.
I. Title.
RC537.N67   1995
616.85'2706—dc20   95-16745

95 96 97 98 99 ❖/RRD 10 9 8 7 6 5 4 3 2

For my mother,
Catherine,
and the memory
of my father,
Donald

ACKNOWLEDGMENTS

I wish to thank a number of exceptional people who helped make this book possible. Joseph Reiner for his valued contributions in writing and editing. Judith Regan for seeing the potential of the book and allowing great freedom in its development. All of the talented individuals at HarperCollins/ReganBooks who helped to shape the completed work, most especially Fran Fisher. Special thanks to Dr. Jeffrey Schwartz for help in numerous ways.

I have had the pleasure and privilege of collaborating with Dr. David Avery in a number of projects relating to this book. Mark Rotenberg and Drs. David Avery, Timothy Brewerton, Donald Klein, V. Markku Linnoila, Vernon Neppe, and Norman Rosenthal were kind enough to read and provide feedback on early versions of various material in this book. I have also benefited from the insights and support of a number of other researchers and colleagues, especially Blaine Shaffer, Neil Owens, and Drs. Richard Balon, Gordon Biely, John Brinkley, Charles Czeisler, Emil Coccaro, Stephen Dager, Trang Dao, Lester Grinspoon, David Haynor, Carla Hellekson, William Hewlett, Jr., Eric Hollander, Jan Hillson, Frederick Jacobsen, Siegfried Kasper, Raymond Lam, Mitchel Lazar, Alfred Lewy, Dan Oren, Barbera Parry, Robert Post, Gerald Rosen, Peter Roy-Byrne, Gary Sachs, Alan Schatzberg, Alan Schwartz, Barry Sears, Clifford Singer, Randall Steinman, Martin Teicher, Robert Trestman, Jiuana Su Terman, Michael Terman, Gary Tucker, Nicholas Ward, Ronald Winchel, Thomas Wehr, and Bruce Yankner.

I appreciate greatly the valuable mentoring I have received in both research and clinical work from Drs. Y. S. Choi, David LeBerge, Irving Yalom, and David Spiegel. I would also like to acknowledge the many outstanding clinicians associated with the psychiatric residency training program at Cedars-Sinai/UCLA who contributed greatly to my clinical training.

I want to give my deepest thanks to my patients. I have for the sake of their privacy made every effort to disguise identities in the material presented.

Jennifer Kesseler deserves special recognition for exceptional administrative support.

Finally, of utmost importance have been the love, encouragement, and tolerance of my wife, Mai, and my sons, Jeremy and Justin, over the long course of researching and writing this book.

CONTENTS

INTRODUCTION:
THE STONE AGE BRAIN IN
MODERN TIMES

Twenty thousand years ago, we evolved to meet the conditions of life on the African savanna. Our bodies, our brains, remain virtually unchanged from those of our Stone Age ancestors. Yet in the last few hundred years a bewildering rush of cultural evolution has thoroughly transformed our world.

No longer do most of us live in villages of a few hundred or less, as Stone Agers did, but rather in teeming cities that compose a global village of nearly six billion. It has become a draining task just to empathize with the televised plights of our fellow global villagers. We have built our roofs and walls thicker and thicker to shelter us from the harshness of the natural world, but under the weight of all our creations, our foundations crumble. These cumulative stresses of modern life have set off an avalanche of depression, anxiety, and insomnia. Less obvious are diverse problems such as weight gain and cancer. Most self-medicate, using anything from caffeine to cocaine; virtually no one remains untouched.

Many simply hunch their shoulders against the strain of modern life, believing it is inevitable and must simply be weathered, or, worse, feeling that their depression or anxiety is a mark of personal weakness. Both views are gravely mistaken. Emotional distress or illness is simply another reaction to modern physical and mental stresses, no more deserving of shame than is heart disease—and more easily treated. Indeed, the treatments discussed throughout this book detail mental *and* physical benefits precisely because the body and mind are so inextricably linked. As you will see, treatments that serve one almost invariably serve the other.

Unfortunately, now that we require *more* tolerance of stress, our brains are *less* able to help us cope. Evidence shows that our modern lifestyles and artificial environments take a costly toll. The way we sleep, the way we eat, even the air we breathe draw on the same account, weakening the specific neurochemical "stress shield" that Prozac is designed to bolster. In a certain sense, our lifestyles have made us "Prozac deficient." Your answers to the questionnaire in chapter 1 will give you an idea of your biochemical vulnerability. I find it no coincidence that Prozac is reported helpful in almost every known category of emotional illness.

That all of us are, to some degree, vulnerable to stress, or are even "Prozac deficient," certainly does not mean that we all need an infusion of Prozac. In the following chapters we will discuss ways to correct many of the stressful aspects of our environments and lifestyles. Further, we'll explore a number of natural remedies that buttress the same brain chemistry and treat many of the same conditions as Prozac does.

Many people will, of course, need the guidance of a health professional, and some will undoubtedly benefit from medication. However, most can use the natural approaches recommended here along with medication for even better results. For readers interested specifically in Prozac, I have included tips gained from my treatment of hundreds of patients. Unfortunately, these techniques are not widely known—especially by primary care physicians, who prescribe most antidepressants. These refinements of treatment help to maximize the benefits of Prozac (or related medications) and to avoid the side effects that befall the majority of users.

This book also covers the many alternative medications now available, some truly remarkable new ones that have just come on the market, and others expected in the near future that I predict will eclipse Prozac.

I also address readers interested simply in seeking greater understanding of the effects of environment and lifestyle on the brain. My research, in collaboration with Dr. David Avery, has resulted in a number of theories relating to stress and heat that explain a range of phenomena: from why sex and violence soar in the heat to why sociopaths and "dreamers" sweat so little; from why baseball players chew gum or tobacco to why Prozac can help people who obsess (think too much) as well as those who are impulsive (think too little).

My goal is to offer all readers—even those with no interest in "self-help"—a look into the intriguing underpinnings of mood and behavior in our time. Amidst the increased challenges of our time, I sincerely hope that better understanding will lessen the shame felt by, and the prejudice against, the millions of people who suffer what are fundamentally stress-induced difficulties.

PART I

"PROZAC DEFICIENCY": THE GREAT BRAIN ROBBERY

CHAPTER 1

IS NEARLY EVERYONE "PROZAC DEFICIENT"?

Mental illness affects not three out of five or four out of five but one of one.
—WILLIAM MENNINGER

John Donne instructed us to "ask not for whom the bell tolls, for it tolls for thee." As we shall see, mental illness now strikes nearly all of us, although with vast differences in form and degree. And the numbers are mounting steadily. In particular, serious depression has risen astonishingly in recent years, as emphasized by the late Dr. Gerald Klerman, a leading figure in American psychiatry. He termed the hunt for the mysterious cause of this epidemic "the search for Agent Blue."

A STIGMA ASSOCIATED WITH GREATNESS

To claim that nearly everyone will suffer mental illness may seem absurd, for many of us still think of it only in its most extreme forms. But let's recast the issue. Let's ask: How many people suffer emotionally or physically from stress? Indeed, the harried, floating anxiety that accompanies stress *is* a type of mental illness, and most of us, even if we do not care to admit it, have experienced it to some degree. However, stress is much more than that harried feeling, which originates in the brain. Biologically, it includes almost anything that puts an extra burden on an organism. For example, extreme heat falls under the heading. Mental illness is certainly stress related, but most people find *stress-related illness* a far more acceptable term, for then their condition joins the respectable company of high blood pressure, ulcers, and the many other stress-caused illnesses.

Ironically, many of the people we most admire are included in this stigmatized group. A study of three hundred biographies of history's most accomplished scientists, politicians, philosophers, and artists found evidence that some three out of four had suffered serious mental illness. For example, two of Western culture's most revered leaders, Abraham Lincoln and Winston Churchill, wrote in detail of their struggle with incapacitating depression. At one point Lincoln concluded: "I am now quite certainly the most miserable man alive."

As the above study shows, the mentally ill are, overall, quite disproportionately gifted and achieving. We fear such illness probably because at some level it reminds us of our own vulnerability. That we don't understand how these conditions develop has made them seem even more frightening. Fortunately, the more we learn about the causes of mental illness and how to treat it, the less stigma is attached to it.

We now know that many mental disorders are actually biological in origin, which puts them on the same plane as angina or arthritis, for example. Apart from biological factors, many psychiatric conditions are simply the result of poor learned responses to life. Fortunately, these can readily be unlearned through cognitive or behavioral therapy. There's nothing terribly mysterious or threatening about such cases.

I believe that making people aware of just how widespread these conditions are, even the most serious ones, will further lessen the stigma. When I first began looking at the puzzle of rising mental illness rates, best estimates were that about one in five people were afflicted at some time during their life. Just as the first large-scale, rigorous study of sexuality in America produced big surprises, the first such study on mental illness produced rather shocking results.

Published in 1994 in *Archives of General Psychiatry,* but curiously receiving little publicity, the study found that among people between the ages of eighteen and fifty-four, nearly half had already met the formal diagnostic criteria for at least one of fourteen serious psychiatric illnesses. These people did not merely feel bad for the occasional few days; nearly one-third of them had had a disorder lasting over a year. The elderly, who were not included in the study, are at particularly high risk for psychiatric conditions. Thus, over a lifetime, clearly a majority of us will undergo serious mental illness.

Mental illness is certainly stress-related but genetics plays a role, as it does with stress-related physical illness. However, a recent study found that stress played the greater role in causing depression.

I cannot emphasize strongly enough that all stress-related conditions are similar, whether manifested as psychiatric or as general medical problems. Indeed, a majority of primary care physician visits concern stress-related illness. This mental-physical overlap is further demonstrated in that roughly two-thirds of those who suffer depression also suffer at least one of the following: hypertension, arthritis, advanced coronary artery disease, diabetes, gastrointestinal disorders, chronic back pain, chronic lung problems, and angina. Insomnia falls somewhere in the netherland between psychiatry and general medicine. The National Commission on Sleep Disorders Research estimates that occasional "tossing and turning" troubles more than 90 percent of the U.S. population, with more than 30 percent reporting the problem as serious and chronic.

Certainly, stress-induced mental illness is no more deserving of shame, fear, or prejudice than are similarly induced medical conditions.

CHARTING THE EPIDEMIC

"Generation X," the group of people born between about 1960 and 1970, has a particularly high depression rate—but so do generations "X − 1" and "X + 1." Since World War II, depression has been increasing steadily across international, cultural, and ethnic boundaries. A national collaborative group recently evaluated these trends in various countries, including Germany, Italy, France, Lebanon, and Taiwan. Some of the studies found that depression in men born after World War II continues to rise, while women's rates have flattened, although twice as many women suffer from depression as men. Disturbingly, suicide rates among adolescents and young adults are also climbing.

According to Paul Greenberg and others, the economic burden that depression inflicts on the United States reaches over $44 billion annually. While other psychiatric conditions have not been studied to the extent that depression has, we see that most other forms of mental illness are certainly increasing. Some, such as anorexia and bulimia, were virtually unknown until recently.

A recent study headed by Dr. Louis Judd, former director of the National Institute of Mental Health, found that many people who do not meet the current diagnostic criteria for depression nonetheless suffer real impairment due to one or more symptoms of the illness. This milder depression, which Judd has labeled "subsyndromal symptomatic depression," befalls four times the number who meet the full definition of depression.

Just how bad is this lesser depression? A recent study found that surprisingly the impairment associated with minor depression often exceeded that caused by medical conditions such as heart disease, diabetes, and arthritis. Further, people with minor depression may use even more psychiatric and other medical services than do those who suffer the full condition. The mildly depressed also take a greater economic toll on society in lost workdays than do their formally diagnosed counterparts.

Curiously, people with minor depression sometimes *lack* the symptom of depressed mood. (The three most common symptoms reported are sleep disturbances, fatigue, and thoughts of death.) Perhaps even more curious, those who do not experience lowered mood account for twice the number of disability days than those who *do* have the symptom.

To understand this, we must first realize that depression often arrives without noticeably lowering one's mood. In order to qualify for the diagnosis of major depression, one need have only five symptoms, and depressed mood need *not* be among them.

I developed the following mnemonic as a diagnostic aid and use it when I lecture on depression.

ASSESSMENT OF DEPRESSION

(APES SWIM)

• •

Physical Symptoms

A: Appetite and/or weight (e.g., 5 percent in a month) reduction or increase
P: Psychomotor retardation or agitation
E: Energy reduction (fatigue)
S: Sleep reduction or increase

Psychological Symptoms

S: Suicidal ideas or thoughts of death
W: Worthlessness or feelings of excessive/inappropriate guilt
I: Interest or pleasure-marked diminution in most activities
M: Mental ability diminution (difficulty thinking, concentrating, or deciding)

The *Diagnostic Statistical Manual IV* diagnosis of a major depressive episode in adults requires either loss of interest or depressed mood plus four other of the above symptoms to be present nearly every day during the same two-week period, and that these symptoms represent a change from previous functioning (suicidal ideation need not meet the nearly-every-day requirement).

Ask the right questions, and diagnosing depression is usually easy enough. So, *why isn't it happening?* I have come to suspect that primary care doctors, perhaps from fear of offending their patients, actually avoid inquiring into their state of mind.

The survey finding that nearly half the U.S. population had undergone a serious, diagnosable psychiatric condition also determined that only 40 percent of them had ever sought professional help. So, perhaps the most common psychiatric "condition" of modern times is massive denial. While some do engage in effective self-help programs, many resort to self-medication, which rarely cures anything and often leads to greater problems. Those who drink heavily often know quite well that they do so to quell the stresses of work and personal life. A study of smokers found that those who could not quit generally suffered a high incidence of mood disorders, suggesting that smoking is too valuable a coping device for them to abandon.

It is now clear that mental or physical stress-related illness, and even serious, formal psychiatric disorders (usually involving anxiety, depression, or drug/alcohol abuse), afflict the vast majority of us. And these problems are rapidly growing worse, making the task of identifying Agent Blue even more critical.

PROZAC DEFICIENCY AS THE NUMBER 1 SUSPECT FOR AGENT BLUE

What lies behind this epidemic? Experts have offered various theories on the identity of Agent Blue, but my own research and direct experience with patients point to what I have termed Prozac deficiency.

As mentioned earlier, I do not mean literally that most people need to take Prozac, but that serotonin, the brain chemical that Prozac affects, has been depleted. Fortunately, the serotonin system can be strengthened through a variety of natural means. To consider the plausibility of Prozac deficiency (i.e., serotonin deficiency) underlying many of our modern maladies, take a look at the following list of stress-related conditions.

CONDITIONS REPORTED TO RESPOND TO PROZAC OR A SIMILAR MEDICATION

Alcoholism/drug dependency
Anorexia nervosa (refusal to eat enough)
Anxiety
Arthritis

Attention deficit/hyperactivity disorder
Autism (severe developmental disorder)
Bipolar disorder (cyclic episodes of severe mania and
    depression)
Body-dysmorphic disorder (imagined ugliness)
Borderline personality disorder (extreme instability of
    mood and behavior)
Bulimia (binge eating/purging)
Cataplexy (sudden attack of extreme muscle weakness)
Chronic pain
Depersonalization disorder (feeling detached from reality,
    as if in a dream)
Diabetic neuropathy (disorder of peripheral nerves often
    involving the feet)
Dysthymia (chronic low-grade depression)
Elective mutism (refusal to speak)
Emotional lability (uncontrollable displays of emotion)
Enuresis (bed wetting)
Gilles de la Tourette syndrome (muscle and vocal tics)
Hypochondria
Hypomania (mild abnormal mood elevation)
Impotence
Impulsive aggression
Intention myoclonus (spasm of muscle when intentionally
    used)
Late luteal dysphoric disorder (premenstrual syndrome)
Major depression
Migraine
Obsessive-compulsive disorder
Onychophagia (nail biting)
Overweight
Panic disorder
Paraphilia (sexual deviance)
Pathologic jealousy
Posttraumatic stress disorder (P.T.S.D.)
Premature ejaculation
Raynaud's phenomenon (intermittent circulation problem
    in fingers)

Schizophrenia
Seasonal affective disorder (SAD; winter depression)
Self-injurious behavior
Sleep paralysis (inability to move just prior to sleep or on
    awakening)
Social phobia (extreme fear of social situations)
Syncope (fainting)
Trichotillomania (compulsive hair pulling)

Please note that further study is required to confirm the effectiveness
of Prozac-like medications for most of these conditions.

In the 1960s people sometimes joked that a person was
"Valium deficient." While one should generally avoid Valium, for
reasons discussed later, it's interesting to note that a few years ago,
researchers found naturally occurring molecules in the brain
identical to Valium. This indicates that our bodies may have a natural need for this substance. I strongly doubt that we will ever
find naturally occurring Prozac molecules in the brain, but the
same principle of a natural requirement seems to apply to serotonin.

An optimal level exists for just about every chemical inside us.
Thyroid, for example, can be too low or too high; the ideal range
is quite narrow. We do not know the desired level for serotonin
because we have no conclusive way to measure it. Of course, we
can measure serotonin in the blood, but that is different from
serotonin in the brain, which is most relevant to mood and behavior. A number of tests exist at the research level, but none is reliable enough to justify widespread clinical use. We can, however,
roughly measure the *function* of brain serotonin by various indirect means. It is this I refer to in discussions of laboratory assess-
ments of brain serotonin levels.

Why should our brains have suddenly become deficient in
serotonin? The short answer is that while our physical evolution
fitted us well for life on the plains of Africa, our cultural evolution
demands far more of us, especially in the last century. Evidence

suggests that our suspicions must logically fall on the lifestyle and environment we have created, and for which we were not designed.

Have you fallen prey to the onslaught of our serotonin-depleting times? The following questionnaire is designed to help you determine that. However, until the test is standardized on large populations, your answers can serve only as an initial guide to identifying a deficiency. Although most of my patients would answer yes to at least three of the questions, even one yes may indicate some weakness in your serotonin system.

ARE YOU PROZAC DEFICIENT?

1. I am frequently irritable.
2. I am much more impatient and given to acting impulsively than most people.
3. I often engage in binge eating or crave carbohydrates.
4. I have felt suicidal at some point.
5. I have a problem or a potential problem with alcohol.
6. I have problems with insomnia or have a "night-owl" pattern (preferring later bedtime).
7. I seem to have trouble with low blood sugar.
8. I have been in at least one fight since age 18.
9. My functioning is significantly impaired in winter or by other conditions of light deprivation.
10. I have a close relative who is alcohol/drug addicted.
11. I do not handle stress well.
12. I sweat less than most people. (See chapter 3 for a discussion of sweating and serotonin.)
13. I have a low tolerance for heat.
14. I tend to be overly dependent in my significant relationships.
15. My moods are highly changeable.
16. I have experienced chronic pain for more than three months.
17. I have had more sexual partners than is usual among my peer group.
18. I am very sensitive to criticism or rejection.
19. I smoke cigarettes.
20. I have significant premenstrual symptoms.

● ●

SUMMING UP

Even by the strictest criteria, most people undergo a significant psychiatric illness at some point in their lives. Milder forms of stress-related mental or physical illness are nearly universal. Prozac and similar medications, which act selectively on serotonin, have proved remarkably effective in treating anxiety, depression, compulsiveness, and many other conditions. These and other findings suggest that serotonin deficiency is the cause of our epidemic of stress-related illness. Chapter 2 focuses on this powerful substance, building a foundation for our discussion of "natural Prozac" and the ways in which you can strengthen your mood chemistry naturally.

CHAPTER 2

SEROTONIN: VIRTUAL MORALITY AND THE BRAIN'S SURROGATE PARENT

*What is moral is what you feel good after and what is
immoral is what you feel bad after.*
—ERNEST HEMINGWAY *DEATH IN THE AFTERNOON*

Arguably, we can gain as much insight into the human condition from a basic understanding of serotonin as we can from reading Freud—and the insights have perhaps the added advantage of being true. But to give credit where it is due, Freud himself predicted that his psychoanalytic concepts would someday give way to biochemical explanations, and he laid much of the groundwork for understanding these unconscious processes.

The ancient Greeks also believed that biochemistry controlled moods. They believed a substance called black bile explained depression. While the ultimate explanation will surely not be as simple as a single substance, neuroscientists have in a way returned to the Greek paradigm. Tremendous advances have been made in understanding the chemistry of mood. Partly in recognition of this, Congress has declared the 1990s the Decade of the Brain. And serotonin stands at center stage.

As it would take more than an act of Congress to interest most people in neurochemistry, rest assured that we can tell the serotonin story without getting too technical.

Following is the first of several case histories of my patients.

BRAD'S CASE

Brad, in his late thirties, is a truly brilliant architect. Unfortunately, his talent has become part of his problem. An engaging man, he tries to be a good husband and father. But he allowed his recent career success to impose impossible demands on his time and energy. He came to me in late winter, feeling utterly overwhelmed. Although his moods tended to fluctuate widely—soaring high in the spring and leading at times to wildly uninhibited behavior, then crashing down in the winter—he paid little attention to his feelings, noting only that he was tremendously creative and productive sometimes while at others it was a real struggle to get anything done. His sleep was often the focus of his concern. Even in the winter he often could not get to sleep until 3 or 4 A.M. and then had to drag himself painfully out of bed in the morning to set to work. He used alcohol and cigarettes to help him cope with stress, but apparently he had not yet succumbed to a family tendency toward alcoholism. He felt his stress physically and had on occasion ended up in the ER for evaluation when his heart beat became irregular. Although he had never consciously felt suicidal, he was aware that his car racing in earlier years when he was depressed often was essentially suicidal. Brad was also extremely sensitive to heat and during stressful times would break out in a rash following a hot shower or even exercise. Brad illustrates well the variety of problems that presumably stem from a single underlying problem—low serotonin. We will come back to his case from time to time as we look at various forms of treatment.

Serotonin, like the better known neurochemical adrenaline, functions in part as a neurotransmitter. (Neurotransmitters convey messages from cell to cell throughout the central nervous system.) If you choose to understand only one of the hundreds of chemicals that influence the brain, make it serotonin—for as serotonin levels change, so does behavior.

Although the amount of serotonin in the brain is small compared to some other neurochemicals, no other one impacts more of the brain. That serotonin has such a broad presence indicates that its task is not limited to a specific duty, but rather that it serves as an overseer. Serotonin neurons set the overall tone or activity level of other regulatory systems. The slow rhythmic firing of serotonin neurons (nerve cells) and their location in an evolutionary old part of the brain further suggest that they are not engaged in rocket science but are busy with the more basic tasks of physical survival.

The action of this slow rhythmic firing can be compared with a conductor's baton: The information conveyed to the orchestra is simple but critical, and the same signal can simultaneously sound the trumpets and quiet the strings.

Well over a dozen types of serotonin receptors have been identified, some of which interpret serotonin's messages in quite the opposite way from others. While our description of serotonin is offered in simplified terms, keep in mind that in fact it is highly complex and poorly understood. Serotonin influences important aspects of physiology, including body temperature, blood pressure, blood clotting, immunity, pain, digestion, sleep, and circadian (i.e., daily) body rhythms.

After millions of years of evolution, our bodies have grown incredibly complicated. To devise simple explanations of our mental biology, it helps to refer back to the basics, to chemistry present at the dawn of life. Apparently that chemistry is so important that evolution never abandoned it but only expanded its role.

SEROTONIN SYNAPSE

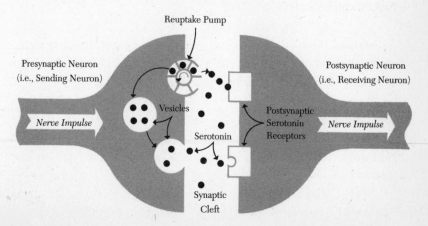

Serotonin is one of life's most ancient components, found in man but also in the most primitive one-celled organisms. Over millions of years of evolution, serotonin has acquired more and more functions, including many that are critical to survival.

In the central nervous system of higher organisms, serotonin often inhibits the firing of brain cells (neurons) that it influences. This results in inhibition of many of our behaviors; indeed, one might think of serotonin partly as a chemical restraint system. The higher cortical areas of the brain are also largely inhibitory, and their impairment can cause extremely uninhibited behavior. This is how alcohol, which cuts off input from the cerebral cortex, causes those regrettable acts at company Christmas parties. Thus, serotonin's action frequently parallels higher brain function, battling other "primitive" brain centers such as the hypothalamus, which generates urges concerning aggression, eating, and sex.

Obviously, the human cerebral cortex is much more highly developed than that of other animals, so we generally transcend "baser instincts" more easily. But not always. Where inhibitory function fails, we can get violent, impulsive criminals in whom, not surprisingly, we often find reduced serotonin activity. For this reason, serotonin has been described by some as the brain's police force, sometimes as its vice squad, since it helps us "just say no" not only to aggression but to alcohol and drugs, sex, binge eating, and other sometimes questionable impulsive behavior.

SURROGATE PARENT

No matter how old a mother is, she watches her middle-aged children for signs of improvement.
—FLORIDA SCOTT-MAXWELL

Serotonin's regulatory tasks are much broader than the police metaphor suggests. A better analogy might be "surrogate parent." Like a good parent, serotonin both discourages behavior that might get us in trouble and comforts us when trouble nevertheless arrives—soothing worry, pain, and, as we'll see, most forms of stress. Serotonin has other parental duties as well, hovering over us as we sleep, eat—even move our bowels.

It seems that a lack of good parental care while growing up causes a greater need of serotonin's surrogate parenting to weather life's challenges. A child born into a family that provides effective guidance and support, however, may do fine with a weaker serotonin system, because life stresses would less often exceed the capacity to cope. Unfortunately, in extreme cases, those most in need of serotonin may be deprived of it early in life by the effects of abusive parenting or other trauma. We have evidence that trauma, especially early in development, can permanently damage the serotonin system. If life is particularly gentle after that point, the increased vulnerability to stress may never be of much concern. But in those not so lucky, the stage has been set for potentially serious psychiatric illness. The chart below illustrates the type of problems that appear to arise most directly from low serotonin. Note that although depression and anxiety are highly associated with abnormalities of serotonin function, the connection is not as strong or as direct as with the following.

WHEN SEROTONIN IS DEFICIENT

● ●

Behaviors:

Increases in:
Irritability/aggression
Impulsivity
Violent suicide
Alcohol/drug use
Eating and bingeing
Sexual activity

Medical Problems:

Increases in:
Chronic pain
Seizures
Hypoglycemia (low blood sugar)

Insomnia
Disruption of circadian body rhythms

This list shows the building blocks from which serotonin-related psychiatric conditions arise. "Low serotonin" is a short-hand phrase for various ways in which the serotonin system shows reduced functioning, such as low neural firing rates, decreased sensitivity of serotonin receptors, reduced availability of serotonin in the synapses (the gaps between neurons), as well as low absolute levels of serotonin in the central nervous system.

VIRTUAL MORALITY

Virtue is more clearly shown in the performance of fine actions than in the nonperformance of base ones.
—ARISTOTLE

Perhaps serotonin will not cause performance of Aristotle's "fine actions," but it will help shape up various morally dubious behaviors. Healthy serotonin function—a strong "parental presence"—makes restraint easier. This is more in keeping with the view of nineteenth-century British statesman John Morley: "The essence of morality is the subjugation of nature in obedience to social needs." This concept of morality hinges on restraint. Of course, lack of restraint in people who have low serotonin activity can sometimes be good, leading to lively, adventurous characters who sometimes are of great benefit to society. For some, however, the dark side will be impulsive acts such as violence, alcohol/drug abuse, and promiscuity. It's intriguing to speculate whether the general decline in serotonin function has contributed to the withering of behavior traditionally defined as "virtuous."

Let's consider a case in point. In San Francisco in 1978, disgruntled city councilman Dan White fatally shot Mayor George Moscone and another city official, Harvey Milk. A jury rendered the verdict "not guilty by reason of insanity," based on White's claim of a crazed mental state due to eating Twinkies. At the time,

I considered the verdict one of the blackest days for both psychiatry and our legal system.

Our growing knowledge of neurochemistry increasingly encumbers our outrage at such crimes. Dan White's later suicide, also by gunshot, suggested that he may well have had markedly low serotonin function. (Studies clearly link violent suicide to depleted serotonin.) Years later, researchers at the National Institute on Alcohol Abuse and Alcoholism found that low-serotonin individuals often develop hypoglycemia (low blood sugar), sometimes suffering out-of-control rages after consuming large doses of sugar or glucose.

Greater understanding of the brain will eventually lessen the helplessness of individuals and thus of society, in the face of chemical dictates. And for those who choose to ignore the new insights—for example, a Dan White, who knows the risk of sugar consumption but ignores it—punishment will have a sounder moral basis. As we learn more in this area, society will close in on a host of thorny ethical questions concerning individuals' responsibility and liberty.

SEROTONIN AND AGGRESSION

Rhesus monkeys make particularly good subjects for studying serotonin and aggression because the structure of their DNA is more than 90% the same as ours, which accounts for many cross-species similarities. In a study of male rhesus, those with the lowest levels of serotonin exhibited the most violent behavior. However, this did not apply to aggression involved in maintaining social dominance; apparently, serotonin does not discourage the aggression required to compete. Monkeys with higher serotonin activity took the trouble to move from branch to branch to shorten leaping distance; those with low serotonin impulsively leaped great distances at heights where falls could prove fatal.

Research on animals bred selectively for nonaggressive temperament shows that they have higher levels of serotonin in the central nervous system. Studies show that drugs that increase serotonin activity lessen aggression, while those that reduce sero-

tonin activity heighten aggression. We also have evidence that
serotonin-boosting drugs such as Prozac can help people prone to
violence. Psychiatric researchers are currently debating just how
greatly serotonin influences aggression itself as opposed to simply
affecting impulsivity—or whether low serotonin is even less
directly responsible for violence, as I suggest, under the theory
that healthy serotonin levels help us, in a yet more general way, to
tolerate stress.

We also see reduced serotonin activity in people prone to
impulsive fire setting, impulsive violent assaults, alcohol/drug
abuse, violent suicide, and bulimia, as well as in those with
Tourette's syndrome (marked by uncontrollable impulses to move
and vocalize rudely, such as shouting an obscenity during a wed-
ding), and in children institutionalized for inappropriate aggressive behavior.

Sometimes, low-serotonin, violence-prone people victimize
society, sometimes themselves. A study following more than seventy psychiatric patients with various diagnoses over fifteen years
revealed that seven of the patients had died by age forty—largely
of suicide, homicide, or accident. All the patients who died young
had shown signs of *very* low serotonin activity. In fact, the highest
level among them still fell well below average for the rest of the
patients.

Obviously, psychosocial factors are extremely important in
determining most complex behavior, especially violence. This
book highlights biology but the importance of psychosocial elements is implicit and should be kept in mind throughout later discussions. Even in terms of biology, however, low serotonin is only
part of the picture. While individuals convicted of violent and
impulsive crimes show signs of reduced serotonin function, brain
imaging studies reveal that the prefrontal cortex (the area behind
the forehead) also has low activity. When the prefrontal cortex,
which is responsible for impulse inhibition, is thus disabled, the
individual has less ability to plan and to anticipate consequences,
less inclination to worry, and, overall, less control of impulses.
Hence, he lacks several of the brain's natural barriers against
crime.

DEPRESSION AND ANXIETY

In the 1960s, the monoamine theory of depression arrived, blaming depression on low levels of either serotonin or norepinephrine (another neurotransmitter). But we now know that the biochemical basis of depression is far more complex. For example, depleting people's brain serotonin by feeding them a diet lacking the amino acid L-tryptophan, from which serotonin is made, caused depression only in those who had special vulnerability. These people either had mild depression already or a clear family history of it. Low serotonin apparently is more of a vulnerability factor, causing depression *only* when other conditions exist.

The relationship between serotonin and anxiety is even more complex. In many types of anxiety, serotonin levels are elevated; however, anxiety can be generated both by drugs that increase serotonin and drugs that stifle it. Whether elevated serotonin during anxiety causes the anxious feeling or is a helpful response to the stress itself we do not yet know. Certainly excessive serotonin can cause agitation. The "serotonin syndrome," the medical term for this in extreme, typically involves confusion, agitation, muscle twitching, sweating, tremor, and diarrhea. It may even include a mild manic reaction (greatly elevated mood), and may be fatal.

WHAT DOES IT FEEL LIKE TO HAVE LOW SEROTONIN?

Although there is little direct evidence to correlate changes in a person's mood with serotonin fluctuation, I believe that the following situation reflects a state of low serotonin. Imagine yourself stuck in rush hour in a hot car on your way to an important meeting after being up all night. Likely you would be quite distressed, irritable, and given to aggressive reactions. Yet, under better circumstances, that state of presumably low serotonin might not be at all troublesome. Lying on a tropical beach, you might still be hot and tired, but feel just fine.

Another good illustration of the effect of low serotonin can, I believe, be seen in the behavioral "meltdown" that young children often exhibit when overtired. The state is extremely changeable, swinging from giddy enthusiasm to tantrum in a moment. A friend of mine observing her two boys in this state remarked for my benefit, "I bet they don't have three serotonin molecules between them right now."

UNIFYING THEORIES OF SEROTONIN

There are several prominent theories about serotonin's main job. One holds that serotonin constrains behavior; more specifically, that it restricts neural information flow and thus constrains behavior. By inhibiting the intensity of signals, especially those from external sources, serotonin ensures that the signals that do get through are the important ones. But someone with reduced serotonin function gets swamped by all kinds of signals, and this may produce erratic behavior.

Others, such as Dr. Barry Jacobs at Princeton, believe that serotonin's primary task is to facilitate motor (muscle) activity and coordinate body processes appropriate to motor activity. He suggests that when the body must act, consistent with the first theory, serotonin helps to avoid confusion by shutting down sensory input. Conversely, when seeking information, for example when an animal listens for sounds and so stands absolutely still, low levels of serotonin quell motor function and boost sensory processes.

The link between serotonin and motor activity probably goes both ways: Not only does serotonin affect motor activity, but motor activity affects serotonin. From this, Jacobs, one of the world's most respected authorities on serotonin, has hypothesized that the repetitive motions of people with obsessive-compulsive disorder might be a form of self-medication: About one-quarter of serotonin neurons increase their activity dramatically—some two to five times—when we engage in repetitive actions like chewing or licking. Another large group of serotonin neurons increase their firing two to three fold with repetitive movement like walking. Compulsive repetitive movement thus likely boosts serotonin, as do medications like Prozac. Chapter 7 explores this type of "natural Prozac" further.

● ●

SUMMING UP

Serotonin clearly plays a central role in our lives. The "surrogate parent" label suggests many of the diverse functions of serotonin, but admittedly the metaphor is rather broad. In contrast, the "unifying theories" are quite narrow. What I hope you have gained from this chapter is a sense of serotonin's complexity and its involvement in many, many varied tasks. In chapter 3 you'll find a new way to view serotonin, based on my ongoing research, which brings together in simple fashion much of what we have discussed and also helps to account for the seemingly paradoxical responses that Prozac and similar medications may cause. The theory further explains why, in the face of modern stresses, our serotonin levels have taken a dive and how we can restore them to healthy levels.

CHAPTER 3

STRESS—THE BRAIN IN HEAT

I pray thee, good Mercutio, let's retire
The day is hot, the Capulets abroad,
And if we meet, we shall not 'scape a brawl,
For now, these hot days, is the mad blood stirring.
—SHAKESPEARE *ROMEO AND JULIET*

THE IMPORTANCE OF BEING COOL

What Shakespeare observed about heat causing us to "lose our cool" reflects something very basic about human beings. Of course, we echo the Bard's observation all the time, though far less eloquently. We say that people get "hot under the collar" or "hotheaded," and in a way these phrases are literally true.

Keeping the brain cool is one of the body's highest priorities, because even a few minutes of high internal temperature can seriously damage our brain. Robert Ornstein and other "bioanthropologists" suggest that evolutionary changes affecting brain heat actually led to human consciousness. The argument goes that our evolution into erect posture raised our brains a few feet more off the baking African earth, in itself a step toward a cooler brain. Standing also demanded a radically changed vascular system to pump blood up to the brain. The resulting bountiful blood supply served as a more vigorous brain-cooling system, efficiently carrying away excess heat from the brain. Larger brains generate more heat, so a species' ability to cool its brain limits its brain size.

Thus, the combined cooling advantages of standing erect allowed our greater brain size, which in turn allowed our greater intelligence. Intelligence that then set about creating the comforts of modern life, which cause so many of the problems this book addresses.

Ornstein and others suggest that the chief advantage of this new, bigger brain was not higher intelligence, at least initially. Even with the improved cooling system, while chasing down dinner under the blazing African sun we inevitably cooked a few brain cells. The bigger brain gave us, in effect, brain cells to burn; thus, we could continue to count on finding our way back after catching dinner. Brain-cell surplus may also explain recent findings that bigger brains seem somewhat protected from the ravages of Alzheimer's: People who have more cells to lose do not reach the impairing level of Alzheimer's until a much later age.

THE HEAT OF ANGER

Aggression is one of the most widely recognized signs of reduced serotonin. Given the link between heat and anger, I wondered if heat somehow lowered serotonin. After all, serotonin plays a role in temperature regulation. Could an intense demand to cool the body cause serotonin to slip up on other duties—such as the restraining of aggression? The first step in checking this out was to verify whether the intuitive connection we make between heat and aggression actually holds up. I invited my colleague Dr. David Avery to help me review the considerable research literature on the subject.

Dr. Avery and I found an amazing amount of statistics collected on violence, some material even quite old. One study, done from 1861 to 1867—well before the advent of air-conditioning— showed a remarkable correlation between monthly temperature and assaults. The correlation was so tight that you could virtually determine the number of assaults by knowing the temperature. Similar findings have been confirmed more recently for many places using yearly, seasonal, monthly, and even daily analysis. Note that only *violent* crime markedly increases in heat; crimes against property, which reflect less aggression, have a much weaker correlation to temperature. Turning to mass aggression, in a study of more than one hundred riots, investigators found that temperatures tended to rise for seven days preceding violence; the heat lasted throughout the rioting, then fell off after rioting ceased.

Finally, consider the most devastating form of human aggression—war. The journal *Nature* recently published a study of all the wars for which we know the start date (there are more than two thousand). A clear seasonal pattern existed in the Northern Hemisphere: Fighting broke out *four times* more often in August than in January, months with highest and lowest temperatures respectively. The same general pattern of warring occurred in reverse in the Southern Hemisphere. Finally, in even-temperatured equatorial regions, remarkably little seasonal variation took place. How strange it is that throughout history, a simple thing like heat has so strongly influenced something as complex as war.

MORE EVIDENCE OF THE HEAT-SEROTONIN CONNECTION

Realizing that many things other than heat-weakened serotonin levels might account for the strong association between heat and aggression, Dr. Avery and I set out to see if any other behaviors under serotonin's control flared up in hot weather. Again, there was a formidable body of literature. We examined the ten behaviors most likely to result from reduced serotonin. What happens to these behaviors in the heat? Here are our findings.

WHEN HEAT RISES

• •

Increases in:

Aggression (war, riots, murders, rapes and other assaults, hostile acts)

Suicides (specifically by violent means; also, failed attempts)

Sexual activity (lost virginity, conceptions, sex crimes, venereal disease)

Impulsive Behavior (automotive and industrial accidents, pilot errors, property crimes)

Seizures (from hot baths or fever)

Pain

Insomnia

Circadian rhythm disturbances

Alcohol/drug use (per capita fatalities, overdoses)

Decreases in:

Eating/appetite

Rarely in the behavioral sciences do we find real-world data that so consistently matches theory. Of the ten behaviors we identified as most clearly inhibited by serotonin, the only one that changed with heat in a manner counter to the theory was eating. The impulse to eat, as most of us have noticed, falls off in hot weather. (For an extended discussion of this and a more detailed look at all of the heat-associated behaviors studied, see appendix I.)

A more serious problem now loomed for Dr. Avery and me. Conventional wisdom had long held that serotonin's temperature-regulating work involved *raising* temperature, not lowering it. Robert Myers and colleagues at East Carolina University laid down this view in the 1960s, and it has stuck despite the growing evidence that serotonin primarily *cools*. The complexity of the relevant laboratory experiments made interpretation of the results ambiguous, so we looked for additional real-world evidence to help settle the matter. Again, the results proved remarkably consistent. Essentially, every time a person does something that heightens serotonin levels, cooling mechanisms kick into higher gear. Dr. Avery and I also examined individuals from groups characterized by low serotonin. What we found were people who tended either to sweat less than normal, to run higher body temperatures, or to tolerate heat poorly, as shown on the next page. (These findings are discussed further in appendix I.)

Low-serotonin groups:	*Our findings:*
Multiple sclerosis patients	Poor heat tolerance (exacerbates symptoms)
Epileptics	Poor heat tolerance; heat often can precipitate seizures
Violent criminals	Decreased sweating under certain conditions
Violently suicidal individuals	Decreased sweating under certain conditions

BRAD'S CASE

If you recall, Brad had great trouble with heat. This dated back to high school, when overheating during exercise led to rashes and at times medically serious reactions. Once, this led to a prolonged period of inability to maintain stable body temperature, accompanied by extreme fatigue and loss of about forty pounds. Extensive workups over the years consistently failed to turn up the cause of Brad's devastating reactions. Of course, at that time, serotonin had not been considered an important factor in regulating body temperature.

When Brad had a similar reaction soon after I began seeing him, we decided to try Prozac. I thought that boosting his serotonin might help him better tolerate heat. Almost immediately the rashes disappeared, and he had only a mild problem after hot showers. Unfortunately, though, he had various side effects from Prozac. We tried the new medication Serzone, which blocks the serotonin-2A receptors, the cause of many often undesirable effects of serotonin, including elevations of body temperature. The Serzone helped even more with Brad's heat tolerance, and so far he has had little trouble with side effects. He finds that his stress tolerance is much improved, and he no longer feels the need for alcohol to relieve his stress.

STRESS AND SEROTONIN

As we can see, serotonin's cooling function sets up a symmetrical relationship: Serotonin reduces heat, and heat reduces serotonin. Although, as mentioned earlier, we don't yet have any reliable way to measure brain serotonin levels, this heat sensitivity suggests the possibility of using body temperature to check serotonin functioning (more on this in chapter 16). For now, however, we may conclude that heat appears to reduce serotonin's ability to handle other duties while simultaneously attending to that highest priority job, maintaining proper body temperature. This relationship sets up a major point of this book, what I term the Serotonin Theory of Stress.

THE SEROTONIN THEORY OF STRESS

Most of what we call stress causes a measurable increase in body temperature, whether it's the stress of physical exertion or of anxiety-provoking situations. Thus, if serotonin's cooling action helps protect us from this aspect of stress, we can view the serotonin system as a stress-adaptation mechanism. This comports well with the earliest known role for serotonin in primitive one-celled organisms. Serotonin and its chief metabolite (by-product), melatonin, protect organisms from "oxidative stress," the biological equivalent of rusting. So, serotonin seems to have buffered stress since time immemorial. But all this is theory. What do we actually *know* about serotonin and stress?

According to preclinical studies (lab work, animal research—all but human research), physical and psychological stresses immediately signal serotonin neurons to heighten the release of serotonin. If the stress lasts too long, it leads to serotonin depletion, according to recent work published in *Brain Research*. Dr. Barry Jacobs's work with cats reached different conclusions, but then, as anyone familiar with cats might agree, they are not necessarily representative of other animals. Depending on your viewpoint, they are either incredibly cool or are the sociopaths of the animal world, or both.

Other research, by Dr. Naesh and colleagues in Sweden, showed that mental stress in students facing exams reliably raised levels of blood serotonin. Finally, one study found that serotonin metabolites also increased in marksmen facing the stress of a shooting competition. But, as stated earlier, blood serotonin is not a good indication of brain serotonin activity.

Not all of serotonin's stress responses benefit us. For example, rising *blood* serotonin causes more blood clotting, which can lead to heart attack. However, the ancient hunter-gatherer faced more physical danger from wounding, so at least back then, increased clotting well served us. With an average life span of fifteen to twenty-five years, heart attacks were the least of our ancestors' worries.

We have good laboratory evidence that medications that boost serotonin function reduce the biochemical effects of stress. So, when we take something like Prozac to raise *brain* serotonin function, we decrease *blood* serotonin. For example, one investigator and his colleagues in a preclinical study administered the medication Anafranil (clomipromine), which has Prozac-like effects, for several weeks and found it prevented the increase in blood serotonin normally caused by chronic stress.

All this research strongly implies that boosted brain serotonin serves as a "stress immunizer." Given the countless ways in which modern life stresses our Stone Age brains, we certainly need a robust serotonin system. But, as we've seen, we do not draw serotonin from a bottomless well. When the bucket comes up light, our "inoculation" against stress may falter, and life's traumas then hit that much harder. Of course, this generates further stress, becoming a vicious cycle.

ENTER PROZAC

Early on, I was fascinated by Prozac's effectiveness with so many conditions. I kept searching for the common thread in my patients' responses. Eventually, it came to me that, more than anything else, Prozac improved people's stress tolerance. Prozac might take weeks to lift their depression, but their resilience to stress usually improved within days. It seemed that no matter how I classified the patients diagnostically, if they were stressed, as most of them were, their stress tolerance often improved rapidly.

One aspect of Prozac's broad treatment range was particularly intriguing. Not only did the medication help overly impulsive people restrain themselves, as expected since it raises serotonin levels, but Prozac also helped the opposite sort of people—the *overly* inhibited individuals suffering obsessive compulsive disorder. This was hardly expected, for those with OCD were believed to have too much restraint and, perhaps, too much serotonin.

That Prozac's serotonin-boosting function helped both sets of people seemed a paradox.

With the model of serotonin as a broad stress-reducing agent, however, the paradox evaporated. Prozac helps impulsive people tolerate the stress of waiting, the discomfort in not obtaining instant gratification. In the case of OCD, Prozac relieves overly inhibited individuals of the crippling stress of worry and anxiety, thus freeing up their ability to take action.

We can even put this into Freudian terms. Prozac shields the ego from both the distress caused by libidinal or id impulses and also from stress caused by a rigid or demanding superego.

With these ideas in hand, in 1989, in the *Harvard Mental Health Letter*, I published an article noting Prozac's stress effectiveness across diagnostic boundaries. Back then, as Prozac was relatively unknown, I drew a highly skeptical response from some professional quarters. Now, however, the versatility of Prozac is widely accepted, as more conditions are found to respond.

● ●

SUMMING UP

Our world is a stranger to the one from and for which we evolved. We are not quite fish out of water, perhaps, but certainly fish in a strange aquarium.

Except in times of war, never has stimulation so bombarded us, and stimulation, whether enjoyable or not, stresses. All change, good and bad, imposes stress, and never has the rate of change approached today's. Our grandparents lived in what now seems a quaint and antiquated world. Our struggle to cope with today's increased stress itself undermines serotonin and thus our stress adaptation capacity. The result? Over half of us develop a serious psychiatric condition at some point, and almost everyone eventually suffers some stress-related disorder, whether hypertension, cardiovascular disease, or cancer. A landmark article in the *New England Journal of Medicine* in 1985 termed these the "diseases of civilization."

Obviously, it is vital that we buttress our natural stress fortification, the serotonin system. The next part of this book looks at how we can do so naturally.

PART II

"NATURAL PROZAC"

CHAPTER 4

LIGHT THERAPY: THE END OF THE MODERN DARK AGE

A cloudy day, or a little sunshine, have a greater influence on many constitutions as the most real blessings or misfortunes.

—JOSEPH ADDISON

Our brains evolved under "field conditions" of long daily sunlight exposure, subject to rhythmic lengthening and shortening by seasons. Now, however, most of our days are unnaturally dark and our nights are unnaturally light. We have lost our strongest connection with the daily rhythm of nature. Dr. Thomas Wehr of the National Institute of Mental Health calls this "a massive uncontrolled experiment." The long-term risks are unknown, but we are starting to understand some of the short-term effects.

The ancient Greeks, dating back at least to Hippocrates, knew quite well how therapeutic light could be. In the early twentieth century, doctors used light widely for both psychiatric and general medical purposes. Solariums were popular in hospitals of all types, and sunlight was used to treat infectious diseases such as tuberculosis. But with the advent of modern medications, light lost its aura. Not until truly seminal work, in the early 1980s by Drs. Alfred Lewy, Norman Rosenthal, and others, under the auspices of the National Institute of Mental Health, did the medical community see its broad interest in light rekindled.

Dr. Lewy demonstrated that people respond to light on a hormone level. Dr. Rosenthal went on to conduct the first controlled trials of light therapy in winter depression and led the crusade to gain mainstream acceptance. Now, bright light therapy is included in therapeutic recommendations of the American Psychiatric Association. Recently, some insurance companies began covering light therapy as a medical expense—the ultimate badge of acceptance as mainstream treatment.

A LIGHT-STARVED ERA

Light levels in a house average about 200 to 300 lux (a measure of brightness roughly equal to one candle flame). A well-lit office may have a mere 500 lux, whereas a sunny day offers 50,000 to 100,000 lux. Even the winters of Seattle, Washington, where I live, typically register several thousand lux; which is much more light than that obtainable indoors.

Modern light starvation occurs even in the midst of plenty; in sunny San Diego, Dr. Daniel Kripke and colleagues put light meters on residents' wrists and found that young adults averaged no more than one or two hours of light over 1,000 lux. The little light we get today hardly bestows its full benefits.

LIGHT AND THE BODY

Therapeutic lighting, or phototherapy, is now well established in general medical practice. It is highly effective in treating a variety of skin conditions from acne to psoriasis. These treatments employ the ultraviolet (UV) spectrum. The UV is also known to be required for the production of vitamin D in the skin and in the treatment of neonatal jaundice. Premature babies often develop a buildup of a chemical called bilirubin, which turns the skin yellow. Their immature livers are not yet capable of breaking down this neurotoxic chemical, but phototherapy can do it for them and thus can be lifesaving.

THE SEROTONIN CONNECTION

Not long ago Dr. Rao and colleagues in Germany showed that both high- and low-intensity light raised blood serotonin levels. Elevation of brain serotonin may well explain light therapy's success in treating winter depression, an illness in which lack of light clearly plays a role. As mentioned before, serotonin deficiency has long been implicated in depression, and Dr. Rosenthal and colleagues have begun to amass evidence in support of a critical role for serotonin specifically in winter depression.

While the evidence certainly supports the idea that light boosts brain serotonin, this is undoubtedly not the only neurochemistry that light affects. In chapter 5 we will discuss light's important interactions with melatonin. Further, some evidence suggests the amphetaminelike neurochemical dopamine may play a role—evidence certainly consistent with light's well-known energizing and activating effects.

LIGHT AND THE MIND

Light entering the eyes apparently accounts for most of the beneficial psychological effects of light treatment. Dr. Wehr and others performed a small experiment, testing blindfolded subjects wearing bathing suits against people wrapped up mummy-fashion except for their eyes. Only the group who could see the light showed an antidepressant response. Certainly this benefit itself is not surprising, as the eyes are a direct physical extension of the brain; light stimulates the brain as surely as Prozac or any other psychotropic drug. Perhaps someday, however, we will find that the mood benefits of light do not reside exclusively in the "eye of the beholder."

In Dr. Raymond Lam's study of bulimics, light reduced binge/purge episodes by an impressive 50 percent. Dr. Kripke, in San Diego, has found that even nonseasonal depressions appear to benefit from light treatment. We even have some preliminary evidence from Dr. Barbara Parry's work that light can ameliorate the symptoms of premenstrual syndrome—a malady that, you may recall, is associated with low serotonin. Light treatment can also boost energy levels. Writing this book in the evenings after seeing patients, I often felt tired and so put a bright light box on my desk. Noticeable elevations in energy resulted—so much so that I had to start turning the box off at least two hours before I wanted to go to sleep!

WINTER DEPRESSION, A.K.A. SEASONAL AFFECTIVE DISORDER (SAD)

Winter changes into stone the water
of heaven and the heart of man.
—Victor Hugo   *Les Miserables*

Much of what we know about the therapeutic use of light has been learned during the course of treating winter depression, so it is useful to understand more about this important condition. My colleague Dr. Rosenthal deserves a great measure of the credit for developing our understanding and treatment of SAD.

As estimated by the questionnaire on the next page, winter depression affects about 6 percent of the U.S. population, although with major differences between North and South. Along the Canadian border, up to 10 percent of the population suffers SAD, while the incidence in Florida is less than 2 percent.

Winter depression differs from other depressions. Typical symptoms include both excessive sleep and appetite coupled with extremely low energy. Nonseasonal depression more often brings insomnia, agitation, decreased appetite, and suicidal ideation. Taking into account milder forms of SAD, as much as 20 percent of the U.S. population is believed to have a significant problem with winter functioning.

You'll get an idea of your own seasonal profile by answering the following questions, excerpted from the Seasonal Pattern Affective Questionnaire, developed by Dr. Rosenthal and colleagues at the National Institute of Mental Health.

TO WHAT DEGREE DO THE FOLLOWING CHANGE
WITH THE SEASONS?

● ●

	No Change	*Slight* Change	*Moderate* Change	*Marked* Change	*Extremely Marked* Change
1. Sleep Length	0	1	2	3	4
2. Social Activity	0	1	2	3	4
3. Mood (overall feeling of well being)	0	1	2	3	4
4. Weight	0	1	2	3	4
5. Appetite	0	1	2	3	4
6. Energy Level	0	1	2	3	4

A score of four to seven is average. A score of eight to ten may mean that you have subsyndromal seasonal affective disorder (a milder form of SAD), especially if the seasonal changes cause a problem for you. A score of eleven or more may earn you a formal diagnosis of SAD if you also rate the seasonal changes you experience as at least a moderate problem for you.

I must emphasize that if you are significantly depressed, you should seek professional help. I have evaluated numerous people who had self-diagnosed seasonal depression only to find that they had something quite different. Professional evaluation helps to ensure not only correct diagnosis but optimal treatment. Not everyone responds fully to the standard treatments, so your treatment may well need some experienced tailoring. I have found that combining multiple treatments is usually required for optimal results.

USING LIGHT THERAPY

The Light Dose for SAD

Light, like medication, requires proper dosage. Too little won't work, and too much can cause side effects. Our knowledge about dosing for winter depression continues to evolve. We have come a long way since the initial recommendation of three hours' sitting in front of a light box both morning and evening. More than ten years ago the standard dose dropped to two hours at 2,500 lux at a distance of two to three feet. This was still a lot of time to spend sitting; especially since researchers often recommend getting the dosage first thing in the morning.

People with SAD generally have a great deal of trouble getting out of bed, so asking them to get up earlier for the treatment was asking a lot. Too much, I felt. I wondered if a more convenient, head-mounted light device that generated a small amount of light close to the eye would match the effect of greater lux at a distance. I began developing prototypes, and even engaged a lawyer for a patent application, but I soon learned that Dr. Rosenthal and others at the NIMH were already developing such a device. Placing second at the patent office offers no silver medal. It's a lot like losing an election: All you have to show for it are bills and odd memorabilia . . . in my case, a goodly collection of small but remarkably powerful flashlights.

However, losing the race may have been for the best. Developing any new product is an incredibly expensive gamble. I had had doubts about how well accepted such a unit would be, especially after a friend kept calling my grand invention a "happy hat." Further, my colleague Dr. David Avery, looking at a prototype, had inquired, "Could anyone with sufficient self-esteem to actually wear that be all that depressed?" Sure enough, these devices did not exactly take the world by storm, although the reasons are not necessarily aesthetic. Today's light visors are more visually pleasing than my early, and arguably unfashionable, design. (See photo on the next page: a currently marketed light visor.)

The light visors fared well enough in early trials so that a multicenter, placebo-controlled study was conducted to test effectiveness. Three intensities of light were used. The lowest, at a mere 30 lux, was meant to be the placebo, since light box studies had found light below about 500 lux ineffective. However, all three light levels worked quite well. So, either dim light close to the eye

or a light visor at any light level is a very good placebo. We don't yet know which is the case.

Another reason for the low demand for light visors was that light boxes had become easier to use. Drs. Michael and Jiuan Su Terman at Columbia had developed a 10,000-lux light box. They found that by using four times as much light, subjects could get by with four times shorter exposure. Most of the boxes today deliver 10,000 lux, although they require that you sit closer than before—some sixteen to twenty inches. To make the closer distance more comfortable, some suggest raising the unit so that the light slants down at the eyes, as pictured on the next page.

This method re-creates the effect of bright sky in the upper visual field and reduces glare. Understand that you do not have to stare at the light directly; merely sit so that your eyes are not shielded from it by your hair or any other obstruction. You can look at the light directly as often as you want, but doing so is not

required. Thus, you can take your treatment while reading, watching television, talking. Some people even mount their light boxes on stands so that they can work out on a stationary bicycle or a stair-climber while getting their treatment.

Brighter light also reduced treatment time to a more manageable level. Although treatment time varies according to the individual, in the middle of winter some people may still require two hours. Further, researchers began showing that, in most cases, timing the light dose was not critical, although on average morning light has been superior and vital for some individuals. Thus, most people can take the light at their convenience, although not in the last few hours before bedtime, as the light may interfere with sleep.

With the briefer, more convenient light-box treatment, the light visor's portability became somewhat less impressive. However, convenience was soon to take a further leap as another innovation appeared—one that allowed people to get a form of light treatment as they slept.

THE CIVILIZATION OF DAWN

For what human ill does not dawn seem to be
an alleviation?
—THORTON WILDER   *THE BRIDGE OF SAN LUIS REY*

Beginning with the false hope of learning a language while one slept, the promise of using sleep time "productively" has beckoned Americans. As we'll see in chapter 6, this general lack of regard for sleep is a shame. However, use of dawn simulation—a special light exposure at the end of your sleep time—seems both to help sleep and improve mood.

In nature, light gradually decreases at dusk and slowly increases at dawn, giving most living creatures important cues upon which to entrain their body rhythms. Sunrise is nature's wake-up call, but most of us wake to a blaring alarm, and then, at least in winter, abruptly and harshly transform the darkness with the flip of a switch. Researchers have found healthier hormonal rhythms in animals exposed to gradual dawn and dusk transitions. It may seem surprising that we can detect dawn through closed eyelids, but our eyes, when dark-adapted, so increase in sensitivity that some people can literally detect a single light photon. This is one reason why we need curtains at night. Modern life's rude awakenings certainly contribute to the daily stress we face, but, more specifically, they may fail to support our fragile body rhythms.

Dr. Michael Terman introduced the first therapeutic use of dawn simulation to the scientific community. He built an elaborate lighting device capable of creating the gradual transition of light at dawn in the exact pattern found at any place on earth at any time. Thus, you could pattern your dawn after April in Paris or summer in Sioux City. The initial findings were extremely encouraging, but Dr. Terman's device was huge and cost thousands of dollars. Blaine Schaffer had independently developed a more practical simulator. Having personally struggled with winter mornings in Seattle for many years, he was determined to find some way to relieve his misery. Finally, he perfected a practical unit (Sun-up Dawn/Dusk Simulator) and made it available to researchers and eventually to the public. I was fortunate to be asked to become research director for his fledgling company, Pi Square, Inc.

DAWN SIMULATION AND SAD

In a series of five studies, Dr. David Avery and colleagues at the University of Washington conducted the first controlled trials of dawn simulation and found it to be an effective treatment for winter depression.

In 1993, along with Dr. Avery, I published a controlled study of dawn simulation in people who were not depressed but never-theless had various complaints about their winter functioning. Subjects showed marked improvement in energy, mood, social interest, productivity, quality of sleep, and quality of awakening. All sixteen subjects preferred waking to a simulated dawn over their usual approach. Most of the improvement occurred the first night, with maximum benefit reached within three days. On average, subjects reported cutting their energy and mood deficits by about half when using natural dawn simulation. The needed "time to get out of bed" dropped from 25 to 10 minutes, and the time to reach a reasonable level of alertness was cut by *more* than half. Which meant that by the time people arrived at work, they were generally functional.

My experience with patients reflects these results. Carol, a highly accomplished lawyer, had experienced recurring depressions since her early teens—once requiring hospitalization—and had been in therapy with me for several years. Each winter she would gain ten to fifteen pounds, finding sweets irresistible, sleeping about twelve hours per day, and, dragging her listless body through the day, barely able to concentrate. Moreover, she felt horrible and cried frequently. Mornings were the worst. This all began to change when she started using dawn simulation. Where previously she absolutely dreaded awakening on winter mornings, she now finds that she wakes up "chirping." Her depression, like that of most of my patients, also benefits from an antidepressant, but the simulator alone had already transformed her winters greatly. She intends never to go through another winter without a dawn simulator. Now planning a trip abroad, she told me that she will get an adaptor for her unit so that it will work on European current.

I often use one when traveling. When attending scientific conferences, I and a number of colleagues routinely pack a dawn simulator to aid alertness at early morning meetings. Without doubt the simulator is an improvement over the dreaded alarm clock, providing a far gentler herald of morning. However, as we'll see in chapter 6, you shouldn't need any help awakening in the first place!

DAWN SIMULATION POINTERS

Today's dawn simulators are compact, relatively inexpensive devices. They can be used with any incandescent lighting fixture, even multiple fixtures. Halogen bulbs, like the Sylvania Capslite, emit no humming noise and the light is a natural color. However, a few highly sensitive people may get a mild sunburn, as halogen bulbs emit a small amount of UV. Like natural sunrise, the light increases extremely slowly, then gradually accelerates to the point at which most people spontaneously awaken. However, someone deep in the throes of winter depression may want a backup alarm, just in case.

UV OR NOT UV?

Most people familiar with therapeutic lighting think first of "full spectrum lighting." That resonates well with our intention to re-create a more natural treatment, for clearly the sun is a full-spectrum lighting fixture. However, research has not shown a need for full-spectrum light in treating SAD. Here, quantity matters more than quality. Some wavelengths, such as green, do seem to work better than others, but basically one just needs lots of lux. Thus, light box manufacturers have for several years excluded the UV spectrum, due to proven risks to the skin and eyes.

Yet, it may be premature to dismiss UV. As we've noted, UV light falling on the skin stimulates vitamin D production and effectively treats several medical conditions including psoriasis. Further, isolated studies continue to report benefits of full spectrum lighting, such as a recent report from New York showing improved school performance in children. The final word is not in. For now, however, the current recommendation must be to use UV-shielded units. Given man's evolution under full-spectrum light, however, you may wish to hedge your bet and get at least a moderate amount of sunshine while continuing other treatments. We can never be certain that our re-creations of nature's recipes include every vital ingredient.

WHAT ABOUT SIDE EFFECTS?

All treatments that work produce side effects in some people, and light is no exception. However, nearly everyone tolerates light treatment quite well. As noted, dawn simulators are particularly well tolerated. People find light box or light visor sessions similar to their experience with sunshine: some get relaxed, others get energized. As with sunshine, some people get headaches or eye strain, especially at first. If this happens to you, simply back off the dosage by reducing either the time or the brightness. (In some units you can adjust the brightness; in others, you can adjust the distance from your eyes.) Then, gradually work back up to full exposure over the course of a week or so, as your tolerance increases.

Light treatment is usually stimulating, but if it reaches the point of agitation, simply reduce the dosage. Occasionally insomnia can develop, especially with light taken late in the day. If you experience this, try taking your treatment at an earlier time. If that does not work, again reduce the dosage.

Individuals with winter depression sometimes exhibit mild mania or hypomania in the spring, and some experience similar elevations of mood with light boxes and even dawn simulators. Generally this will be in proportion to the amount of light used, so I encourage people to reduce their exposure if they have any signs of excessive mood elevation. People with a history of true mania should be extremely cautious with anything that might cause a manic reaction; thus, they should use light therapy *only* under close supervision.

EYE DAMAGE RISK?

In the more than ten years that light therapy has been actively studied, we have no reports of eye damage. In Canada, Dr. Chris Gorman followed seventy-one patients who had been treated yearly with light therapy for five consecutive years and found no evidence of retinal damage in any patient.

Eye damage seems unlikely given that the summer sky can be ten times brighter than a 10,000 lux light box. However, some argue that the relatively more constant exposure of light treatment might be a concern. People who have retinal disease may be particularly at risk, and some practitioners recommend that, to be on the safe side, patients be examined by an ophthalmologist before starting light treatment. Eye damage is not an issue with dawn simulation, because standard low-level bedside lighting is employed.

GETTING THE LIGHT: BUYING, RENTING, OR AU NATUREL

Those considering light treatment have four choices: (1) use the sun; (2) build a light device; (3) rent light equipment; (4) buy a unit.

Oddly, we have much more evidence on the effectiveness of artificial light than we do on sunlight. A Swiss study by Dr. Anna Wirz-Justice found that walking outdoors was therapeutic, but that's hardly surprising. Of course sunlight works—when you can get it. But in many places, sunshine is a rare commodity. Also, if you respond best to morning light, in winter the sun may not rise early enough for you. In addition, rain and cold may cause you to skip needed sessions. With even a patch of blue, the sky probably offers 10,000 lux, which means you may need only about 30 minutes outside. But gray days provide only a few thousand lux, and at this level you'd likely have to spend several hours outdoors. For all these reasons, most people find light devices the treatment of choice.

For safety's sake, I recommend against building your own unit. Anyway, some models now cost less than $200, rivaling the expense of building your own. Certain companies will rent out light boxes, and some of the better-established companies have liberal return policies if the unit does not meet your needs. Sources for light boxes, visors, and dawn simulators are listed under Resources in appendix III. Those interested in learning more about seasonal depression will find Dr. Rosenthal's book *Winter Blues* eminently readable and informative.

•••

SUMMING UP

Most of us today are grossly light deprived. Light therapy has recently been rediscovered and it appears effective in the treatment of a number of disorders including depression and various circadian rhythm disturbances. The effectiveness of bright light therapy in winter depression is firmly established, and well-controlled study also supports the efficacy of dawn simulation. While light therapy may well boost serotonin, we know with certainty that it can control the release of serotonin's intriguing derivative, melatonin. Melatonin, which we will be discussing in chapter 5, is the chief emissary of the pineal, the long-mysterious gland at the center of the brain termed by Descartes as "the seat of the soul."

CHAPTER 5

MELATONIN:
THE NATURAL HEIR TO
SEROTONIN

The eyes are the windows of the soul.

—SHAKESPEARE

Let's now take a look at another stress-related neurochemical: melatonin. Actually a neurohormone, melatonin affects the entire body. In recent years scientists have discovered how, often in tandem with its "parent," serotonin, melatonin exerts its considerable influence.

Melatonin helps us adapt to basic environmental rhythms, such as night and day, bringing home the message that night has fallen and signaling the start of various mental and physical restorative processes. Without melatonin, these critical processes would fall out of sync with our periods of activity and rest. It also likely accounts for almost half of the body's temperature rhythm, producing much of the nighttime temperature drop required for sleep.

Melatonin is often confused with melanin, which produces the darkness of the skin and is essentially unrelated.

Melatonin enters any cell easily and is able to pass through the so-called blood brain barrier that stops serotonin, and many medications, cold. Thus, as is not the case with serotonin, we can boost brain levels simply by taking a melatonin pill. People have already started using melatonin to advantage—from battling cancer to simply getting a good night's sleep.

THE PINEAL—SOURCE OF MELATONIN

By converting serotonin, the pineal gland generates most of the brain's melatonin. Centuries ago Descartes labeled the pineal "the seat of the soul." Some Eastern philosophies consider it highly spiritual or mystical, associated with the so-called Third Eye. All of this suggests something of the intrigue surrounding the gland. By the 1800s scientists knew that a particularly elaborate blood vessel system favored the pineal. Yet, the gland's work itself remained mysterious until recently.

We now know that the pineal gland serves as a key modulator of the entire neurohormone system, gearing us to adapt to shifting environmental conditions. The pineal gland is light sensitive, allowing the brain to perceive the time of day. So, in a sense, the eyes truly are the windows of the soul!

THE SEROTONIN CONNECTION

A preclinical experiment, reported in the journal *Science* in 1968, determined that melatonin administration raises brain serotonin levels. In turn, melatonin levels increase when serotonin is given. Melatonin and serotonin interact, sometimes intensifying each other's effect on the body, at other times opposing each other. While scientists disagree about serotonin's effect on body temperature, it is clear that melatonin produces cooling—which, as I discussed in chapter 3, is a key stress-relieving function.

MELATONIN IN PSYCHIATRY

Melatonin is a critical antistress hormone. It inhibits the sympathetic nervous system, which generates the fight-or-flight response. It seems also to stimulate the opposing parasympathetic nervous system, which is associated with calming. Like Valium, melatonin increases the effect of GABA, an important neurochemical in mood regulation. Again, similar to serotonin, we see melatonin plays an overseer role, adapting the central nervous system to the environment and thereby reducing stress. Like serotonin, melatonin affects prostaglandins, but likely to an even greater extent. We will discuss the potentially critical role of prostaglandins in depression in chapter 11.

There is much interest about melatonin's role in psychiatric disorders. A recent preliminary study has shown that a skin medication (5-methoxypsoralen) known to have no significant biochemical action other than to boost melatonin was effective in relieving depression. Evidence also suggests that melatonin dysfunction plays a part in the type of depression known as melancholia, a depression so severe that sufferers often show almost no interest in anything. Other common symptoms include sleep disruption, disturbed body rhythms, agitation, and high body temperature. These symptoms certainly suggest a possible deficiency of melatonin in melancholia. Several studies have found that melancholics have low melatonin levels, though not all studies confirm this. More research is needed to determine whether low melatonin results from depression or perhaps causes it. In theory, however, melatonin has great potential for treating melancholia.

Low levels of melatonin are associated with PMS. We have seen a similar association for serotonin. As yet, melatonin has not been studied as a treatment, but studies using light therapy to treat PMS have shown clearly beneficial effects on the rhythm of melatonin release.

In studies of alcoholism, a condition thought to be genetically related to depression, some researchers have found lowered melatonin. Even in abstinent alcoholics, melatonin levels in the urine were depressed.

Melatonin probably plays a role in seasonal affective disorder (SAD), too. But rather than a simple deficit, it is more likely a matter of poor timing—too much released during the day, when melatonin should be almost completely suppressed. Since light suppresses melatonin, winter with its late sunrise may cause the melatonin rhythm to drift forward into the early morning hours, making it hard for people to awaken on time. In 1988, Dr. Norman Rosenthal and colleagues tried suppressing melatonin by administering Atenolol, a so-called beta-blocker, in an attempt to duplicate the therapeutic effects of light. Only a few patients benefited. Obviously, the technique needed refining.

In 1994 Dr. David Schlager took the next step, administering a short-acting beta-blocker first thing in the morning. He believed that the suppressant would simulate the natural light suppression of melatonin without going on to suppress melatonin later at night. This produced a good antidepressant response, but further trials are needed to confirm the work.

Dr. Wirtz-Justice, in Switzerland, found that administering a small dose of melatonin either in the morning or at night did not relieve winter depression. Though some did have improved sleep.

I recently began using melatonin on a limited basis in my practice. Some patients reported excellent improvement in their sleep. More exciting, some found that melatonin also reduced their stress and improved their mood. These anecdotal observations certainly make me eager to see further investigation of melatonin therapy for a range of stress-related conditions.

There is already substantial support for the use of melatonin in sleep disorders, jet lag—even cancer (see p. 55). But perhaps you will find the most exciting potential to be the fact that, in preclinical studies, administered melatonin slowed aging and lengthened life span.

MELATONIN: THE FOUNTAIN OF YOUTH?

Life would be infinitely happier if only we could be born at the age of eighty and gradually approach eighteen.
—MARK TWAIN

Melatonin levels correlate strongly with aging. In fact, age accounts for 90 percent of the variance. Think of these levels as the body's calendar. The timing and amount of the nightly surge of melatonin essentially tells the body how old it is. Or so several research groups studying melatonin and aging have concluded.

Probably no other factor accounts for as many aging effects as simply and elegantly as does degeneration of the pineal gland and the resulting drop in melatonin levels. Melatonin indirectly stimulates repair and maintenance throughout the body. Administration of melatonin can also delay puberty, delay menopause, and even extend longevity. All this points to the pineal as the *single best explanation* for the effects of aging.

Melatonin controls the release of a substance called arginine vasotocin (AVT), which is important for sleep. Very small doses of AVT cause rapid onset of slow-wave sleep—probably the body's most restorative sleep stage. As we age, we get less slow-wave sleep, possibly due to the falling melatonin levels. However, the pineal gland produces other hormones and neuromodulators involved in regeneration and repair, and their weakening may cause similar deterioration.

We also find substantial age-related drops in nighttime melatonin levels in laboratory animals. This melatonin deficiency in aging, across species, is accompanied by significantly greater sensitivity to oxidative stress, specifically the damaging attacks of free radicals, which are unstable molecules capable of stealing electrons from neighboring molecules. The damage caused particularly by hydroxyl radicals, which are strongly implicated in brain degeneration, builds horribly, exponentially, with aging.

Progressive neural damage by hydroxyl radicals might be regarded as one of the most significant irreversible processes of aging. Our "melatonin shield" against free radicals seems most important to the DNA in our cells, where, studies indicate, melatonin provides on-site protection. This DNA damage can not only kill the individual cells but may also lead to cancer or Alzheimer's.

Thus, boosting melatonin levels may help prevent these diseases and other effects of aging, including heart disease, poor sleep, and increased risk of depression.

MORE EVIDENCE ON THE MELATONIN/ AGING CONNECTION

Extensive research demonstrates that a low-calorie diet greatly increases the life span of various animals. Restricting calories helps preserve the melatonin rhythm against the tide of aging. This pineal effect is particularly striking since prolonged food restriction *decreases* the output of almost every other gland.

These findings encouraged researchers to attempt to slow the process by transplanting the pineal glands of young animals into old ones. This caused a 25 percent increase in life span. Other investigators simply added melatonin to the animals' drinking water, which resulted in a 20 percent increase in life span.

Taking melatonin also increases the release of growth hormone. Growth hormone remarkably improved the vigor of elderly men, causing a *fifteen year* decrease in apparent age in a famous study published in 1990 in the *New England Journal of Medicine*. This miraculous effect lasted the entire year of the trial but disappeared when the hormone treatment was stopped.

A true antiaging hormone should be effective throughout life, which melatonin is. Melatonin delays the onset of menopause in female rats when administered at midlife. It has even delayed adolescence in rats. Melatonin's role in triggering adolescence likely relates to one of its few ultra-high-dose side effects: contraception. Indeed, a melatonin-based contraceptive is currently under study.

MELATONIN AND THE BODY

Melatonin boosts immunity and so has drawn the attention of cancer researchers eager to explore the hormone's antioxidant powers.

In its role as an aggressive free radical scavenger, melatonin donates to "hungry radicals" an electron that they would otherwise steal from surrounding molecules. These molecules would in turn steal electrons from other molecules and the result would be a destructive chain reaction. Thus, melatonin prevents serious cellular disruption. Because it is extremely electroreactive, melatonin can donate an electron without starting a similar chain reaction. In this way, Melatonin is able to neutralize free radicals, which are generally thought to contribute to a range of conditions including arthritis, cancer, and heart disease. In one study, the highly potent carcinogen safrole, a powerful generator of the hydroxyl radical, could not produce *any* DNA damage after a small dose of melatonin (one thousand times lower than the carcinogen dose).

MELATONIN AS TREATMENT FOR CANCER

Clinical investigation of melatonin as a cancer treatment is only a few years old, but more than a dozen studies have already shown encouraging results. Hormonally dependent cancers, such as breast cancer and melanoma, have received much attention. Melatonin directly suppresses the growth of cultured melanoma cells in the laboratory. A number of clinical studies have found high melatonin levels in patients with various types of cancer; further, the highest level was found in those who had the best prognosis. Presumably, the pineal gland, faced with cancer, turned up melatonin production, and this led to the body's success in fighting the cancer.

The most remarkable cancer study, by Lissoni and colleagues, looked at eighty patients with advanced cancers of various types treated with a standard chemotherapy, Interleukin 2. Half the patients received 40 mg of melatonin daily for four weeks. Three of the melatonin-treated patients achieved complete remission. None of the control group did. Eight of the melatonin group showed partial improvement, compared to only one of the control group. The net result? Survival at one year was more than *three times greater* for the melatonin group.

Similar results turned up in a study of nonoperable brain cancers. Subjects received either supportive care alone or supportive care with daily supplements of 20 mg melatonin. Again, the survival at one year, as well as other objective measures, significantly favored the melatonin group. In addition, the quality of life was rated significantly better in this group. The beauty of melatonin, particularly when compared to other cancer treatments, is its lack of side effects. Although with very high doses, some patients reported fatigue—certainly a small price to pay.

HOW TO RAISE YOUR MELATONIN LEVELS

With melatonin at only a few cents a dose, most of us are extremely unlikely to resort to the ancient, though still used, Indian yogic practice of "amaroli"—the drinking of morning urine. Morning urine does contain a lot of melatonin metabolites, resulting from high nighttime levels. That the claimed health benefits of the practice (treatment of skin problems, cancer, etc.) might derive from melatonin is bolstered by the traditional Eastern teaching that the urine of prepubescent children works best. As we know, young children have the highest melatonin levels. At any rate, scientists have not investigated the effects of amaroli, so there may be a down side apart from the obvious.

Fortunately, there are many alternatives for raising melatonin levels.

DIETARY APPROACHES

Food deprivation raises melatonin levels in all tissues investigated, particularly those in the stomach and the brain. Researchers found that to produce this result in rats, a 40 percent reduction in food intake was effective. (For people to cut their consumption so drastically is a daunting if not impossible task. However, chapter 13 contains some suggestions.) In other studies of rats, it was found that a diet deficient in fish oil suppresses melatonin release. Thus, taking fish oil supplements or eating several servings of fish each week may be important. Other nutritional approaches include magnesium supplements, as magnesium stimulates the production of melatonin.

There are many other ways to raise your melatonin levels, such as by taking amino acid supplements, certain antidepressants but notably *not Prozac,* and various other medications. However, by far the most direct method is simply to take melatonin supplements.

MELATONIN SUPPLEMENTS

Currently, you can get supplements without a prescription. However, the FDA is pressuring manufacturers to stop the sale of melatonin supplements. This is because the FDA has not evaluated them for safety or effectiveness. However, dozens of clinical trials have clearly shown that melatonin supplements get good results and cause remarkably few side effects.

People have been taking melatonin since the 1960s, in some cases in doses one thousand times greater than that required to produce healthy blood levels for as long as four months (as a contraceptive) without ill effects. Some mild fatigue may be noted with these higher levels or with inappropriate daytime administration. In addition, extremely high doses result in sexual suppression, which is one of melatonin's natural roles in the body, as falling levels are believed to cause the onset of puberty. (However, at low doses, some of my patients have reported an increase in sexual response.) In another study, a daily 50 mg dose of melatonin (about one hundred times the amount needed to briefly reach youthful melatonin levels), taken for a week, produced only an increase in self-rated fatigue and a tendency to fall asleep more quickly. And the fatigue bothered only those subjects who took their dose in the morning. Finally, the cancer studies have often employed high doses over months of treatment with no ill effects.

Further study is needed to determine whether melatonin supplementation has long-term negative effects. Melatonin is, after all, a powerful hormone. While we have found only positives so far, treatments without significant side effects are rare in medicine. Determining the risk-benefit ratio for any treatment is a highly personal matter. For someone with advanced cancer, the dramatic potential of melatonin to extend survival and improve functioning will certainly outweigh fears of unknown long-term complications. Many elderly people facing degenerative conditions will probably feel the same.

I certainly hope that the choice remains with the individual, rather than the government withdrawing access until the FDA-required large-scale trials occur. I'm afraid that those trials simply may not take place. Melatonin supplements are not patentable, though special long-acting forms may be, and these would better simulate the body's nighttime melatonin levels. So it is possible that pharmaceutical companies might undertake the immense costs involved in testing and marketing.

LIFESTYLES AND MELATONIN

Exercise increases melatonin as long as it's not in the evening. Those committed to bulking up their melatonin should also avoid alcohol in the evening. One study found that drinking alcohol at night reduced melatonin levels by more than 40 percent—echoing folk wisdom that "hard living" speeds aging. Alcohol suppresses nighttime melatonin in animals, too.

Exposure to electromagnetic fields also seems to disrupt melatonin rhythms.

So living close to high-voltage power lines may be hazardous. Further, some household appliances may pose a risk, most notably electric blankets.

● ●

SUMMING UP

Good evidence supports the effectiveness of melatonin supplements in treating jet lag, insomnia, and even cancer. Preliminary findings suggest exciting potential for treating depression, stress, and various degenerative effects of aging. Further work is needed to replicate these results in controlled trials and to better establish the safety of long-term treatment. Melatonin deserves to join serotonin in the public's awareness. Together, these two provide protection against the onslaught of modern stress, helping us cope both emotionally and physically in the body's own natural way. Chapter 6 addresses many methods for optimizing sleep, including a detailed discussion on melatonin's role in this much neglected but vital component of stress relief and basic brain maintenance.

CHAPTER 6

SLEEP AS IT WAS MEANT TO BE

Sleep that knits up the raveled sleeve of care,
the death of each day's life, sore labor's bath,
balm of hurt minds, great nature's second course,
chief nourisher in life's feast.
—SHAKESPEARE *MACBETH*

Most of us rather enjoy sleeping, but too often we fail to take it seriously. Sleep seems a luxury, expendable in the face of life's demands. Once again our lifestyles impose a penalty—and a costly one.

OUR NATIONAL SLEEP DEBT

Early to bed and early to rise is a bad rule for anyone who
wishes to become acquainted with our most prominent
and influential people.
—GEORGE ADE

This type of advice reflects our general disregard for the importance of maintaining a natural sleep pattern and getting an adequate amount of sleep. Some estimate that our average sleep time has dropped a full 20 percent since the invention of the electric light.

Although some of the sleep deficit is assumed voluntarily,

insomnia plagues the United States. About one-third of all adults report a period of insomnia during the previous year, and half of these consider their sleeplessness "serious." Mary Carskadon, a professor of psychiatry at Brown University and one of the nation's leading sleep experts, says that most adults need eight hours of sleep. Yet, fully half the population gets less than this, with a quarter of us getting fewer than seven hours. According to other experts, more than 100 million Americans are sleep deprived. Teenagers now average two hours less sleep per night than they did a mere eight years ago—although they reportedly use school as a bedroom to make up for some of it.

According to recent data, four out of five psychiatric patients complain of insomnia. Despite the seriousness and prevalence of insomnia, however, few people mention this problem to their regular physician. Perhaps this is because telling a primary care doctor often causes little to happen.

SLEEP AND GENERAL MEDICAL PROBLEMS

Family doctors sometimes reassure patients that "no one ever died of not sleeping." Actually, in rare cases, sustained sleep loss *can* kill; several years ago, the *New England Journal of Medicine* reported a fatal condition called "familial insomnia." Sleeplessness can also lead to death in cases of untreated mania. Regular sleep loss may cause earlier death, according to research by Dr. Daniel Kripke.

Sleep difficulties are routinely missed or ignored by doctors. Dr. William Dement, head of the National Commission on Sleep Disorders, has estimated that 95 percent of cases of sleep disorders go undiagnosed. In the pages of *Science,* he despaired that a "river of patients are flowing past the unseeing eyes of doctors."

Doctors may not consider the indirect medical implications of sleeplessness, such as the increased likelihood of accidents. The National Commission on Sleep Disorders found that drunk driving causes *fewer* fatalities than sleepiness. Both the Chernobyl and Three Mile Island nuclear disasters occurred in the early morning hours, when the body wants, and needs, sleep. Such potentially devastating accidents are now frequently blamed on sleep-impaired worker performance. It's not just the rare Homer Simpson; about half of nuclear power plant shift workers fall asleep on the job at least once a week, according to Harvard's Dr. Charles Czeisler, director of neuroendocrinology at the Brigham and Women's Hospital in Boston.

While most people think that a captain's drunkenness caused the *Exxon Valdez* oil spill, the National Commission on Sleep Disorders says otherwise. The real problem was the severe fatigue of the ship's third mate, who was in charge at the time. The commission noted generally that sleep problems cost society about $50 billion a year, yet largely go unrecognized.

A study of more than five thousand Finnish men found that short sleepers had significantly more symptoms of coronary artery disease. An American Cancer Society study of more than a *million* people reported higher rates not only of cancer but of fatal coronary heart disease and stroke in the habitual short sleeper.

SLEEP AND THE PSYCHE

Depression is strongly tied to inadequate sleep. A major study reported that insomniacs had a forty-fold increased risk of developing major depression, compared with good sleepers. While studies show that we can adequately perform tasks with less than the optimum amount of sleep, our performance suffers if we lack too much sleep. Most of us feel the effects of even minor sleep loss on our mood. The majority of untreated insomniacs report being easily upset, irritated, or annoyed. Recall that irritability is one of the most consistent features of apparent serotonin deficiency.

The consequences of our national sleep debt are far ranging: damage to physical health, impaired sense of well-being, work-related injuries, even catastrophic accidents. Moreover, as suggested above, sleep loss is likely yet another of modern life's drain on serotonin.

SLEEP DEPRIVATION AS ANTIDEPRESSANT

Paradoxically, although insufficient sleep appears to be an important cause of depression, acute sleep deprivation is a well-established *antidepressant*. More than sixty studies have found that about 60 percent of depressed patients feel significantly better after a night without sleep. Hard to believe, but there is essentially no controversy about this—it works. The problem is that it doesn't work for very long. In the vast majority of cases, depression returned after the first period of sleep. However, preliminary studies show that the effect may be sustained by the use of medications such as lithium. If this is confirmed, the technique may catch on, but it is now rarely used.

A note of caution: Sleep deprivation is also one of the best ways to precipitate mania, so people who have a bipolar disorder should *not* try this except under extremely close medical supervision. This cannot be recommended as a self-help technique.

We know ongoing sleep loss can lead to depression. What could account for the implausible lifting of depression following a single sleepless night? I have proposed the theory that sleep generally interrupts the natural recovery process by shutting down serotonin activity. This has the same effect as giving people recently recovered from depression a serotonin-depleting mixture of amino acids (devoid of L-tryptophan), which will cause an immediate relapse. Not sleeping, in effect, leaves the system "on" overnight, allowing this recovery process to continue into the next day, without an interruption in serotonin function.

THE SEROTONIN CONNECTION

According to preclinical data, sleep deprivation can produce a 20 percent decrease in brain serotonin. Depriving animals of REM sleep, the sleep stage in which serotonin neurons are almost completely at rest, caused increases in appetite, sexual and locomotor activity, and fighting. We know that adequate serotonin inhibits all these behaviors. Serotonin neurons, like all of the body, require rest to recharge. Robbing ourselves of REM sleep forces the serotonin system into overtime, exceeding its ability to renew its stores. Of course, sleep deprivation is irritating in and of itself and may explain some of the behaviors mentioned above, but in a 1989 study, preliminary evidence suggested that sleep deprivation in people directly leads to lowered brain serotonin. Clinically, the serotonin depletion may also underlie the enormous increase in depression attributed to sleep loss.

BRAD'S CASE: SLEEP DIFFICULTIES

My patient Brad, mentioned earlier, has had terrible problems with sleep throughout his adult life. An extreme "night owl," he often finds himself out of sync with society and with the demands on his schedule. Even the strongest sleeping pills have consistently failed him. Brad's problem is called delayed sleep phase syndrome; his body rhythms are delayed several hours from the norm. Brad fails to fall asleep because he is trying to do so during his body's "forbidden zone"—the time of day when his body most wants to keep him awake. For most people, this would fall during the period known in television as "prime time."

To treat this type of insomnia, he must advance his body rhythm several hours. Melatonin is a key part of this body rhythm because it in turn entrains other body rhythms. Bright light, which suppresses melatonin, is capable of advancing this rhythm when taken in the morning. So, I instructed Brad to sit for twenty to thirty minutes in front of his light box first thing in the morning, and to carefully avoid bright light exposure at night when he wanted his melatonin rhythm to begin (around 8 P.M.). He was amazed at how effective this was; in fact, he found that if he got too much light, his rhythm advanced too far and he would fall asleep too early.

Still, he sometimes had trouble falling asleep. We found that melatonin supplements of approximately 1 mg in the evening were quite

> effective at helping him get to sleep. He observes that often, if he skips either part of the treatment, "there is nothing I can do that will get me to sleep."

NAPPING, EXERCISE, AND MELATONIN

The amount of sleep required by the average person is about five minutes more.

—MAX KAUFFMANN

How much sleep should you get? Some people need less than eight hours. Your daytime alertness will tell you this. If you get sleepy during the day, as many people do, you probably need more sleep. One clear indication is if dull repetitive work causes you to doze. Also, look at what happens when you wake up. If you need an alarm clock or a cup of coffee to get going, see if this is still necessary after you get another half hour or hour of sleep.

If your schedule requires a short night, try to get extra sleep the night before. Or, nap. (Some call this "power napping" to avoid any connotation of laziness.) Many famous achievers were blessed with the ability to nap midday, including Winston Churchill. Studies of international airline flight crews revealed that forty-minute naps by crew members halved the number of "microsleeps"—brief involuntary dozing—during the end of flights, that critical period of aircraft descent and landing. Consider yourself fortunate if you can nap.

Napping can make up sleep deficit, but timing is important. Usually, regular naps are best if they do not exceed thirty minutes. If you have been significantly sleep deprived, however, a longer nap is appropriate—especially if you take it during your body's natural "siesta time," between about noon and 4:00 or 5:00 P.M.

If you cannot nap, you may be able to counter drowsiness with physical activity. Exercise works well. Exposure to outdoor or bright light as soon as possible after you wake up will also help. Avoid alcohol and high carbohydrate foods, and in general eat lightly.

Protein-rich foods generally raise alertness, but don't stuff yourself.

You might also consider trying melatonin supplements. Several studies, including one by Richard Wurtman and colleagues at the Massachusetts Institute of Technology, have found that some poor sleepers, even those with chronic insomnia, benefited from supplements. However, remember that melatonin is a hormone and without FDA approval as a medication; thus, it must be considered somewhat experimental.

SPECIAL SLEEP PROBLEMS

While this section focuses on jet lag and shift-work-related sleep problems, reading it will no doubt provide useful ideas to anyone who has sleep difficulties or an irregular schedule.

Jet Lag

If you anticipate sleep problems caused by time zone changes—i.e., jet lag—on trips of only a few days, I recommend that you stay on your home time schedule. On longer trips, adapting to the new schedule usually works best. Travelers who get a lot of outdoor light adapt twice as fast as those who do not. If the new time zone requires earlier rising, exposure to bright light first thing in the morning will shift your internal clock to an earlier setting. Similarly, if you need to stay up later, exposure to bright light at the end of the day will adjust your body's circadian rhythm to a later time. Whichever direction you take, couple it with avoiding exposure to bright light at the opposite end of the day. Dawn simulation should also help you gear up to the new time zone.

If these natural methods fail, Ambien (zolpidem) or other sleep medication may be needed.

Several studies have confirmed that melatonin helps with jet lag. As with light dosing, the effect varies depending on when you take the hormone. Dr. Alfred Lewy has shown that melatonin administered in late afternoon or early evening advances the circadian rhythm, convincing the body that night has fallen earlier. Administered in the morning, melatonin delays this rhythm.

Several preliminary studies show marked relief of jet lag symptoms with dosages from 0.5 mg to 5 mg per day. The trials involved taking the melatonin supplement while still in the original time zone, but at the time of day when one would be going to bed in the destination time zone, and continuing bedtime dosage for several days following arrival.

Shift Work: Avoiding the Waking Nightmare

One out of five Americans maintains a schedule different from typical work hours.

As with jet lag, shift work disrupts the body's rhythms. But shift work is a lot worse. With jet lag, dawn and dusk signals in the new locale help entrain you to the new schedule. For the shift worker, however, nature and society collude to make entrainment to the night schedule virtually impossible. Even if one manages to adapt partially to the schedule over several weeks, most shifts rotate so frequently that significant adjustment is impossible.

How stiff a toll does shift work exact on society? We've already touched on some of the problems caused by fatigue, but in her excellent book *Bodyrhythms,* Lynne Lamberg echoes the estimate made by Martin Moore-Ede of Circadian Technologies Incorporated, a shift-work research and consulting firm, that shift-work problems specifically cost the United States more than $70 billion annually in medical expenses, property damage, lost productivity, insurance premiums, and so on. Researchers at the Karolinska Institute in Stockholm monitored railroad engineers driving trains equipped with sleep monitors; the men, who were often sleep deprived, fell asleep at the wheel for several minutes without realizing they had done so. Truck drivers, who are often on schedules that allow them little sleep, garner three times their share of accidents.

When authorities released the black box from the Korean Air Lines 747 jetliner shot down over Russian airspace, the tape revealed audible yawns. An obviously sleepy crew had made the apparent navigational error. On U.S. airlines, the schedules of international flights demand that pilots fly during their normal sleep period about half the time. A voluntary, confidential hot line for pilots to discuss "close calls" and other flight dangers receives more than 3,000 calls a month; one in five callers blames fatigue for the problem.

The most common shift-work schedule is one week on nights, then two days off; one week on evenings, then three days off. Two-thirds of shift workers complain of disrupted sleep and average a full hour less sleep than their day-shift counterparts. Night-shift workers are twice as likely to report gastrointestinal problems. They also self-medicate more, with caffeine and alcohol, and are twice as likely to smoke as day-shift workers. After being on the job for five years, a shift worker's odds of heart attack are double that of a day worker's. After fifteen years, the incidence is tripled! A final grim statistic: One in four shift workers report falling asleep behind the wheel, leading to a crash rate double that of day workers. Although there is no reliable data for humans, animal studies that simulated shift-work conditions showed a 20 percent reduction in life expectancy.

Help for the Shift Worker

Studies have shown that melatonin may improve both the sleep and the alertness of shift workers. In one study, police officers on night shift took 5 mg of melatonin at the desired bedtime (generally immediately after work). They experienced better quality sleep and felt more alert during their waking hours. However, performance tests generally showed little change. Perhaps fine-tuning the timing and the dosage, or combining melatonin with other approaches, will provide even better results.

Another problem for shift workers is that their internal temperature rhythm doesn't change to match their nighttime waking period because they still see enough daylight to keep them on a daytime rhythm. However, when Czeisler and colleagues exposed eight workers to bright light during their night shift and then had them sleep in bedrooms with blackout shades from 9:00 A.M. to 5:00 P.M., the workers' temperature rhythms adapted within a mere six days—despite the natural sunlight they got during their commute. A control group of shift workers without bright light or shades showed no adaptation.

The eight study subjects found the bright lights more enlivening than coffee. Further, the lights held off the grogginess that usually hit them between 4:00 A.M. and their 8:00 A.M. quitting time. Daytime sleep also improved. If you work nights and want to try using blackout shades, you must darken every part of the house you walk in during your "night" (dim light may be used so that you can navigate to the bathroom). Your sleep period should pass quietly and without interruption. After getting a full "night's" sleep, which for most people means eight hours, use the dawn simulation techniques described earlier.

You might first try using a sleep mask, a less expensive approach than blackout shades. You will need a mask that blocks out light completely, which means that you cannot use dawn simulation, at least for now. A sleep mask with tiny lights to provide a dawn light signal to entrain your rhythms is under development. You will really lock in the proper rhythm if, immediately following the simulated dawn, you get a good twenty or thirty minutes of bright light. Natural light is best, so if it's still light when you rise, go outside and walk or exercise for a while. Exercise itself helps to entrain the body to the rhythm of the day. Or, use a bright light box for thirty minutes.

Now, to solve the problem with the commute home from work. In an ideal world, companies would provide chauffeur service from work to home after a night shift with workers wearing welder's goggles to and from a darkened vehicle to avoid all bright light. Perhaps someday employers will realize the cost effectiveness of such a step, but don't hold your breath. In the meantime, try to get a friend or family member to drive you home under these conditions.

If all this sounds like too much trouble, remember that the cost to you, and to society, may be steep. We will all benefit when more attention is paid to the shift worker's need for a good "night."

NOT AS EASY AS IT LOOKS:
STEPS TO BETTER SLEEP

Whenever asked if he has slept well, the Canadian comic Steven Wright likes to reply, "No, I made a few mistakes." It may seem a joke that one could make mistakes in sleeping, but many of us do. So, sleep experts have developed a set of rules for "sleep hygiene." Remember, though, that insomnia is not an illness. Rather, it is a *symptom* of various underlying health, environmental, or behavioral problems. Practicing good sleep hygiene should help insomnia caused by the last two categories. If it does not, you may have a medical problem that requires attention.

Important elements of sleep hygiene;

1. Use the bedroom only for sleeping and sex.
2. Set a time for going to bed and a time for rising that stays the same weekdays *and* weekends (if you must go to bed late on weekends, try to get up at the same time and take a nap at midday).
3. Develop a relaxing bedtime routine—a light snack may help; avoid stimulating TV, reading material, or conversation.
4. Exercise regularly, preferably in the late afternoon or very early evening. Be sure to leave enough time (five hours, ideally) for your body to cool off; if you exercise within a couple of hours of bedtime, your sleep will be poor, since you'll still be in the overheated mode.
5. Avoid substances that alter physical or mental states—caffeine and even cigarettes—near bedtime. Among the worst is alcohol, which can disrupt sleep all night. You might try a traditional relaxing ritual from Japan—the evening hot bath; but be careful to allow enough time to cool off before retiring.
6. Make your bedroom "sleep central," quiet and dark. Fabric stores sell blackout material, or you can buy ready-made shades. A simpler solution, though it doesn't allow dawn simulation, is to wear a sleep mask.

Don't overlook that last item, making your bedroom "sleep central." It's critical. Your room should have no extraneous light sources (although natural moonlight is okay). Room temperature should be cool. A cool head tends to promote good sleep. Quiet is the rule. Alarms should be as gentle as possible—the anticipation of a jarring alarm works against peaceful sleep. Waking to the natural light of dawn is best. If you must get up in the night, use the least amount of light needed to navigate safely.

If despite these steps you still cannot sleep, after about fifteen minutes get out of bed, go to a different room, and involve yourself in nonstimulating activity until you feel drowsy. Then, and only then, return to bed. While waiting for drowsiness, avoid all stimulation, most particularly bright light and snacking. If you simply stay in bed tossing and turning, you may come to associate your bed with this struggle, and this unpleasant association will not help.

Bright light treatment promises to improve sleep. Particular situations call for more specific timing of light, however. If you have trouble falling asleep, avoid light in the later part of the day because it tends to stimulate, as noted in the discussion of shift work. If you have trouble rising, try a strong dose of light early on to rekey your waking rhythm.

Avoid sleeping pills. If you must use them, limit the period of use generally to no more than a week or two. Sleeping pills are best for isolated sleep difficulties such as those due to travel or to stressful events. In any case, most sleep medications lose their efficacy when taken steadily, except perhaps for the relatively new Ambien. I find it by far the least likely to cause trouble with habituation, withdrawal, and rebound insomnia. For those suffering severe chronic insomnia characterized by abnormal sleep-wake rhythms, case reports indicate that vitamin B-12 may help.

Persistence and patience with sleep hygiene will usually produce results. Again, unresponsive chronic problems require medical evaluation. Your doctor may refer you to a sleep specialist. The names of specialists in your area may be obtained by writing to the National Sleep Foundation, 122 South Robertson Boulevard, Los Angeles, California, 90048-3208.

• •

SUMMING UP

Many people simply do not appreciate the importance of sleep, although, as we have seen, it is vital to both mind and body. Without adequate sleep, rates of depression soar, as do other often lethal conditions such as heart disease. Yet, millions of Americans spend more time each day watching television than sleeping. Add to this the millions who want to sleep but can't, and we see that inadequate sleep is clearly one of America's leading health problems. Having covered a variety of ways to improve sleep, ranging from basic sleep hygiene to use of therapeutic lighting, we now see that it's usually possible to avoid the use of medications for this purpose. Exercise is another such ally of a good night's sleep. In chapter 7 we'll explore other benefits of exercise, including some novel ideas about its "sedentary" forms.

CHAPTER 7

EXERCISE AND YOUR BRAIN: PUMPING NEURONS

Whenever I get the urge to exercise, I lie down
until the feeling passes.
—ROBERT MAYNARD HUTCHINS

"Sure," you say, "exercise is supposed to be good for me. But margarine was supposed to be good for me too, and now, after years of culinary compromising, I hear butter may be better after all." If you think that nutritionists can't be trusted, you might suspect that the conventional wisdom on exercise is wrong too. Wasted effort or worse. Maybe the human heart has only so many beats; perhaps it's best to bang the drum slowly.

Is there hard evidence that exercise is good for you? Does it improve your mood or help you deal with stress? In this chapter you'll find that exercise can indeed be very beneficial, especially certain types of exercise—including one that may surprise you, which I term "sedentary exercise."

THE SEROTONIN CONNECTION

Exercise has a clearly established ability to raise serotonin. Indeed, exercise may briefly raise serotonin levels to a point of mild "overdose." We think that excessive serotonin levels contribute to the sensation of fatigue that follows heavy exertion. High levels might also account for the nausea sometimes felt, especially by those who are out of shape, after extreme exertion. These symptoms match those found in those people who take high doses of Prozac.

Ninety minutes on a treadmill doubles brain serotonin levels, according to one preclinical study. Another similar study revealed that chronic exercise increased not only serotonin production but also serotonin activity in the cerebral cortex; further, this improvement lasted for weeks after training stopped. This is important because, as we've seen, any stress can acutely stimulate serotonin release, but exercise produces *lasting* elevations. A study of athletes exercising to the point of fatigue found that those who took Paxil, a serotonin booster similar to Prozac, became fatigued 20 percent sooner than the group taking a placebo, supporting the idea that excessive serotonin levels may generally play a part in causing fatigue.

That serotonin rises in response to exercise makes sense, because a primary function of serotonin is to prepare the body for physical activity. Since physical activity inevitably generates body heat, if serotonin can indeed cause cooling, as I have argued, serotonin's greater presence to handle this heat would then be expected.

Dr. Barry Jacobs of Princeton University has discovered that some types of muscle movement generate more serotonin than others. The most effective motions are repetitive ones, especially chewing or licking. Jacobs originated the suggestion that repetitive motions commonly engaged in by those with obsessive compulsive disorder may be a form of self-medication via the serotonin system.

Perhaps the finding that repetitive movement stimulates serotonin explains the calming effect of activities such as knitting. Indeed, one wonders if the movement of a nervous toe, or foot tapping, is not only a symptom of anxiety but nature's cleverly engineered antidote. Given the extra effectiveness of repetitive mouth movement such as chewing in stimulating serotonin, I was struck by a recent report of one of my patients. Carol clearly recognized a connection between chewing and stress reduction. She had given up gum chewing more than forty years ago, deeming it an unpleasant habit. However, in the throes of an unusual combination of stresses in her life, she started chewing again. She found it so effective as a stress balm that she kept it up until her life settled down.

Indeed, since learning of this "jaw connection," it is hard for me to look at baseball players' famed gum or tobacco chewing without making the serotonin connection. Baseball certainly provides more opportunity for waiting and worrying than most sports, and baseball players are noted for an assortment of repetitive ritualistic behaviors in addition to chewing.

A SEDENTARY SOCIETY

Americans are in the habit of never walking
if they can ride.
—LOUIS PHILIPPE, DUC D'ORLÉANS

It has only gotten worse since Philippe made this observation back in 1798. Fewer and fewer Americans get regular exercise, including young people. Today, only 37 percent of our high-school kids get even moderate regular exercise. That's a decline of more than 60 percent since 1984. Once again we see modern life sharply diverging from ancestral life. Our forebears could chase an antelope across the hot savanna plains till the prey collapsed from exhaustion—a feat of which some aboriginal peoples remain capable. Luckily, we do not depend on such superb conditioning for our dinner. Instead, most of us earn our dinner by driving to work, sitting in a chair all day, then going home to eat and read or watch TV. This lifestyle clearly contributes to today's serotonin deficiency.

Not only do we get less exercise these days, even compared to the 1970s and 1980s, but recent advice even encourages this. The latest government recommendations are that thirty minutes of even mild activity, such as housework, meets most health requirements. While this gentle exercise may avoid the most drastic health conditions, it is simply not enough to get optimal serotonin-enhancing effects. However, for those unhappy at the idea of tiring exercise, any exercise is better than none, and if nothing else, you can always take up gum chewing—a time-tested but at this point scientifically unproven stress reliever.

DEPRESSION, ANXIETY, AND STRESS

Almost anyone who has worked out knows firsthand the melting away of tension and aggression that exercise provides. Dozens of studies confirm that exercise fends off depression and anxiety and improves stress tolerance. In some cases, exercise has matched the effectiveness of standard therapies. Although aerobic exercise has the best established effect on mood, an increasing number of studies point to similar benefits from nonaerobic exercise, specifically weight training.

The effect of exercise is immediate. Research indicates that twenty to forty minutes of aerobic exercise temporarily lessens anxiety and improves mood, an effect that lasts several hours. Regular exercise somewhat elevates the mood of "normal" people, but it is of most benefit to those who have significant anxiety and depression. Energy and concentration also increase. Both aerobic and nonaerobic exercise reduce anxiety, but it seems that aerobic exercise does the better job. However, it may be a different story with self-esteem. A study comparing aerobic exercise with weight training found them equally effective at reducing depression but concluded that weight training resulted in greater enhancement of self-image.

Perhaps you're thinking, "Oh, I'm too old for weight lifting." Forget it. Weight training helps folks as old as ninety! Both men and women at this age were shown to respond to training with a greater than 200 percent increase in strength.

In a study comparing exercise with psychotherapy and medication, all three methods were found to cause significant improvement in depressed patients treated for twelve weeks and then followed for nine months. The group who walked and jogged did as well as or better than those who received psychotherapy. A second study duplicated these findings, again shedding a less favorable light on psychotherapy; on follow-up, more of the psychotherapy patients reported relapse of their symptoms.

Long-term exercise programs in conjunction with medication have also helped seriously depressed patients. Therapists treating alcoholics have successfully used exercise as supplemental therapy. Not surprisingly, given the serotonin connection, an important exercise dividend is improved ability to cope with stress. In a study of adolescents, stress produced debilitating effects on physical and emotional health among those who rarely exercised. Comparable stress levels did not affect those who exercised regularly. Thus, we see exercise serving as a stress "immunization."

Many of my patients find exercise a critical part of their recovery. Recently I saw a man named Sean, who for years had used running as an antidepressant until an injury took him off the road. While he couldn't run, Sean's depression had grown quite serious, so he came to me. We found that Prozac worked as well as the natural antidepressant of running, but Sean clearly preferred running.

Some mental health practitioners believe that exercise can increase anxiety or even induce panic attacks. On the contrary. While it is true that direct infusions of lactic acid can cause attacks in those suffering panic disorder, the body handles the lactic acid that builds up in muscles after exercise very differently. The concern is shown in error by a report on some seventy thousand exercise stress tests at the Cooper Clinic in Dallas. Not one instance of panic attack occurred. Indeed, highly anxious individuals typically experience a *reduction* in anxiety following vigorous exercise.

When highly stressed, many people find solace in eating. The biological explanation for this remains unclear. We now have evidence that eating carbohydrates temporarily improves serotonin function, but this occurs too slowly to account for an immediate mood benefit. At any rate, eating carbohydrates is no solution— you may feel better briefly, but the blood sugar effects from eating such foods will cripple your feeling of well-being over the long haul—as explained later, in the chapters that address nutrition.

Perhaps the comfort derived from eating stems in part from the chewing motion, which, as noted earlier, enhances serotonin.

It's important to understand that these exercise benefits are separate from what has been called the runner's high (although no doubt achieving the runner's high will temporarily improve mood). The high is described as a sense of euphoria occurring typically after running many miles; it is typically only the well-conditioned, "serious" runners who experience the high.

The best known physiological explanation for the runner's high concerns the body's endorphin system, through which natural opiumlike substances are thought to be released during exercise. However, the relationship between mood change and endorphin secretion is unclear. Naloxone, a drug that eliminates the effects of opiate drugs, has failed to reverse exercise-induced mood peaks. Since Naloxone is the gold standard for identifying the effects of narcotics, including ones produced naturally in the body, this failure probably means that endorphins do not tell the whole story. Further, some researchers question whether endorphins can even cross the blood-brain barrier. If endorphins cannot, they are unlikely to affect mood, so the high remains a bit of a mystery.

PHYSICAL WELL-BEING

Obviously, exercise promotes health. How much exercise is the question. The new government recommendations contain some good news for those who dislike exercise. The old standard of thirty minutes a day, five days a week, can now be accomplished through walking, vacuuming, gardening, and the like. In other words, daily activities. What's more, this activity need not take place at one time. It just has to total 30 minutes per day.

These relaxed guidelines may in part simply reflect the government's belief that more-obtainable goals will encourage people to make the effort. But more than a dozen studies support this low level of exercise as sufficient to affect longevity, general health, and risk of heart disease or stroke. Further, in a Stanford study, subjects exercised on stationary bicycles for either half an hour continuously or, in a second group, for two fifteen-minute periods. Surprisingly, the two groups showed virtually identical improvements in their levels of fitness. I'm afraid, however, that studies do not support the idea that vacuuming relieves depression; studies focusing on mood effects have generally used more rigorous activity.

Another physical benefit of exercise is lowered insulin levels. Keeping insulin low is one of the most important things you can do for your body. Among other unsavory behavior, insulin stimulates fat storage. Note that exercise is one of the few things consistently associated with reducing body fat—unlike most dieting.

We have not yet heard the final word on how much exercise is required for the best physical health. One study, which appeared after the release of the new government guidelines, followed a large group for twenty-three years and found benefits only among those who had the greatest amount of physical activity. These subjects averaged five and a half hours of physical activity per day, generally due to jobs that involved physical exertion.

Thus, it may still turn out that the ideal amount of exercise for both brain and body is similar, and that more is better . . . up to a point.

A NOTE OF CAUTION

Athletes generally score higher than any other population segment on such factors as emotional adjustment and sense of well-being. As with medication therapy, it is possible to "overdose" on exercise. This is common among competitive endurance athletes but also occurs in recreational athletes. Overdose results from intensified training or "overtraining," a routine part of preparing for competition. The athlete intentionally overtrains for several weeks, then rapidly tapers off. Generally, athletic performance surges beyond normal during the tapering phase, but in some cases performance either plateaus or deteriorates. This is known as "staleness" and often results in behavioral problems, sleep disturbances, and emotional distress. Depression is the primary psychological problem. The only known cure is rest, sometimes for several weeks, although staleness can last up to six months. Some regular exercisers become "exercise abusers," people who place too high a priority on exercise, compromising their work, family, relationships, even health. Whether endorphins could explain this "addiction" is unclear. But, as with other kinds of addiction, exercisers forced to interrupt their program for whatever reason may experience withdrawal symptoms such as depression, anxiety, restlessness, irritability, nervousness, guilt, muscle twitching, and bloating.

Of course, exercising poses some risk of injury, so we might consider relative injury rates as well. In a study undertaken at the Center for Sports Medicine at Saint Francis Memorial Hospital in San Francisco, the injury rates of a thousand people involved in physical fitness programs at local health clubs were evaluated. The injury rates for sports like running were more than ten times greater than those for weight lifting. Outdoor runners also face a significant threat from automobiles—a danger not generally found in a weight room.

TIPS FOR A SEROTONIN WORKOUT

1. Find an exercise you enjoy. No surer path to failure exists than forcing yourself to engage in exercise that you find unpleasant.
2. Although we have more evidence on mood improvement resulting from aerobic exercise, it appears that any form of exercise is helpful. Again, weight training may be more beneficial for self-esteem, not to mention the safety aspect.
3. Avoid exercising within two or three hours of bedtime, especially if you have insomnia.
4. The more the better—up to a point. Moderate exercise for thirty to sixty minutes every other day should produce a marked improvement in your sense of well-being. To ensure good results, aim for at least two and a half hours per week. You probably need to reach the point of fatigue to get the maximum stimulation of serotonin, so you must weigh this benefit against the disadvantages of getting stale,

overheated, becoming prone to injury, exercise addicted, or just plain tired.

• •

SUMMING UP

Extensive evidence shows that exercise relieves stress-related conditions and aids general physical well-being. We've seen that a strong, direct connection exists between exercise and higher serotonin levels. Our lack of exercise almost certainly explains some of modern life's serotonin drain. Yet, for many, exercise is a bitter pill to swallow; for them, perhaps the more sedentary approach to exercise may hold some appeal. Most of the techniques we will discuss require little if any exertion. In chapter 8, for example, you'll find one that requires you to do nothing more than breathe. Indeed, treatment can even take place while you sleep.

CHAPTER 8

THE BODY ELECTRIC

*It was one of those hot dry Santa Anas that come
down through the mountain passes and curl your hair and
make your nerves jump and your skin itch. On nights like
that every booze party ends in a fight. . . .
Anything can happen.*
— RAYMOND CHANDLER *"RED WIND"*

Like most things today, our bodies run on electricity. It should
come as no surprise, then, that the electromagnetic forces that
bathe the earth affect us profoundly. Yet, it is always hard to accept
the role of the invisible—witness the initial resistance to the germ
theory. We now accept that electromagnetic waves might be hazardous. Cancer rates among electric-line workers and those with
similar jobs appear elevated. That electromagnetic waves may also
affect our behavior is quite distressing, especially given that we are
constantly exposed to types of electrical power that have no prece-
dent in nature, and to air nearly devoid of vital negative ions.
Nonetheless epidemiologic data suggest that electromagnetism
and the related influence of ionized air can cause the sort of
impulsive, moody states discussed throughout this book.

ELECTROMAGNETISM

While mysterious in influence, electromagnetism is easily measured. For example, we know that levels leap during the forma-

tion of sunspots—dark patches of relative coolness on the sun's surface—which peak every eleven years or so. The sun's electromagnetic waves also affect the earth's electromagnetic field, which varies in intensity according to latitude and longitude and which occasionally undergoes fluctuations called geomagnetic storms. After peaking, electromagnetic levels drop, and the day of the falloff is often the most dangerous period in terms of associated self-destructive behavior.

The Serotonin Connection

While no studies have measured changes in serotonin during electromagnetic influence, so many behaviors directly related to serotonin rise following electromagnetic upheaval that I believe a serotonin connection is strongly implicated. Statistics show that in addition to accidents and migraines, seizure activity, circadian rhythm disturbances, alcohol abuse, and other self-destructive behaviors, including suicide, all increase in association with sudden changes in electromagnetic levels. Further, after a lag of a week or two following geomagnetic storms, we see increased hospital admission rates for certain psychiatric disorders. Since these storms are known to affect the ions in our air, later in this chapter we will review evidence of the ions' effects on serotonin.

Researchers have documented alterations in the structure of the nerve synapse within the pineal gland during geomagnetic storms. Geomagnetic activity clearly decreases nighttime melatonin levels, and electromagnetic influences in general can disrupt melatonin rhythm. Recall the important role the pineal plays in manufacturing melatonin and the many tasks this hormone performs, including direct interactions with serotonin.

The Mind and Electromagnetism

The psychological influence of electromagnetism can be deadly. Along with increasing accident rates and alcohol/drug abuse— obviously a potentially fatal pair—one study showed that suicide rates doubled on days of falling geomagnetic activity compared to days of rising levels.

Other associations prove more cheerful, however. A few years ago, William Randall analyzed births from 1909 to 1985, in both the United States and New Zealand, and found that the rhythm of human conceptions correlated with the rhythm of the eleven-year sunspot cycle. Perhaps this helps create a sort of human generational rhythm. Electricity can also help nonsexual performance. A recent study exposed thirty volunteers to a 60-hertz electromagnetic field, which invoked changes in the brain's electrical state and resulted in fewer errors on a timed performance test.

A fascinating set of findings suggests that electromagnetic influences at the time of birth affect adult behavior. Two separate groups of investigators have confirmed this unlikely association, linking adult anxiety levels with high geomagnetic activity around the time of birth. Studies of rodents exposed briefly to electromagnetic waves at the time of birth demonstrated similar permanent "character change."

Psychiatric researchers exploring the therapeutic potential of electromagnetism have had encouraging results. Dr. Mark George and colleagues at the NIMH have reported that alternating magnetic fields were able to produce elevated or depressed mood depending on which side of the brain was exposed. Applications in the treatment of depression are being investigated. Radio waves have helped patients with chronic insomnia. The treatment involves placing a tiny radio receiver under the tongue for about twenty minutes. This may sound somewhat bizzare, but evidence indicates that it may be a better treatment than sleeping pills. This same approach is being studied by Dr. Gary Sachs and others at Harvard as treatment for anxiety. The device is currently under review by the FDA and may be available for clinical use in the near future. However, this does not mean you cannot benefit now from our growing knowledge of electromagnetism. One of the principal ways electromagnetism is believed to affect behavior is through changes in air ions: devices designed to generate small negative air ions, which are believed to be beneficial to mood and health, are discussed later in this chapter.

Electromagnetism and the Body

Electromagnetic influence on the body, as on the mind, may be fatal. A review of hospital deaths over a period of fourteen years, particularly deaths involving cardiovascular disease, showed a highly significant correlation with monthly electromagnetic levels. As in the area of psychology, physicians have also found therapeutic uses for electromagnetism. Possibly electromagnetic fields, such as those created by some electric blankets, may be related to certain cancers. But such fields may also *treat* cancer. Preliminary data from a recent study suggest treatments utilizing electrical currents can aid in controlling malignancy. A recent review article in the *Journal of Cellular Biochemistry* summarized other medical applications: the treatment of diabetes, heart attacks, and strokes, and faster nerve regeneration and wound healing. Numerous reports document effectiveness of pulsing electromagnetic fields in treating osteoarthritis and in postsurgical orthopedic healing.

NEGATIVE IONS

One thing we do know about sunspot activity: It affects the ionization of our air. Sometimes we witness this in the form of bad radio or TV reception. We consider air "ionized" when the air molecule either loses or gains an electron, which leaves the air particle either positively or negatively charged. The journals *Science* and *Nature* have published studies demonstrating the biological activity of the so-called small ions. Only the *small* negative ions actually change us biologically. Although exactly how they do so remains controversial.

Once again, modern life has revised natural conditions. Industrialization has polluted our air in two ways: by adding electromagnetic waves from machines and wiring, and by sullying the air with particulate matter. The latter robs our air of the beneficial small negative ions. This, in combination with our breathing recycled indoor air, lowers our intake of biologically active air ions to nearly nothing. Measurements taken alongside major roadways find only *one-twentieth* as many negative ions as are found in clean country air, which, even without knowing of studies showing the benefits of these ions, we think of as "good" and healthful.

If the beneficial effects of negative ions are so well established, why don't we see more ion generators in homes and office buildings? Possibly because until recently ionizers failed to reliably generate biologically active small negative ions.

Nature also provides another type of ion. Warm wind moving over dry land produces positive ions—which are far from "positive" for us. One famous example of such a wind is the foehn of Europe, which when blowing brings irritability, suicide, violence, and accidents. The Santa Ana winds of California cause similar effects. By now these behaviors should be a familiar calling card: that of disturbed serotonin function.

The Serotonin Connection

Positive air ions actually have a fairly complex effect. They can increase serotonin, but only in the blood, and high blood serotonin often produces undesirable effects such as agitation, fatigue, and nausea—as do overly high Prozac levels. In contrast, negative ions apparently augment brain serotonin function, which likely explains their good effect.

An article in *Science* stated that ions specifically altered serotonin metabolism in humans. Japanese findings that subjects exposed to negative ions had consistently lowered rectal temperature also suggests to me serotonin involvement, given serotonin's proposed role in cooling. Further evidence supporting a role for serotonin is the significant reduction in seizure threshold among humans and rats during heightened geomagnetic activity accompanying a solar eclipse. A lab study published in *Brain Research* reported that neuron responsiveness to serotonin increased with exposure to negative ions but fell with exposure to positive ions. This likely explains the beneficial effects of negative ions on critical central nervous system function. If we look merely at the blood, we see the opposite picture—but, as mentioned before, blood serotonin is almost worthless in assessing serotonin activity in the brain.

A recent study exposed subjects to positive air ions. Most subjects underwent mood changes characterized by increased tension and irritability—reactions typical of reduced brain serotonin function. Notably, in relation to the cooling theory of serotonin, these "ion sensitive" subjects, in contrast to the others, showed depressed sweat rates.

CARMEN'S CASE

As a dancer, Carmen listens to her body. She readily feels the impact of her environment, but for most of her adult life that impact had been devastating. Each year around October she would brace herself for the onslaught of winter. Finally, several years ago, she arrived at my office in early March, feeling that without help, she could not endure waiting any longer for spring to arrive. She had gained ten pounds, had uncontrollable cravings for carbohydrates, and often slept much of the day. When she was up, her usually limber body felt leaden. It was hard for her even to move, but most of the time she didn't want to anyway. She was extremely apathetic, especially when it came to any kind of social activity. Not only had her body betrayed her, but her mental powers were similarly impaired. This was more than just a state of hibernation; she was in extreme emotional pain, feeling at times that she didn't want to live with such pain, but, as a parent, she rejected suicide as an option.

She began an integrated program of medication, nutrition, and light therapy, and within several days she was feeling much better (rapid response is typical with SAD). However, over the next few years, despite the combined treatment, she still at times dragged herself through winter. This past year, thirty minutes of exposure each morning to a negative ion generator was added to her program. She found that this not only seemed to help her mood but was generally energizing and refreshing. For the first time in more than a decade, Carmen has actually enjoyed winter.

Mood and Ions

Waterfalls and the seashore, which are dense with negative ions (because moving water ionizes air), are pleasant places to be.

Similarly, the high negative ion content of air after a thunderstorm often engenders a feeling of well-being. Conversely, positive ions, associated with certain winds and with certain electromagnetic activity, make us feel irritable, destructive.

An analysis of more than two thousand crisis evaluations at a walk-in clinic revealed that rape increased with solar flare activity. A 1992 study found increased psychiatric admissions for depression in men only, following geomagnetic disturbances. This is strange because most evidence shows that women are far more likely to be "ion sensitive." Researchers have linked positive ions to increases in suicide, crime, industrial and automotive accidents, and impairment in central nervous system function.

Conversely, some controlled studies in humans have found that negative ions reduce irritability and depression and improve cognitive performance and energy. Moreover, a pilot study of manic patients yielded extremely encouraging results—seven of these normally agitated patients actually fell asleep during ion exposure. Sleep is a rare and precious commodity in manic patients. This report, in *Biological Psychiatry,* also found a calming effect induced by negative ions, along with a sense of well-being.

Yet other research reveals no effects from the use of air ionizers. This might be caused by unreliable ion generators, used until recently, or by employing too low a dose.

In early 1995, ion therapy gained new stature with the publication of Michael and Jiuana Su Terman's work at Columbia Presbyterian. Having become interested in ionization from recent work of another prominent investigator, Dr. Charmane Eastman, the Termans designed an elegant study comparing light therapy with various levels of ion exposure. They found that ion treatment wrought antidepressant benefit equal to that of light therapy. Moreover, they found that only higher levels of ionization could cause this effect—which helps explain the failures of some previous studies. The ineffective low-level ion dose made a superb placebo because subjects could not tell what level of ion generation they were getting. This study, if confirmed in other studies such as those of Eastman, suggests that we will see an increase in the use of negative ions in the treatment of SAD and other conditions.

Ions and the Body

Preclinical work has established the beneficial effect of negative ions on healing gastric ulcers. Effectiveness has also been shown in healing skin conditions. Studies of the bacterial killing action of negative ions have been published in both *Science* and *Nature*. Preclinical studies have demonstrated quicker recovery from respiratory infections with exposure to negative ions. One air ionizer has been approved abroad as a medical device for the treatment of respiratory problems. This and similar units are also available in the United States but are sold as air cleaners rather than as medical devices.

The early findings with ulcers were replicated in a 1988 study of twenty-eight students who had a history of ulcers when undergoing stress. Using an ion generator, 75 percent of the subjects avoided an expected crisis of gastrointestinal pain when taking their winter exams. These effectively treated twenty-one patients were followed for one to two years, and the preventive treatment was again applied a month before winter exams; in most, the treatment maintained its efficacy.

The New Generation of Ion Machines

As mentioned, levels of biologically active ions in city air are almost 90 percent lower than country levels, and in an air-conditioned office, levels decrease another six fold. A good ion generator can restore the kind of air we are designed to breathe. Appendix III, Resources, provides sources for air ionizers. Older units might do little or no good other than simply to clean the air, because they may not generate sufficient small negative ions.

Even with the new small-ion generating machines, one must sit within a few feet to garner any benefit. The Termans' successful antidepressant results were based on subjects receiving nearly three million ions per cubic centimeter and sitting three feet from the ionizer for thirty minutes daily for nearly three weeks. None of the subjects reported any side effects. The unit they are now using is much more affordable, but subjects must sit only a foot and a half away to get the same ion dose.

●　●

SUMMING UP

The response of our bodies to electromagnetic energy of various sorts is only beginning to be explored. Much more research in needed, but already well-controlled studies have established the considerable potential of such treatments for mood disorders. Most of these technologies are not yet available in the United States. However, units that appear to generate biologically active negative air ions reliably are now available, and good research is beginning to support their effectiveness. Ionization therapy research remains preliminary but shows tremendous potential without significant safety concerns. Rather, the major safety concerns lie with the air we breathe normally. Once again, our modern lifestyles seem the greater risk.

CHAPTER 9

VITAMIN, MINERAL, AND AMINO ACID SUPPLEMENTS

Food is an important part of a well-balanced diet.
—FRAN LEBOWITZ

VITAMINS

Today we hear a range of opinion, often strident, about vitamins. It brings to mind Bertrand Russell's remark: "The most savage controversies are those about matters as to which there is no good evidence either way." However, this void is slowly filling.

Drawing conclusions about a given nutrient is difficult when nutrients often work effectively only as part of an ensemble. For this reason, isolating the clinical effects of a single nutrient takes considerable time and extremely large numbers of people. The data now trickling in greatly challenge the adequacy of the government's recommended daily allowances (RDAs).

RDAs were meant to be only the amounts of nutrients needed to prevent deficiency diseases, not to promote optimal health. In 1993 leading experts held a symposium evaluating the RDAs and concluded that enough new evidence had surfaced to indicate that some RDAs were too low. For example, the RDA for vitamin C is a mere 60 mg per day. Yet, a recent study found that over a ten-year period, men who took 400 mg or more had 70 percent less mortality than those who consumed less than 50 mg.

Seventy percent less mortality! Moreover, we need vitamin C to make serotonin.

As for vitamin E, preclinical studies published in the *Journal of Neurochemistry* show that an E-deficient diet will, in as little as two weeks, actually damage serotonin neurons and significantly interfere with the functioning of the system.

Many multivitamin pills sold over the counter, particularly those for "stress," incorporate adequate amounts of C and E with many other vitamins needed for healthy serotonin function, including all the B vitamins, especially B-6, folic acid, and biotin. Optimal doses are certainly controversial, but it seems we have a wide margin of safety at least with the B's and other water soluble vitamins. In contrast, excessive amounts of the nonwater soluble vitamins A and D can readily cause problems, so it's best to limit yourself to the RDAs for those two. We quickly eliminate many vitamins from the body; thus, it is very important to divide your total supplement intake into at least two daily doses to maintain benefits over the entire day.

Vitamin B-6

The role of vitamin B-6 in heightening serotonin function is well documented; the body needs it to make serotonin from L-tryptophan. B-6 also inhibits the destruction of brain L-tryptophan, thus encouraging the production of serotonin. This action on serotonin may help explain B-6's reported success in treating premenstrual syndrome as well as autism and certain seizure disorders. A recent study found that high-dose vitamin B-6 treatment in children reduced infantile spasms, one such seizure disorder. In a group of children whose seizures were otherwise uncontrollable, almost one-third were completely seizure-free within a month after starting the B-6 treatment. The Autism Research Institute notes that seventeen published studies showed that vitamin B-6 and magnesium helped almost half the autistic individuals studied.

The best known application of B-6 is for premenstrual syndrome. Many studies have reported success, including one particularly well controlled study published in 1992 in the *Journal of Internal Medicine Research*. However, other studies have found the vitamin no more helpful than a placebo. My clinical experience has mostly been positive, although the effects are generally less complete and less reliable than with Prozac. The most common worry with B-6 is peripheral neuropathy, a nerve problem that can develop at dosages of more than 600 mg per day. Any numbness or tingling following high doses of B-6—usually more than about 600 mg a day—is a clear sign to decrease the dose. Successful PMS treatment has been reported with doses as low as 50 mg per day.

Please note that the body can use vitamin B-6 only in its active "co-enzyme" form, pyridoxal-5-phosphate. Some people have a metabolism that can convert B-6 to the active form, but many do not; it then becomes critical to consume the active form, about 10 to 100 mg daily. It is preferable to take enteric-coated B-6, which is less likely to be destroyed by stomach acid.

Vitamin B-6 may also beef up the action of some antidepressant medications, an effect also reported with folic acid.

MINERALS

Lithium, the standard treatment for bipolar patients (manic-depressive), clearly boosts serotonin. Lithium is a naturally occurring salt. Years ago, after learning that lithium was toxic at certain levels, manufacturers were forced to remove it from most commercial products. This may have added to our modern serotonin drain. Several states, Texas among them, have communities with high, naturally occurring dietary sources of lithium—chiefly from the water supply; thus, the residents effectively avoid the lithium ban. Remarkably, preliminary findings indicate that certain areas with higher lithium levels actually have lower than expected rates of psychiatric admissions, suicide, homicide, and arrests relating to drug addiction. These are all likely associations of improved serotonin levels.

Another important mineral is chromium, critical in lowering insulin requirements. Lower insulin levels aid healthy function of many body systems, including the serotonin system. Experts recommend 200 mcg per day, but it's unlikely that most Americans get anywhere near that level without supplementation. No problems have been reported even with high doses of chromium. Some authorities consider chromium chloride the best form to take, but considerable debate, with proprietary overtones, exists about this.

Other minerals critical to serotonin manufacture include magnesium, zinc, copper, manganese, and iron. Americans are commonly deficient in many of these, especially magnesium, in which as much as 40 percent of the U.S. population may lack the proper level.

The dosages typically available in standard multivitamin/mineral supplements are probably both safe and helpful and can be used along with almost any other form of treatment. One cautionary note: Although many women are iron deficient, people other than children, teens, and menstruating women should generally avoid supplemental iron. In excess, iron is toxic and difficult for the body to eliminate. Most multivitamins still include significant iron, so people who don't need it should choose bottles labeled "without iron."

L-TRYPTOPHAN AND OTHER AMINOS

The amino acid L-tryptophan is *the* building block of both serotonin and melatonin. Supplementation will definitely raise brain serotonin levels, and it has helped as an adjunct in certain antidepressant therapy. On its own, L-tryptophan has relatively little effect on depression, but then simply raising serotonin levels probably does not cure depression either. However, studies do show that L-tryptophan supplementation lowers aggression, which is more directly related to serotonin. Preliminary evidence also supports a role in controlling mania.

While side effects of L-tryptophan are generally mild—occasional drowsiness, nausea, headache, and dizziness—in 1989 retailers yanked L-tryptophan from the market when thirty-eight users died from eosinophilia myalgia syndrome (EMS). Investigation traced the illness to a specific manufacturer in Japan that had apparently introduced a contaminant into its L-tryptophan. Thus, most researchers do not believe that L-tryptophan causes the syndrome. The FDA is not convinced. Perhaps given the deaths and another fifteen hundred seriously affected by EMS, an extra bit of caution may be called for.

Note, however, the following excerpt from a report by the FDA, which casts a different light on its own motivations:

> The Task Force considered various issues in its deliberations, including . . . *what steps are necessary to ensure that the existence of dietary supplements on the market does not act as a disincentive for drug development* [emphasis added]. (FDA Dietary Supplement Task Force Report, June 15, 1993)

This language so enraged many in the alternative medicine and nutrition supplement communities that they began using L-tryptophan as a rallying cry. After all, not only does pure L-tryptophan apparently not cause EMS, but, by an all too strange coincidence, a study by Dr. Christopher Caston showed that the substance makes a very effective *treatment* for EMS—and it's about the only one. Yet, overall, the strengths of L-tryptophan are few, and people might better spend their energy on other issues. However, it is worthwhile to describe the research on L-tryptophan because you can likely do as well or better with a newly emerging substance, discussed below, which I have dubbed "son of L-tryptophan."

As little as a gram of L-tryptophan can help to promote sleep. But you will get a similar sleep-inducing effect with a bedtime carbohydrate snack, although that effect is smaller and shorter-lived. And if even 4 percent of that bedtime snack is protein, it can block the effect—which means no milk with your cookies. However, this type of snack should generally be avoided, as we will discuss in chapter 13. A number of studies, largely uncontrolled, have shown L-tryptophan's modest mood-enhancing effect when used with certain antidepressants. *A note of caution:* Such combined therapy can cause a serious serotonin overdose.

Further, it takes several grams a day for most clinical purposes. While L-tryptophan is the building block for serotonin, it also produces many other chemicals in the body, at least one of which has carcinogenic potential. According to Dr. Ray Fuller, one of the principal developers of Prozac, a substance produced from L-tryptophan is probably a central nervous system toxin. All in all, even if the FDA recants and L-tryptophan makes it back onto the shelves, I strongly suggest that you leave it right there.

That said, perhaps we should reintroduce *small* quantities of L-tryptophan in certain products. I published a warning in this regard in the *Archives of General Psychiatry*. Experiments have established a marked decrease in serotonin levels, and resultant depression, when some people consume an amino acid mixture lacking L-tryptophan. After manufacturers exiled L-tryptophan, some amino acid supplements completely devoid of L-tryptophan became available, which posed a real danger to some users. In theory, large doses of aspartame, the artificial sweetener used in most diet products, might similarly deplete L-tryptophan, since aspartame contains a competing amino acid (phenylalanine). Indeed, very preliminary evidence has linked high intake of the sweetener with depression.

Most makers of combination amino acid supplements have remedied this problem by using allowable natural sources of L-tryptophan. But people who make their own amino acid mixtures from individual supplements must take care to get L-tryptophan in their diet and not consume excessive amounts of amino acids, which compete with tryptophan. Turkey and milk are two very good food sources. Moderate quantities of L-tryptophan, *appropriately balanced with other amino acids,* are vital and do not pose a problem.

At any rate, there's a direct descendent of L-tryptophan that seems free of these problems.

Son of L-Tryptophan

My patient Sara had been burdened with chronic anxiety and depression for most of her forty-four years. But it seemed the pill had not been made that did not give her intolerable side effects. With the few medications that proved marginally helpful, even my determined attempts to minimize dosage were of no avail. We kept coming back to natural treatments. In addition to ongoing psychotherapy, we had some success in layering various treatments, incorporating nutrition, light, stress reduction, and exercise. But what made the biggest difference was L-tryptophan, which Sara had purchased in Canada, where it remains available by prescription. But even with L-tryptophan she still struggled most of the time.

After years of little further improvement, I learned of the availability of the metabolite of L-tryptophan, 5-hydroxytryptophan (5-HTP). We stopped L-tryptophan and substituted 5-HTP, 800 mg twice a day *on an empty stomach*. Suddenly life got much better for Sara—not perfect, of course, but remarkably better. Both her anxiety and her depression lessened considerably. She mentioned with astonishment that Christmas songs had always greatly annoyed her, but suddenly she was finding them "almost listenable." Many elements contributed to Sara's recovery, but 5-HTP seemed the most important.

A European study of twenty-five depressed patients treated with 5-HTP found unusually fast response (within three to five days), and the percentage of people helped was typical of that helped with standard antidepressants. Anxious and agitated depressives benefited particularly. A 1993 study of fifty patients who had fibromyalgia—a difficult to treat disorder often involving depression and characterized by "tender points" spread all over the body, accompanied by muscle aches and fatigue—found that fully half showed significant improvement. If this success is replicated, 5-HTP signifies a major advance in treatment. Preliminary evidence also suggests that 5-HTP eases alcohol withdrawal and drug-induced psychosis. A well-controlled study found that this metabolite also lowered appetite and improved weight loss over a five-week period. In other work, 5-HTP caused moderate improvement in anxiety and it reduced migraines. The migraine study involved one hundred patients; 70 percent got benefit equal to that of the standard drug treatment, but with much fewer side effects. The investigators concluded that 5-HTP could become the treatment of choice for migraine.

"Son of L-tryptophan" has undergone numerous studies, though mostly in other countries. A number of leaders in the field of psychopharmacology consider 5-HTP to be one of the most promising of all agents now under investigation. Unfortunately, 5-HTP may remain simply promising. Once again, we have a non-patentable therapy, which means that pharmaceutical companies have little incentive to research its usefulness.

The cloud of L-tryptophan still hangs over 5-HTP, even while evidence mounts that L-tryptophan does not cause EMS. After all, Canada has been selling L-tryptophan continuously in recent years by prescription without report of any EMS. The FDA even claims that EMS could result from 5-HTP—distinctly a minority opinion. Still, until this is settled, 5-HTP must be approached cautiously. Currently, you can get the medication in this country by prescription through certain compounding pharmacies willing to prepare it (see appendix III, Resources).

• •

SUMMING UP

A number of vitamins, minerals, and amino acids show real promise as treatments for a wide variety of modern ills. Unfortunately, unequivocal evidence in support of their benefits is generally lacking. However, as a rule the treatments appear quite safe and can generally be used to advantage in conjunction with more standard therapies. I hope that recent trends toward greater acceptance of nutritional approaches by mainstream medicine will result in more study of this important area. In chapter 10, we'll look at a supplement that we all take rather liberally—cholesterol.

CHAPTER 10

CHOLESTEROL'S GOOD SIDE

The great tragedy of Science—the slaying of a beautiful hypothesis by an ugly fact.

—Thomas Henry Huxley

The nice, neat story about cholesterol that nutritionists have been telling us has increasingly strained against the facts. Evidence now suggests that most people can relax about the cholesterol in their diet. Actually, writing this chapter makes me a little uneasy, because to call cholesterol a form of natural Prozac, which many people may need *more* of for physical and mental well-being, may so jar the reader's worldview as to cause the very sort of stress this book aims at defusing. But one way or another, the cholesterol news will reach you soon enough, if you haven't heard the rumblings already.

Since we have been making a point of relating our concerns to the natural lifestyle of our Stone Age ancestors, it is notable that a report in the *New England Journal of Medicine* calculates that cholesterol intake was quite high. In fact, the diet is believed to have derived 20–80 percent of its calories from meat.

We are a people who know our cholesterol levels. But most of us do not really know what this level means—except that if it is high, one is apparently marked for death. In referring to cholesterol, we are talking about total cholesterol, which includes HDL (high density lipoprotein), the so-called good cholesterol, and the dreaded LDL (low density lipoprotein).

Yet of all of the trials of cholesterol reduction conducted, only one has been able to show lower overall mortality. Moreover, this study, published in *Lancet,* used only patients who were at great risk for heart attacks, and showed only a modest improvement in survival. So that's really all we have for the proven benefits of cholesterol reduction on *overall* mortality. One larger study, not confined to those having suffered heart attacks, found that overall mortality was more than twice as high for those who were taking cholesterol-reducing medication.

The association between dietary cholesterol and *any* disease is very poor. The French eat four times the milk fat we do, and twice the animal fat, yet they have less than half our rate of heart disease. The French are not the only ones getting away with this. The Swiss, whose life expectancy falls short only of the Japanese, eat more cheese, cream, and sausages than the French! The reason is that *dietary* cholesterol—the cholesterol we eat—has relatively little effect on blood cholesterol levels. The body makes most of its cholesterol in the liver, and the cholesterol we eat has little, if any, influence on that process. In fact, the *New England Journal of Medicine* reported the case of a man who ate over a dozen eggs daily for many years while maintaining normal blood cholesterol levels.

At any rate, the evidence suggests that nutritionists have exaggerated the dangers of cholesterol. Studies further show that too *low* a blood cholesterol level poses risks easily as severe as those of high cholesterol, resulting in greater rates of depression, accidents, and even suicide. In some twenty studies of people at less risk than the heart attack survivors of the *Lancet* study, while lowering cholesterol often decreased heart attacks, it never lowered overall mortality, and not infrequently increased it.

CHOLESTEROL AND THE MIND

A recent study of several hundred thousand people uncovered the rather grim fact that those with low cholesterol—levels below 160 (the level found in about a quarter of the U.S. population)—faced significantly higher risk of suicide. A 1991 study of 50,000 people by Swedish researchers confirmed these higher suicide rates and also found that low-cholesterol subjects suffered three times more injuries than normal subjects over several years. This accident rate brings to mind the higher rate of impulsivity associated with depleted serotonin levels, discussed in chapters 2 and 3.

Another study, this one comprising hospitalized psychiatric patients, also found that low cholesterol in males was accompanied by increased risk of suicide. After adjusting for many other factors that might contribute to or otherwise explain the increased suicidality, the researchers concluded that men whose cholesterol fell in the bottom 25 percent of the normal range for their age were *twice* as likely to make a serious suicide attempt. Finally, a survey published in *Primary Psychiatry,* also comprising 50,000 subjects, but this time men only, found a four-fold increase in suicide risk for those in the lowest 25 percent of cholesterol levels. These findings suggest that high cholesterol seems to immunize against suicidal impulse—however, only at levels so high as to increase the risk of heart disease.

Early on we mentioned that suicidal behavior is associated with serotonin depletion. Also suggesting a connection with low serotonin function are research findings linking depression with low cholesterol. A California study found that men over the age of seventy with low cholesterol had three times the depression rate of those with more typical levels.

Some have dismissed the depression-cholesterol link, arguing that the low cholesterol resulted simply from the already-depressed person's poor appetite and subsequent decreased eating. But this appears not to be the case. For one thing, evidence suggests that low cholesterol actually precedes depression. Further, studies have shown that the cholesterol-depression link is independent of subjects' weight loss. Thus, we cannot blame the low cholesterol and depression on simple lack of food.

THE SEROTONIN CONNECTION

The picture painted by the above certainly has the signature of low serotonin. We also routinely find low cholesterol in some alcoholics and in people who are habitually violent or impulsive.

Of course these groups show low serotonin levels as well. But association cannot prove causation, so we need more evidence to establish the serotonin connection.

In one recent study, monkeys fed high cholesterol diets showed reductions in aggression, thus establishing a cause-and-effect relationship between cholesterol and serotonin-related behavior. Specific serotonin involvement has also emerged. A 1994 study found that cholesterol makes more serotonin available in the nerves' synapses—which is similar to what Prozac does.

Thus, even modern nutritional advice apparently contributes to the drain on serotonin. Natural enhancement of serotonin means, in part, making sure cholesterol levels don't fall too *low*. As we'll see, this probably means keeping cholesterol above 160 and not worrying about moderately higher levels except in people who are at special risk for heart disease.

CHOLESTEROL AND THE BODY

Doubt is not a pleasant state but certainty is a ridiculous one.

—Voltaire

Not all groups are equally threatened by high cholesterol levels. High cholesterol poses little risk of heart attack in premenopausal women, who are at low risk anyway, nor does it particularly endanger the elderly, who are at high risk in any case. A recent study reported in the *Journal of the American Medical Association* tracked 997 people over the age of seventy for several years and found no difference in mortality or even heart attacks between those with high cholesterol levels and those with levels to brag about. Make no mistake, however: For many people, mainly middle-aged men, high levels of cholesterol—though not necessarily dietary cholesterol—*do* pose a heart risk.

Since for some people a high cholesterol level puts the heart at risk, and a low level poses psychological risks, we have a conflict. Is it a case of "what's good for the heart is bad for the soul" (or at least the brain)? If so, that violates a comforting notion of mutuality. The ideal prescription, as emphasized throughout this book, benefits us across the board. However, while extremely high levels are risky, it turns out that keeping your cholesterol above 160 is a good prescription for *both* body and soul.

To further complicate the issue, it appears that excessively low levels may be associated with an increased risk of cancer and even heart disease. This heart disease finding, emerging from a massive longitudinal study in Russia, was most unexpected. Some believe that it may be explained by other factors such as lifestyle. This same degree of scientific skepticism should be directed at *all* of the findings on cholesterol. Various dangers statistically associated with high cholesterol may best be explained by other factors as well.

Even if some people with high cholesterol may be at increased risk of heart disease, other dangers rear their head when cholesterol falls. Remember, in more than twenty studies examining lowering cholesterol, while coronary deaths were often lower, no net improvement in death rates resulted. The reduction of mortality from heart attacks was completely offset by the increased mortality rates from other causes. Indeed, reducing cholesterol in some groups, like young men, who face little risk from heart disease, increases the death rate.

It is probably premature to recommend elevating cholesterol to prevent other health problems. Yet, those with cholesterol below 160 should consider it safe to bring their level up to this low normal level. Conversely, those at risk for depression should carefully weigh any treatment that involves reducing cholesterol—even if they face significant cardiac risk.

● ●

SUMMING UP

No doubt the cholesterol gurus will be a long time in admitting that they have oversold cholesterol and led people on a major public health campaign to no clear benefit. Admitting error is never enjoyable, especially if it means rendering your professional expertise obsolete. But already the tide has turned. It may seem a revelation that up to a quarter of our population has so low a blood cholesterol level that they put mood and health at risk. Nonetheless, when cholesterol levels fall below 160, a red flag should go up. One has increased the risk of suicide and other mortality or, surviving that, magnified the risk of depression many fold, without any gain in cardiovascular protection.

Fortunately, through diet one can lose weight, reduce heart disease risk, and improve physical and mental well-being without tampering with cholesterol. How? The answer lies in the way nutrition controls a group of powerful hormones called prostaglandins.

As the next few chapters show, supplementing a properly balanced diet with certain fats puts the reins of these powerful hormones in your hands.

CHAPTER 11

PROSTAGLANDIN POWER: THE UNEXPECTED ROLE OF FOOD

Tell me what you eat, and I shall tell you what you are.
—ANTHELME BRILLAT-SAVARIN

I certainly don't believe that food is quite as revealing as Brillat-Savarin claimed, but I have found that you will profoundly feel what you eat. I want this and the next two chapters to get you thinking of food not only as nutrition but as a *hormonal adjustment*. Because what you put in your mouth kicks off hormonal changes just as surely as if you'd taken a drug.

THE WORK OF PROSTAGLANDINS

Prostaglandins, named for the prostate gland, where they were originally found, often control the release of serotonin. Serotonin in turn heavily influences the production of prostaglandins. We already know the importance of serotonin, but the importance of the prostaglandins goes well beyond their interaction with serotonin. Understanding prostaglandins enhances our understanding not only of depression, alcoholism, and premenstrual syndrome but of general medical conditions such as arthritis, multiple sclerosis, even AIDS. Prostaglandin research may very well result in a genuine medical revolution.

Although scientists discovered prostaglandins more than sixty years ago, it was not until the mid-1970s, with the advent of sufficiently developed research techniques, that serious study began. Within a few years, these hormones became one of the hottest areas of research. Prostaglandin researchers received the 1982 Nobel Prize in medicine, in part for showing that aspirin works through the prostaglandins.

Such a powerful system—and you can consciously control it, for prostaglandins are heavily dependent on what you eat.

Prostaglandins are produced from only one source—essential fatty acids—which you get from ordinary dietary fats, although you can also take supplements, as discussed in chapter 12. You can further control prostaglandins by adjusting the percentages of protein, fat, and carbohydrate in your diet, as explained in chapter 13.

Your body makes two kinds of prostaglandins, which some refer to as "good" and "bad." You need a balance of both to survive, but you want to keep the bad ones relatively low. The so-called good prostaglandins promote immune response, quiet inflammation (helping prevent arthritis), inhibit cell proliferation (protecting against cancer), and inhibit platelet aggregation while promoting blood vessel dilation (protecting against heart disease). The bad hormones act as a check on these good deeds. After all, if the good ones had completely free run of the place, your blood wouldn't clot when you need it to. We need the bad hormones to balance effects.

Nonetheless, in many diseases the balance has shifted in favor of the bad. Conditions such as cardiovascular disorders, for instance, are linked to too much platelet aggregation, too much cell proliferation, and too much vasoconstriction. Aspirin's recommended use in preventing heart disease stems from its ability to block the effects of these bad prostaglandins. Unfortunately, it blocks the good ones too.

Just what ratio of good to bad hormones your body makes from the essential fatty acids in your diet depends on factors such as age, illness, stress, and the presence of one key essential fatty acid, eicosapentaenoic acid (EPA), which is found in high concentrations in fish oil. But perhaps your insulin and glucagon levels are the most important factor. These two hormones work in tandem and are controlled by the foods we eat at every meal. In turn, insulin and glucagon help control which type of prostaglandins our bodies produce at any given time.

THE PROSTAGLANDIN THEORY OF DEPRESSION

Researchers are not exactly fighting each other off to be first to show that prostaglandins may cause depression. The few interested investigators however have discovered that depressed people produce high levels of bad prostaglandins—levels two to three times those of nondepressed subjects. The finding is quite reliable. Originally reported by researchers at the National Institute of Mental Health in 1983, another group replicated these results a few years later, as did a third group—through the use of a simple saliva test—a few years after that. Not exactly a stampede, given that such results suggested a possible cause of depression.

MAKING PROSTAGLANDINS

The Role of Insulin and Glucagon

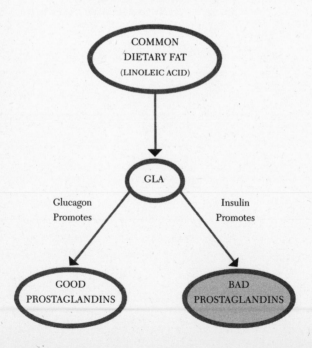

I suspect several factors explain this relative indifference. Historically, isolated lab findings in psychiatric patients often failed to prove helpful. Furthermore, no theoretical framework was elaborated along with the findings to support their significance. Finally, the last laboratory test for depression that got psychiatrists enthusiastic turned into a high-profile bust.

Having been burned, the field is wary. Yet the practical implications are great: By easily and cheaply sampling some saliva, we might reliably diagnose depression! You might not find that too exciting, but for practitioners, a dependable test for depression is something of a grail. Such a test might convince depressed people to seek the help they may need. A test might also aid in determining the appropriate type of treatment and getting patients equitable insurance reimbursement, thus fighting the discriminatory policies too often in place. Not only do measurements of bad prostaglandins offer a possible diagnosis of depression, but as the levels vary with severity, we could monitor improvement over the course of treatment.

DO PROSTAGLANDINS CAUSE DEPRESSION?

Since levels of prostaglandins so closely follow levels of depression, one cannot help wondering if they actually cause depression. I believe it likely. For years now, when trying to help depressed patients get a grip on what has happened to them, I compare their illness to the flu. The flu shares many symptoms with depression: low energy, diminished appetite, decreased interest in the world, lack of enjoyment—even muscle stiffness and other unpleasant body sensations. As you know, common remedies like aspirin and Motrin which block prostaglandins can relieve such symptoms. The analogy gathers speed when you realize that most core symptoms of depression can also be caused by too many bad prostaglandins. For example, they might cause low energy by constricting blood vessels, thus denying tissues their needed replenishment. Prostaglandins regulate sleep and appetite and can cause too much or too little of either—as can depression. Prostaglandins also regulate sexual activity and might cause the low sex drive so common in depression.

Further clues exist. Depressed people suffer immune system changes. Prostaglandin E2 (PGE2), one of the bad prostaglandins elevated during depression, suppresses natural "killer cell" activity, leaving the depressed more susceptible to conditions such as infection and even cancer. A growing body of evidence supports the idea that depression involves an inflammatory process; for example, depression often brings a higher white blood cell count. Further, we find higher levels of acute-phase proteins in depression, a condition common to infection. Finally, bad prostaglandins also cause the familiar heat of fever and possibly account for the higher body temperatures found in the depressed. However, this does not mean that depression *is* an infection. Many other things cause inflammatory reactions.

We can also account for depression's main symptom, sadness or dysphoria, by noting that good prostaglandins (PGE1) are associated with elevated mood, while PGE2 opposes their action. Many believe that PGE1 causes the initial elation of alcohol as well as the sedation. Further, there is evidence that depressed individuals do not respond as well biologically to the good prostaglandins they do have. Finally, elevation of bad prostaglandins fits together with the decreased melatonin levels frequently seen in depression, as melatonin is believed to inhibit prostaglandin production.

THE SEROTONIN CONNECTION

Another reason to think that prostaglandins cause depression is their interaction with serotonin. PGE1, the classic good prostaglandin, seems usually to magnify the effects of brain serotonin. In addition, it both dampens pain and helps suppress seizures, apparently by its actions on serotonin. In chapter 2, I explained that serotonin had some link to depression but did not appear to cause it directly; here we have an example of a factor that may do so.

Muddying the picture, however, is the fact that a few of the bad prostaglandins heighten serotonin function, too, although they may be less abundant and therefore of lesser influence. Depressed people with *less* tendency to suicide have higher levels of these particular bad prostaglandins. Perhaps the elevation of these bad prostaglandins during depression may in part serve a useful purpose—like inflammatory reactions in general. Unfortunately, as with many kinds of inflammation—for example arthritis—the body goes overboard in an attempt to cure itself, and this reaction itself becomes a problem. As with prostaglandins generally, we need more research to understand this.

THE STRESS CONNECTION

Stress contributes to depression. Indeed, recall genetic researchers estimate that stress plays a greater role in causing the trouble than does hereditary disposition. We can see how stress might do this via prostaglandins. Stress raises insulin, which in turn tips prostaglandin production in the bad direction. This effect also helps explain why depressed people tend to have more than their share of chronic diseases related to elevated insulin—conditions such as hypertension, diabetes, and heart disease. Depressed people suffer rates of heart disease estimated at up to eight times those of the undepressed.

Serotonin acts on the prostaglandin system by helping to lower insulin levels, which in turn promotes production of good prostaglandins and suppresses the bad. The three systems thus intermesh as vital cogs in the brain's mood machinery.

I find the prostaglandin story in depression quite compelling. Prostaglandins should be moved off the back burners of research, for they offer, I believe, the most promising avenue for both diagnostic testing and better depression treatment.

GENERAL HEALTH

Perhaps the needed understanding of prostaglandins will come from nonpsychiatric fields of medicine. One finds prostaglandins at the forefront of research on many diseases. Prostaglandins, and the larger family of similarly diet-dependent hormones, the eicosanoids, are master switches at all levels in almost all organisms. Most medications that treat cardiovascular disorders specifically target prostaglandins. The same goes for arthritis and other inflammatory conditions. Eventually the word will get back to psychiatry, and I expect that similarly powerful medicines for mood will result.

● ●

SUMMING UP

Good prostaglandins are a key booster of serotonin. But prostaglandins with or without serotonin are a force to be reckoned with. The Prostaglandin Theory of Depression advanced here will, I hope, help focus deserved attention in this area. Perhaps someday we will see medications developed that take advantage of the prostaglandins' role in depression. On the other hand, it may turn out that no medications are needed. Recall that for the most part, prostaglandins are controlled naturally through diet. Perhaps no medication will ever be capable of improving upon the body's natural system of regulation—given a healthy lifestyle. In chapter 12 we'll learn how to influence production of these master hormones by consuming essential fatty acids—fats that have long interested alternative health-care practitioners and have now caught the attention of mainstream medicine.

CHAPTER 12

ESSENTIAL FATS

Life is largely a matter of chemistry.
—WILLIAM J. MAYO, M.D.

Much of the most important chemistry in our bodies falls under the influence of prostaglandins, and prostaglandin production depends on diet. Our bodies can generate prostaglandins only from certain kinds of fat. Because we cannot manufacture these fats, we must get them via food—thus, biochemists call them *essential* fatty acids. Some of the most remarkable improvements in depression I have seen in my practice have come from adding essential fatty acid supplements to the diet. However, these supplements must be taken in a very specific way.

The first step in your body's process of making prostaglandins from fats requires the involvement of an enzyme whose activity weakens with age, illness, stress, and certain nutritional factors. Happily, you can bypass this enzyme's increasing stinginess by consuming more of the fatty acid gamma linoleic acid (GLA). Common dietary supplements such as evening primrose oil, black current seed oil, and borage oil contain GLA in abundance.

Alternative health practitioners often prescribe evening primrose oil for a number of conditions, most commonly premenstrual syndrome, and it is reportedly quite effective. As the body generally uses GLA to make good prostaglandins, we can expect such results. Unfortunately, some people's systems accept GLA happily enough but use it to excessively boost the production of bad prostaglandins. That, we don't need. How much GLA goes down each path depends on many factors, including genetics. People whose insulin levels fluctuate widely often have this trouble, as high insulin levels promote production of bad prostaglandins. In addition to genetics, age, illness, stress, and low protein–high carbohydrate diets promote bad prostaglandins. With such people, GLA supplements, while perhaps beneficial at first, can eventually lead to a pile-up of the bad type. In order to funnel production toward good prostaglandins, along with GLA you can take the fatty acid EPA (eicosapentaenoic acid), which is found in fish oil. Salmon is an excellent food source for EPA.

FISH OIL (EPA)

Unfortunately, most researchers have focused on doses of either GLA or EPA but not both. Let's take a look at that research, starting with fish oil.

Reducing cardiovascular risk factors is probably the most established benefit; even the FDA recommends "adequate" fish intake. However, you'd have to eat an awful lot of fish to get much effect. Eight ounces of salmon has about 3.5 grams of fish oil. One study found that fish oil supplementation requires doses of more than five grams per day to markedly improve risk factors. That large a dose could produce a discomforting amount of intestinal gas.

Fish oil can also raise HDL—the "good" cholesterol—although this may occur significantly only in women. Further, in one study, fish oil reversed precancerous lesions of the colon. In addition, it has aided in treatments of psoriasis, rheumatoid arthritis, high blood pressure, and ulcerative colitis. The British medical journal *Lancet* reported that women at risk for premature delivery who took four grams of fish oil per day significantly prolonged their pregnancies and increased infant birth weight and length. The best fish oil story has to be its success, demonstrated in controlled trials, in preventing recurrence of coronary artery blockage after surgery.

Results of fish oil treatment are somewhat inconsistent, however. One well-designed study failed to repeat the helpful effect first reported on psoriasis. This also happened when retesting the oil's ability to lower high blood pressure. One problem with supplementing EPA alone is that while it blocks bad prostaglandins, it may also block the formation of GLA. This effect is relatively small, even in high doses, but even so, it can cause some decrease in the production of good prostaglandins. Therefore, I do not recommend taking fish oil alone, without other dietary measures.

VEGETABLE OIL (GLA)

Some studies find more dramatic results from GLA supplements. However, as with EPA supplementation, large studies have sometimes failed to replicate early good results—for example, on treating premenstrual syndrome. At least nine controlled trials looked at evening primrose oil for premenstrual syndrome and got gener-

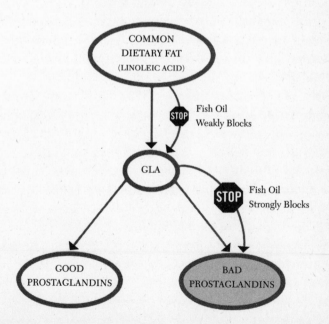

MAKING PROSTAGLANDINS

The Role of Fatty Acids

ally favorable results—particularly, improvement of depressed mood—but a couple of trials failed to replicate these findings. The jury must remain out on this one.

Similar inconsistent results have been shown in the use of evening primrose oil, or GLA, in treating skin disease, mastalgia (breast pain), rheumatoid arthritis, liver cancer, and preeclampsia, a serious pregnancy complication.

So, we can see that despite some successes, when used alone, GLA or EPA cannot generally be relied on. Our hormonal system is simply not that straightforward. However, these essential fatty acids are like the arms of tongs—broken apart, either arm is of limited use; joined together, the two form a truly useful tool.

COMBINED TREATMENT

Alternative health-care practitioners often prescribe fish oil or evening primrose oil, and many claim considerable success, but most practitioners seem nearly blind to the importance of using GLA and EPA supplements together. Remember, all prostaglandins are made from GLA, but the presence of EPA helps ensure that mainly good prostaglandins are produced.

A few recent studies of combined EPA/GLA supplementation have turned up better results. Where evening primrose oil alone gave mixed results against preeclampsia, a combination treatment was found highly successful. In preclinical studies, the combination also proved effective in treating allergies. Combined treatment has not resurrected all the earlier promises, however. A *Lancet* study found that evening primrose oil, with or without EPA, was of no help with atopic dermatitis, despite earlier findings to the contrary. So, possibly there's still something missing.

Dr. Barry Sears and his group, who have treated hundreds of patients with dual supplementation, have had more consistent success. Dr. Sears's work first introduced me to the prostaglandin field. He finds that combined EPA/GLA treatment can be remarkably effective but sometimes requires tricky adjustment. Failing to tailor subjects' doses may explain the mixed results obtained in various other studies. Combined supplementation can

occasionally even work so well that the good prostaglandins over-
whelm the system, causing excessive blood vessel dilation. The
resulting symptoms include diarrhea and fatigue. The opposing
symptoms, caused by too many bad prostaglandins, are constipation, dry skin, and, once again, fatigue. Dr. Sears has developed
the following set of indicators to help in making adjustments to
GLA/EPA doses.

Too Many Good Prostaglandins
(Take fewer supplements, especially EPA)

Increased appetite
Diarrhea
Increased urination
Fatigue
Gas
Headaches

Too Many Bad Prostaglandins
(Take fewer GLA and/or more EPA supplements)

Constipation
Fatigue
Prolonged need for sleep
Grogginess upon waking
Minor skin problems
Muscle or joint soreness
Brittle nails
Brittle hair
Dry skin
Headaches
Lack of appetite
Anxiety or irritation
Return of medical problems

Appropriate Balance of Good and Bad Prostaglandins

Increased energy
Sense of well-being

Reduced need for sleep
Alertness upon waking
Improvement of minor skin problems
Increased athletic performance

While Barry Sears has found encouraging results with physical conditions such as hypertension, elevated triglycerides, and diabetes, I believe that EPA/GLA's most intriguing promise, given the prostaglandins' relationship to serotonin and depression, is for treating depression. Because I consider this an experimental treatment, I have used it only occasionally in my practice, but essential fatty acid supplements have already produced some remarkable responses.

TREATING DEPRESSION

Some time ago I noted with interest a report by researchers who had successfully treated chronic fatigue syndrome with essential fatty acids. Chronic fatigue often causes depression. Indeed, studies have singled out depression as one of the factors most responsive to treatment. Aware of the premenstrual syndrome studies, mentioned earlier, which had concluded that depression responded well to treatment with essential fatty acids, I began to wonder about treating depression directly with GLA and/or EPA. However, the literature contained no studies on the subject. Given the Prostaglandin Theory of Depression, discussed in chapter 11, the use of combination GLA/EPA therapy appeared very promising, so I offered it to selected patients.

GREG'S CASE

Greg, an electrician, suffered severe winter depression. His early morning insomnia left him so listless that his work performance suffered markedly, and he had begun to miss workdays. He scored 25 on the twenty-nine-item Hamilton Depression Rating, indicating a fairly serious level of depression. However, he did not want to take medication, nor could he afford to spend several hundred dollars for a light unit. Despite being so dysfunctional, he was not at all suicidal, and we agreed to try essential fatty acid supplements.

Greg began taking a small amount of GLA combined with a larger amount of EPA. When he returned ten days later, his depression rating score had dropped to one! Within several weeks he was scoring a zero.

This remains the most complete cure of seasonal depression that I've ever seen from a single treatment—and I specialize in treating the condition. Most people with SAD must combine several forms of treatment to approach even 90 percent of their summer level of functioning. But Greg got 100 percent recovery, simply by nutritional means. His work performance zoomed to summer heights, and he began enjoying demanding winter sports—during a season that had once relegated him to despair.

Almost certainly, the EPA/GLA supplements caused the improvement. On three occasions Greg discontinued them, thinking he no longer needed treatment, and suffered a relapse within a couple of weeks. Fortunately, each time he quickly recovered when he resumed taking the supplements. Although at first Greg depended purely on supplementation, ultimately he made some dietary changes (see chapter 13) that likely helped maintain his response.

STEVEN'S CASE

Steven also achieved dramatic results with fatty acid supplements. Another psychiatrist referred this forty-two-year-old executive to me because his chronic depression and fatigue had only partly responded to treatments including combined Prozac and BuSpar.

As was the case with Greg, Steven showed excellent response to the supplements. His depression rating fell rapidly to zero, and he made some rather limited efforts to change his overall diet. I had to adjust the initial dose gradually over the first few months, but it has remained stable for about two years now. Steven too had a seasonal component to his depression. Yet, in the heart of last winter, he stopped using Prozac (but continued BuSpar for anxiety) and declared that he felt completely well and exceptionally energetic. In stark contrast to the old days, after a long day at work, Steven now has plenty of energy to spend on his family.

● ●

SUMMING UP

With all of the effective treatments available for depression, I have used combined EPA/GLA only half a dozen times, usually along with conventional therapies that were not succeeding fully. Administration can be fussy, which puts off some patients. For many people, especially those unable to make dietary changes, the balance of these fatty acids must be carefully adjusted to avoid, for example, constipation, which indicates a need for a higher dose of fish oil. Overall, however, the results are greatly encouraging. In fact, it is largely because this treatment appears so very powerful that I have been so conservative in my approach. Anything that has such strongly positive effects might, under certain conditions, have negative effects as well. Nevertheless, I will continue to use this approach with certain patients as I await the much-needed studies to confirm the effectiveness and safety of this treatment. The area cries out for further investigation. However, scores of preliminary studies have thus far *not* raised significant safety concerns.

Fortunately, you can avoid all significant risk and still move your body into healthier prostaglandin balance through diet alone—without supplementation. Then, if the addition of essential fatty acids is desired, they may be optimally used at very safe, in fact ordinary, dietary levels (the equivalent of a daily bowl of slow-cooked oatmeal, which has about 1 mg of GLA, and a salmon dinner). By this point it is probably not too surprising that this prostaglandin-favorable diet, which is described in chapter 13, mimics the balanced nutrition of our Stone Age ancestors.

CHAPTER 13

THE NATURAL DIET OF HOMO SAPIENS—UPDATED

If you have formed the habit of checking on every new diet that comes along, you will find that, mercifully, they all blur together, leaving you with only one definite piece of information: french-fried potatoes are out.

—JEAN KERR

Now we'll examine the perhaps surprising balance of protein, carbohydrate, and fat that helps us create both mental and physical equilibrium. Eating in the way that nature intended corrects one of the worst physical affronts of modern times, thus addressing another source of our modern serotonin drain.

THE CURSE OF THE PYRAMID

I suspect that no one aspect of modern living hurts us as greatly as our diet. This is especially true for Americans. Today, most of us are unhappy with our weight. A recent survey found that over the course of a year, the average woman goes on two diets and the average man on "half" a diet. Dieters suffer more depression than others, and evidence now suggests that it's not the dreaded weight but the dieting itself that causes this depression.

Despite documented evidence of lowered fat intake and increased dieting, Americans have gotten heavier in the last ten years. Surprisingly, average weights remained steady from the

1960s all the way to the early 1980s, as did the percentage of those considered overweight—about 25 percent. But by the early 1990s that percentage had jumped by more than a third. And, the *Journal of the American Medical Association* tells us, the average weight of these overweight Americans jumped by a hefty eight pounds.

People simply respond by dieting more. It's an important part of the economy now; in one recent year, consumers spent *$10 billion* on commercial weight-loss programs. Yet in a follow-up of five hundred "successful dieters," fewer than one in seven had maintained significant weight loss a year later.

In the last few years researchers have linked heart disease, diabetes, various cancers, and a host of other "diseases of civilization" to our diet. Experts have turned this way and that trying to find the villain. A number of years ago they started pointing at fat. Gradually, Americans grew obsessed with fat, particularly, as we've seen, with cholesterol. Fat was evil. Today, one finds entire supermarket shelves filled with fat-free products—even the breakfast cereals that contain little more than white flour and sweetener trumpet the health-promising "fat free" label.

Not long ago, the government published the food pyramid (see below). You'll note that sugar and fat are near the peak, indicating that little of either should be eaten; next, a narrow band of proteins, followed by fruits and vegetables, which are largely carbohydrate. Then, in the broad base at the bottom—indicating that these should make up the largest component of our diet—grains. Carbohydrates and more carbohydrates!

I suggest that the problem is not that we have failed to follow these guidelines, but that we have followed some of them all too well. We have worried too much about dietary fat, thus encouraging a greater foe of weight loss and overall health.

Ancient man would not recognize this food pyramid. Our bodies were designed for something quite different. In 1985, the *New England Journal of Medicine* published a landmark article outlining the diet of human beings during the Paleolithic period, or early Stone Age. The authors concluded that the diet was 20 percent to 80 percent meat from the apparently plentiful small game—lean but high-cholesterol food. Still more radically differ-

A Guide to Daily Food Choices

Fats, Oils, and Sweets: Use sparingly

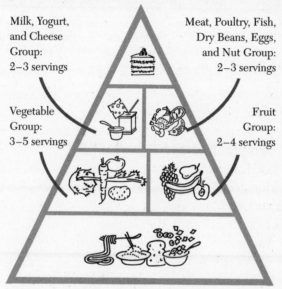

Milk, Yogurt, and Cheese Group: 2–3 servings

Meat, Poultry, Fish, Dry Beans, Eggs, and Nut Group: 2–3 servings

Vegetable Group: 3–5 servings

Fruit Group: 2–4 servings

Bread, Cereal, Rice, and Pasta Group: 6–11 servings

ent, the Stone Age diet had absolutely no grain—the entire base of the food pyramid. In fact, we had virtually no grain in our diet until the advent of agriculture, some 10,000 years ago. Then, grain took over. As we will see, we have good reason to think this was a wrong turn.

Returning to the mystery of America's ill health and recent weight gain, we have seen that fat makes a poor villain. I would point instead to the recent "health food" trends, which overemphasize carbohydrates and turn away from meat, eggs, and dairy, which are at least partly to blame. Dismissing these high-protein, moderate-fat, low-sugar foods from the diet and replacing them with carbohydrates does us no favor. Those foods were indeed kind to our insulin levels. On the other hand, carbohydrates *raise* insulin levels, thus telling the body to store the incoming food as fat.

So, while the body tucks away calories as fat, out of easy energy reach (but not out of sight), the dieter takes a harsh path: trying to eat less. Feeling starved, the body redoubles the message to eat, often issuing an intense, sometimes irresistible craving for carbohydrates. The cycle continues. The raised insulin levels soon cause the dieter's blood sugar to drop. This leaves the dieter in even worse shape, because the only nourishment the brain can use is this blood sugar, known as glucose. The brain grows cranky when its dinner is snatched away—and the dieter pays the price with symptoms not only of hunger but of irritability and poor performance.

THE NATURAL DIET OF HOMO SAPIENS

The diet our metabolism evolved to handle consisted largely of those cholesterol-rich (although generally low-fat) game animals. Fossils can actually reveal evidence that an individual died of heart disease, yet we find almost no sign of this disease in ancient man. Admittedly, most of those individuals died long before the age of fifty, but even in the remains of younger people we find no sign of the early stages of cardiovascular disease so common among us today.

CARBOHYDRATE CRAVING

A VICIOUS CIRCLE

In people "oversensitive" to carbohydrates

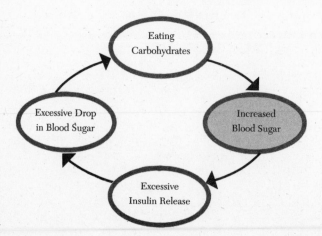

The Paleolithic diet offers other guidance that medical science is gradually adopting. The ancient diet featured many foods rich in vitamin C, with little sugar or salt, lots of fiber and calcium, and fat probably below 20 percent to 30 percent. And consistent with their high meat intake is the fact that we still have not quite reached the average heights of our ancient ancestors, although, as we eat successively more protein than earlier Americans did, we have gained height in recent generations.

Ancient man ate essentially no grain. How can "whole grain" not be in the natural diet, you may wonder; what can possibly be wrong with such seemingly harmless food? After all, we're talking complex carbohydrates. The problem lies in the fact that grains have a very high glycemic index—meaning that they quickly raise blood sugar, thus raising insulin. We know that a chronically high insulin level, called hyperinsulinemia, causes or aggravates numerous degenerative diseases, particularly cardiac disease, diabetes, and cancer. While few until recently have addressed the carbohydrate danger, that is changing. I am far from a lone voice. Many books on this subject are due out soon. It seems a revolution is brewing, and it may mean the end of the long reign of carbohydrates.

FOOD AS A DRUG

Despite the growing attention to insulin, one factor is commonly overlooked: the hormone glucagon. Glucagon tends to counteract insulin effects. Carbohydrates invoke insulin, and protein invokes the beneficial glucagon. Thus, every time we put food into our mouths, we make a positive or negative hormone adjustment. The balance we set at mealtime lasts for the next four to six hours—unless we eat sooner. So, we must think of food like a drug.

The paired hormones insulin and glucagon are heavy hitters both short and long term. Over that four to six hours, these hormones determine whether we get our energy by burning fat or by burning carbohydrates. As mentioned, insulin directs the body to store fat. Low levels of insulin signal low blood sugar, and the body begins to burn fat as fuel. Not only do we lose weight, but when the body burns fat, blood glucose is freed up for the brain. Remember, the brain can use only glucose for nourishment. And it doesn't like sharing. When insulin levels rise and we go to fat storage, body tissues start snatching up blood glucose and the brain starts griping. This explains the fatigue or irritability associated with hypoglycemia (low blood sugar).

The long-term hormonal effects fall on the prostaglandin system. Recall that insulin encourages the formation of bad prostaglandins, while glucagon blocks their production. Barry Sears, a leader in the development of dietary endocrinology, is studying the proper balance of protein, carbohydrate, and fat that will generate the best hormone responses. His research shows that for most people, every meal should consist of 30 percent protein, 30 percent fat, and 40 percent carbohydrate. Not a very radical formula, as exactly this balance shows up commonly both in milk and in Mom's homemade chicken soup.

Yet, most nutritionists feel that 30 percent protein is way too much. Typical recommendations call for half that figure. However, because the hormone-favorable diet dictates eating only about half the usual number of calories, you wind up eating about the same amount of protein as you do now—but *in better proportion* to the carbohydrates and fats. Happily, the diet allows the lower calorie intake to be both satisfying and comfortable. Barry Sears, a six-foot five-inch, 210-pound man, maintains a caloric intake of about 1,250 calories per day. For such a large man, 1,250 calories normally would equal starvation. However, in a diet where fat is burned as fuel and all the critical nutrients are provided, along with enough protein to prevent the breakdown of muscle tissue, calories go a long way.

Stimulating your body to burn fat will also keep your blood sugar stable, thus ensuring that your brain gets a consistent fuel source. With no periods of low blood sugar, the brain does not issue calls for more food.

People may also wonder about the recommendation for fat. Fat slows down absorption of carbohydrates, effectively dampening their troublesome stimulation of insulin. The 30 percent fat is relatively uncontroversial: it's what the American Heart Association recommends as the maximum intake. The average American ate closer to 40 percent until very recently, and most still eat more than 30 percent. Remember, this is 30 percent of a much smaller number of calories. The actual amount of fat you end up eating is about the same as that of the ultra-low-fat Pritikin diet.

It is the insulin-stimulating carbohydrates that take the hit. Notably, the body has no absolute requirement for carbohydrates. However, carbohydrates must at least equal the protein consumed in order to avoid forming ketones, undesirable chemicals produced by many high-protein diets.

WHEN LESS IS MORE

What about the low calorie intake? Is it, in and of itself, unhealthy? In every animal species studied, a reduction in calories (generally about 40 percent) produced better overall health, increased vigor, and greater longevity. But how do humans fare on 40 percent fewer calories? Barry Sears investigated this in one of the most unforgiving of laboratories: the world of elite swimmers.

The Stanford University swim team, which once dominated the field, had in recent years been beaten consistently by the University of Texas. When Sears put the Stanford team on the low calorie, hormonally favorable diet we've been discussing, most of the swimmers took it very seriously and were greatly rewarded. A number of them dramatically cut body fat without losing strength—indeed, their weight training produced greater increases in strength. Various articles in the sports press have since described Stanford's dramatic comeback. Further, Stanford team members won eight Olympic gold medals in Barcelona in 1992 and secured fourteen national individual championships in 1993.

Although this was not a controlled setting, the swimmers of Stanford proved that, at the very least, no impairment comes from the low-calorie diet even when demanding performance is called for. Sears, looking for a controlled setting, next turned to adult-onset diabetics. They were given either the hormonally favorable diet or the standard American Diabetic Association diet. In a sixteen-week crossover study, he found that patients not only gained better blood sugar control and reduced their insulin requirements but also lost weight. Similar results were obtained in a four-center study by Stanford researchers and recently published in the *Journal of the American Medical Association*. This study used the same 40 percent carbohydrate figure in the diet and an even higher fat percentage than Sears's, yet the diabetic patients still reduced their triglyceride levels.

I must note here that while nutritionists are divided on many issues, most do agree that low insulin levels are preferable to high. So, given a choice between high glycemic carbohydrates such as corn or french bread and low glycemic carbohydrates such as broccoli or peaches, nutritionists overwhelmingly favor the latter (see Glycemic Index of Carbohydrates, below).

To agree with this is really to agree with the heart of this diet. Actually, the only unusual feature is not that you eat less but what you eat less of—carbohydrates. Surprisingly, you'll actually feel a decrease in between-meal hunger, because you will avoid the blood sugar crash a couple of hours after eating.

GLYCEMIC INDEX OF CARBOHYDRATES
• •

A. *Rapid inducers of insulin*

Glycemic Index Greater Than 100%

Pasta, Cereals, Grains, Starches, and Breads
Cornflakes
Puffed rice
Puffed wheat
Millet
Instant rice
Instant potatoes
Microwaved potatoes
Millet
French bread

Simple Sugars
Maltose
Glucose

Snacks
Tofu ice cream
Puffed rice cakes

Glycemic Index Standard = 100%

Pasta, Cereals, Grains, Starches, and Breads
White bread

Glycemic Index 80%–100%

Pasta, Cereals, Grains, Starches, and Breads
Grapenuts
Whole wheat bread
Rolled oats
Oat bran
Instant mashed potatoes
White rice
Brown rice
Muesli
Shredded wheat

Vegetables
Carrots
Parsnips
Corn

Fruits
Bananas
Raisins
Apricots
Papayas
Mangoes

Snacks
Ice cream (low fat)
Corn chips
Rye crisps

B. Moderate inducers of insulin

Glycemic Index 50%–80%

Pasta, Cereals, Grains, Starches, and Breads
Spaghetti (white)

Spaghetti (whole wheat)
Macaroni
Pumpernickel rye bread
All-Bran

Fruits
Oranges
Orange juice

Vegetables
Peas
Pinto beans
Garbanzo beans
Kidney beans (canned)
Baked beans
Navy beans

Simple Sugars
Lactose
Sucrose

Snacks
Candy bar*
Potato chips (with fat)*

C. Reduced insulin secretion

Glycemic Index 30%–50%

Pasta, Cereals, Grains, Starches, and Breads
Barley
Oatmeal (slow-cooking)
Whole-grain rye bread

Fruits
Apples
Apple juice
Applesauce
Pears
Grapes
Peaches
Grapefruit

Vegetables
Kidney beans
Lentils
Black-eyed peas
Chickpeas
Kidney beans (dried)
Lima beans
Tomato soup
Peas

DairyProducts
Ice cream (high fat)*
Milk (skim, whole)
Yogurt

Glycemic Index 30% or Less

Fruits
Cherries
Plums
Grapefruits

Simple Sugars
Fructose

Vegetables
Soy beans*

Snacks
Peanuts*

---

*High fat content will reduce or retard the rate of carbohydrate absorption into the body.

THE DIET GUIDELINES

1. Attempt to build *every* meal according to the 30-30-40 formula of protein, fat, and carbohydrate. You cannot "average out" over the course of the day, as each meal is a separate hormonal adjustment, designed to optimize insulin and glucagon levels for four to six hours.
2. No meal should exceed 500 calories, because high calorie meals stimulate insulin, the fat storage hormone.
3. Except during sleep, no more than five hours should pass between meals. This usually means an afternoon and a bedtime snack. Snacks, however, need be only about 100 calories. Long intervals without food stimulate a starvation response and higher insulin release.
4. Carbohydrates should preferably be selected from those with a low glycemic index (see chart, pp. 126-129). High glycemic carbohydrates stimulate more insulin.
5. Avoid caffeine; it stimulates insulin. Decaf beverages are fine, however.
6. At least 8 ounces of liquid should be consumed with each meal or snack. A note of caution: When trying to cut down on sugar, go easy on the use of aspartame-sweetened diet sodas. A recent report indicated that high levels may cause depression in some people.
7. Choose monounsaturated fats such as olive oil over saturated fats. Especially avoid trans-fatty acids such as those found in margarine—use butter instead. Transfatty acids block prostaglandin production.
8. Beef fat and egg yolks should be consumed sparingly, perhaps once per week, as they contain arachidonic acid, the precursor of the bad prostaglandins.

Got it? Admittedly, world class athletes are better motivated to pull this off, but what about the rest of us? A few years ago I became interested in this diet. I'd already been eating less, hoping to shed some weight, but I found it difficult to cut calories. Sears's hormonally favorable diet helped me lose twenty pounds of fat and took fifteen points off my blood pressure—both common results. I have maintained these benefits for the past several years without difficulty, and I find the diet relatively easy to follow—at least compared to other "health conscious" diets.

Perhaps the biggest payoff for me was an improved sense of general well-being, but there have been many others. For example, ever since a high-school sports injury, my knees ached whenever I ran or tried other types of exercise; even crouching was painful. Now, however, I have no problem with my knees. (Others on the diet have also noted the striking ability to withstand strenuous exercise without getting stiff, as well as improved recovery time.) In addition, I gained energy and endurance, and I found I required less sleep.

Mind you, America does not make it easy to limit carbohydrates: They are everywhere you turn, and enthusiastically promoted. Although my patients usually do quite well at first, they tend to have trouble staying on the diet. However, my personal experience has helped me guide them through some of the rough spots and offer suggestions.

Many people are not used to eating much protein at breakfast. I have found good sources in nonfat yogurt topped with a handful of nuts, or low-fat cottage cheese topped with fruit. You may be surprised to find that such a breakfast, totaling about 200 calories, can fully satisfy you. However, if you have been eating a very high carbohydrate diet, it may take several days to reach the fat-burning state that makes such a small breakfast sufficient to sustain you until lunch.

Lunch poses little difficulty, as most meat sandwiches, made with a proper (low glycemic index) bread such as rye or pumpernickel, along with a piece of fruit, fill the 30-30-40 balance requirement. Other lunch options include many soups and chicken salad.

It's important to remember your afternoon and bedtime snacks. Patients love my Häagen-Dazs maintenance phase of the program. I've found that I can eat ice cream on a fairly regular basis if I balance it out with protein. So I put about half a cup of my favorite flavor in the blender, along with some high-protein powder (MET-Rx works well). Other good choices are nuts or cheese (very easy on the crackers). Fruit is fine, as long as you eat some protein along with it.

Dinner is easy. Most people already include enough protein. The trick is to find substitutes for the bread and potatoes. Almost any vegetable or fruit will fill the bill for carbohydrates—and you can eat several cups' worth. However, if you can't live without starch, a modest portion of whole-grain pasta is a reasonable alternative.

Happily, this diet allows you a great deal of flexibility. Occasional high-carbohydrate intake has little negative impact because your system has been primed for low insulin response. So, on special occasions, you can eat basically anything you like.

When my patients fall off this diet, it's usually because of carbohydrate craving. This isn't very surprising, as I treat a lot of winter depression, which, as you may recall, frequently produces this symptom. For those who suffer real carbohydrate withdrawal, I use the Carbohydrate Addicts Diet (Signet) developed by Drs. Richard and Rachel Heller, researchers at the Mount Sinai School of Medicine in New York. My patients come back amazed at the disappearance of their carbohydrate cravings. Yet, during most of their meals, the Hellers' diet forbids carbohydrate almost completely, to avoid stimulating insulin in these particularly overreactive individuals. They do, however, get a "reward" meal, typically dinner.

There are no restrictions on the reward meal except that one must stop eating after sixty minutes. This avoids a second insulin release that might occur after eighty to ninety minutes if one continued to eat for that long. The high-protein meals essentially fool the body into expecting protein, and therefore less insulin is released. For many patients, this diet prevents their usual winter weight gain, although weight loss is definitely rarer—especially if the "reward" meals are particularly rewarding.

Diet is probably the most challenging and most important aspect of modern lifestyle to change. An example of the power of the hormonally favorable diet discussed throughout this chapter is revealed in the experience of my patient Paul.

PAUL'S CASE

For well over a year, Paul had suffered what appeared to be a debilitating case of chronic fatigue syndrome. He had gone to many specialists, but nothing had helped. The condition dramatically impaired his ability to work; he felt so poorly that he became convinced he was dying.

His doctors had suggested that the problem might be depression, but Paul's psychological outlook was as positive as could be expected under the circumstances. I suggested that he follow the hormonally favorable diet and incorporate supplementation with essential fatty acids. The results were rapid and dramatic. Within weeks he felt like his old self, and after several more weeks he recovered fully. Paul, like the Stanford swimmers, had both the discipline and the motivation to follow the diet rather precisely. The payoff was remarkable.

I believe I have provided all you need to know to follow this diet, but you may find it easier with more detailed information on meal planning. A more thorough presentation of the diet, along with recipes and so forth, may be found in the book *The Zone,* by Dr. Barry Sears.

● ●

SUMMING UP

Our standard diet creates a host of problems, and "dieting" creates even more. Weight gain and other medical problems suggested that something was terribly wrong with how we ate, but until recently we lacked scientific guidance on what to change. We now have a new approach to eating that you can put to the test. Once you see what it can do for you, the only other thing to establish is your willingness to permanently change entrenched dietary habits.

For most people, diet, exercise, and the other changes discussed in recent chapters will raise serotonin levels satisfactorily.

However, some will find natural methods insufficient for whatever reason and may consider medication. Part III looks into the most often prescribed antidepressants and includes information on the important new medication therapies available and some others not yet available.

PART III

WHEN NATURAL IS NOT ENOUGH

Medication of
Today and Tomorrow

While nearly everyone self-medicates stress with some psychoactive substance, we tend to imagine great differences between medications like Prozac and perennial favorites like coffee, chocolate, or alcohol. Understandably, people worry about unknown long-term effects from psychoactive medications, and there is some basis for concern. But for many the concern is really with the very idea of taking them, and what they fear it may say about them. Yet few would hesitate to correct a low thyroid level. We see again the double standard.

These medications, just as the people they treat, deserve to be free of stigma. While we can often reasonably question the long-term safety of medications, we know quite well the frequently devastating short- and long-term results of depression, anxiety, and even stress itself. Clearly, there are no paths free of risk, and doing nothing is often the riskiest path of all.

The view I take is that effective natural treatments in general are preferable because they are likelier to complement the body's own efforts at healing, easier to tolerate and safer—especially over the long term. However, since we often do not have adequate evidence of their effectiveness, in serious conditions such as major depression, we can better rely on more established treatments and use natural approaches as supplements. Natural treatments alone often are not enough for many people, and in these cases medication can prove invaluable.

This section of the book looks at the choices we have among various medications, noting briefly the strengths of each and describing trouble spots. Chapter 14 discusses in depth the concerns raised about Prozac, establishing why many should indeed move beyond this medication, which has become the reference standard of treatment. For the legions who take Prozac now or might in the future, we look at both how to get more out of it and how to avoid problems that commonly arise.

Recently, new medications have become available that in key ways appear to surpass Prozac. Chapter 15 explores these new arrivals, particularly the extremely promising Effexor and Serzone, and a couple of remarkable medications that actually came out around the same time as Prozac but were largely overlooked. Chapter 16 looks to the future. A deluge of important developments, some involving medication, some not, will radically change the treatment picture in coming years.

Older medications such as the tricyclic antidepressants and Valium are discussed in appendix II. I consider most of them somewhat over the hill. The "old guard" still has a place, but generally it will not be the treatment of choice, especially for depression. In the many years since Prozac's introduction, I have watched expert opinion very *slowly* turn away from these older antidepressants.

This may be due mainly to the inertia of established opinion. I suspect dinosaurs didn't think much of mammals when they first came on the scene.

CHAPTER 14

PROZAC: THE REFERENCE STANDARD

*You don't need a shrink. There's nothing wrong with you
that can't be cured with a little Prozac and a polo mallet.*
—WOODY ALLEN *MANHATTAN MURDER MYSTERY*

We have seen that Prozac (fluoxetine) relieves a vast array of
psychiatric conditions. This impressive range of effects stems
from its action on serotonin, and on what I believe to be the
resultant increase in resistance to psychological and environmental stress, the underlying engine of much psychological
illness.

"BETTER THAN WELL"

Dr. Peter Kramer wrote in *Listening to Prozac* that his Prozac
patients often felt "better than well." I would agree that occasionally people may feel this way, but typically only at first.
Some do experience something like elation as Prozac raises
their serotonin levels to normal and thus, relatively abruptly,
unyokes them from the sensation of grinding stress—sometimes
for the first time in many years. But, like one growing accus-
tomed to the sweet smell of a bakery, people soon realize that
feeling good is simply wellness, and the sense of excitement
quiets.

WILL PROZAC CHANGE WHO I AM?

Some people, no matter how depressed or anxious, fear that psychoactive medications will change them—a concern voiced even by those who regularly self-medicate with cigarettes, alcohol, or assorted illegal substances. The concern is a bit paradoxical in that one does not contemplate any psychotherapy, medication-based or otherwise, without hoping for real change. At any rate, my patients who take Prozac—even the ones who initially worried about this issue—have never complained of any loss of identity.

Back in 1989 I published a paper that examined Prozac's ability to alter personality. I described a dozen patients with borderline personality disorder, a difficult-to-treat condition whose symptoms include suicidality, impulsivity, and irritability. Typically, the sufferers tolerated stress terribly. Such symptoms no doubt strike you as similar to those that indicate low serotonin function, and, sure enough, these patients responded dramatically to Prozac's serotonin enhancement. Since my paper, several research groups, both here and abroad, have similarly found Prozac effective in borderline personality disorder. As many as one in five patients seeking psychiatric care suffer this troubling affliction, and only the Prozac-like medications have been shown to help significantly. Stopping so many of a person's symptoms could be termed a real personality change, but it strikes me that what emerges is the patient's true personality, which the illness had previously smothered.

CARLA'S CASE

Carla's life seemed a continuing crisis; more precisely, one long series of crises. Often suicidal, Carla at twenty-seven was married—but just barely—and similarly poorly employed. This was many years ago, and at the time there was no medication known to be effective in treating borderline personality disorder. Carla's treatment consisted initially only of cognitive behavioral psychotherapy (talk therapy aimed at developing new, positive ways of thinking about life's problems and developing more helpful responses).

Carla worked exceptionally hard at this and actually made considerable headway. However, every time a new crisis exploded, the stress seemed to steal away her hard-earned gains. Very simply, her strong emotional reactions short-circuited her ability to think clearly. She seemed somehow emotionally raw, often experiencing intense pain with little provocation.

Recognizing that improved serotonin function might help Carla, I started her on Prozac. Within days, to our mutual amazement stress no longer seemed to carry quite the old weight, and her mood reflected a new stability. As she said: "It felt like I stepped off an emotional roller coaster." Carla could now truly apply what she had learned in cognitive therapy, and she made significant changes in her approach to problems and her interactions with others.

However, her road to further recovery was not trouble-free. Carla did not like taking medication; she saw it as a sign of weakness or defect. In the next few years, she discontinued Prozac more than a dozen times, always against my advice, and always within a few days finding herself once more emotionally raw and overwhelmed, sometimes even suicidal. Fortunately, restarting the medication resulted in a good recovery within a day or two. A few years ago, Carla had finally had enough and was convinced that she must stay on Prozac. Over the last few years, she has told me that despite Prozac's expense, it is not an item subject to budget cutting.

Carla's case seems one of transformation by Prozac. She now has a happy marriage and a good job where she is both well liked and valued for her contributions. But asking Carla whether, given her dramatic change, Prozac has changed her personality, she answers "no." She tells me that she doesn't feel like a different person but simply feels like she did on the occasional good days she had before Prozac.

Carla does not find her new calmer state unfamiliar. What is different is that she can trust her calm to last, for stress that once turned her life upside down no longer derails her.

Many might say that Carla's personality has changed. It's a matter of definition, I suppose. After all, many of the "changes" are reversible when medication is stopped. At any rate, what we can take from Carla's story is that Prozac, even in extreme cases, usually leaves one's fundamental sense of self unaltered.

In rare cases, this decreased reactivity to stress can reach the point of clear unwanted "personality change." I have never seen this but the psychiatric literature contains a number of cases including a woman on Prozac who, quite out of character, expressed a desire at a company party to serve cocktails in her bra "like Madonna." Of course, such essentially toxic reactions by rare individuals can occur with almost any medicine.

Change stemming from any kind of therapy can upset those around you. Someone may become more assertive, for example, less "codependent," or intimidated, and annoyed spouses or coworkers will fault the medication. However, the individuals themselves almost always perceive these changes as a welcome relief from distress and a chance finally to act more powerfully.

SIDE EFFECTS OF PROZAC

The Suicide and Violence Question

Despite the rosy picture painted by effectiveness studies and the overall positive clinical experience of psychiatrists like myself, reports of violence and suicide by those taking Prozac have understandably captured the attention of the media and the public. The first report of such an occurrence was actually contained in my 1989 paper on borderline personality disorder. One patient became intensely suicidal, but this resolved after a few days, and notably this patient ultimately benefited greatly from the addition of Desyrel (see appendix II). This is especially significant because Desyrel blocks the serotonin-2A receptor, which is the one believed to be overactive in suicidal individuals. By increasing serotonin, Prozac generally opposes suicide, but to the extent that it also acts on this suicide-related receptor, conceivably it might occasionally be dangerous in predisposed individuals with overly responsive serotonin-2A receptors.

The original media concern about a suicide connection arose from a later Harvard report by Dr. Martin Teicher and colleagues on six patients who acted intensely suicidal after taking Prozac. If indeed Teicher's patients were experiencing a reaction to Prozac, as opposed to suicidality due simply to depression, it may be accounted for in part by the fact that a number of these patients had recently taken a monoamine oxidase inhibiter antidepressant (MAOI). Suicidal behavior possibly might be related to a failure to clear MAOI antidepressants from the body before taking Prozac. Evidence indicates that the effects of MAOIs on the brain persist for four weeks or more after cessation of treatment. The literature further contains a few other case reports suggesting a cause and effect relationship between Prozac and an urge to harm oneself.

Some of the incidents reported could also relate to high dosage and/or rapid escalation of dose. In a study comparing one-, two-, and three-capsule consumption per day for depression, the high-dose group experienced an initial worsening of symptoms. Further, one high-dose patient made a suicide attempt. However, other studies in which patients were gradually built up to high doses have not found either induced depression or suicidal ideation.

Therefore, it may well be true that a person with a special predisposition can become more suicidal because of Prozac. But all this really means at present is that Prozac should be avoided for perhaps a month or more after MAOI treatment has stopped, dose increases should not be too rapid, and that if anyone on Prozac becomes more suicidal, reduction or elimination of Prozac should be considered.

To put these suicide reports in perspective, one must realize that 3 percent of the U.S. population attempts suicide at some point. Further, most depressed people have some suicidal thoughts. Thus, a better group for studying this possible side effect would be nondepressed people. One such study, involving more than 3,800 patients taking Prozac experimentally for weight loss, suggested that Prozac does not cause suicidal behavior. This particular group had been screened for depression and was likely less depressed than the average population. The only instance of suicidal behavior occurred in someone taking a placebo well after Prozac was discontinued.

A number of studies have now concluded that an analysis of the available literature indicates that in general, Prozac-like medications exercise a *protective* effect against the emergence of suicidal thoughts and behavior. Notably, it has emerged that certain of the older tricyclic antidepressants are associated with higher rates of suicide than Prozac.

The gist of all this? Considering all the evidence, a depressed person who avoids Prozac for fear of suicide has generally placed him- or herself in greater danger of self-harm. Remember nothing increases suicide risk as much as depression itself. The only course of action that may ultimately prove to be preferable would be a better antidepressant. Given what we are now learning about the serotonin-2A receptor, it is possible that such a medication may now be available, in the recently introduced Serzone. Notably, the related medication Desyrel, which also blocks this troublesome receptor, is the only medication that appears associated with lower rates of suicide/suicidal ideation than Prozac. Desyrel, however, is not generally favored as a first-line antidepressant. Time will tell if this will apply to the generally more favorable Serzone. (See chapter 16 for more on this medication.)

As for the question of violence while taking Prozac, keep in mind more than four million acts of violence take place in the United States each year. In this sea of violence, it is difficult to attribute to Prozac occasional acts of violence by people who take the medication. The scientific community has looked for evidence of Prozac-caused violence or aggressive behavior. Eighteen separate studies of Prozac, testing efficacy on various problems besides depression, were evaluated. This provided a good sized database of about four thousand patients. All the various aggressive behaviors documented were *four times more common* in those taking a placebo. This and other research demonstrates Prozac and similar medications have great potential in *treating* those prone to violence. Still, "paradoxical" reactions cannot be ruled out in rare individuals. Prozac's potential to cause agitation could certainly contribute to violence, but then so could a little too much coffee. Nothing is completely safe.

Mania: Too Much of a Good Thing

Although we often use Prozac for manic depressive (bipolar) patients, we cannot use the medication to treat pure mania, which is a dysfunctional state of irritability or, more commonly, excessively elevated mood. There are reports of people who were taking Prozac for depression turning manic, although causation is very difficult to prove because lifting depression by any method may result in mania.

Winter depression patients often undergo a mild mania called hypomania in spring or summer. Strikingly, in a number of such individuals Prozac has appeared to quiet the hypomania. I find it interesting that a medication can energize one in winter and be sedating in the warmer months. Yet this is like the reaction that winter depressives have to carbohydrates; in contrast to most people, they find carbohydrates stimulating in winter, but in summer their response matches others' in producing sedation. Similarly, winter depressives respond to medications that stimulate serotonin receptors in an opposite fashion from others—but only during winter. While serotonin might well have antimanic properties, given that lithium and most other known antimanic medications promote serotonin, for the time being the use of Prozac or similar drugs for bipolar patients must generally be restricted to treating only the depressed phase or recognized as a clearly experimental treatment.

The Melatonin Question

Many antidepressants have been found to boost melatonin—which, as we have seen, may have very important benefits in its own right. However, a couple of Prozac studies have failed to show this elevation, and, more disturbingly, a recent study of seasonally depressed patients showed a significant drop in melatonin levels. All things being equal, given the importance of melatonin especially for long-term use, this may become an important reason to select an antidepressant other than Prozac. Most of the newer agents have not yet been evaluated for this, but the Prozac-like medication Luvox clearly elevates melatonin levels, and the promising Wellbutrin,

Effexor and Serzone, on the basis of their mechanism of action (in part boosting norepinephrine), are predicted to stimulate melatonin.

Lesser Side Effects

Prozac's greatest advantage over old-guard antidepressants is its easy toleration. Further, Prozac and similar medications tend not to impair motor or cognitive skills, which are important when driving or "operating heavy machinery." However, a few people will find themselves somewhat impaired, so care should be taken when first starting medication.

A handful of lesser side effects include mild nausea, headache, or insomnia, which usually disappears after a couple of weeks. Occasionally, individuals get a rash, generally regarded as an indication to stop Prozac. Some people undergo reduced appetite and subsequent weight loss, especially at the beginning of treatment, but this rarely persists (much to the dismay of many).

Surprisingly, studies also reveal the opposite side effect: many people gain weight on Prozac. A substantial number of my patients have complained about this. Why this happens, or even whether it is truly caused by the Prozac, remains unknown.

A more persistent side effect is agitation, or jitteriness. This sometimes forces people off the medication because agitation, unlike most other side effects, usually does not go away simply by reducing dosage. Another "opposite" side effect is sedation. In my experience, this almost always disappears with reduced dosage.

Far and away the most common side effect, although originally reported as rare, is sexual dysfunction. Estimates now are that nearly half of patients can expect some form of sexual problem, typically delayed ejaculation or orgasm. In addition, Prozac often causes decreased sexual interest, although very rarely erectile difficulties (erectile improvement has also been reported). Ways in which to lessen or eliminate these and other side effects are discussed a little later.

Avoiding Side Effects

The metabolic process for Prozac varies widely. Because of differences in metabolism, one person may have ten times the blood level of another on the same dose of a given medication. For many years, people using Prozac took one or more 20 mg capsules, which until recently was the smallest dose available. This was more than many really needed. Most tolerated this well enough, because, as discussed, the side effect profile is generally low. Now lower dosage forms are manufactured (a 10 mg capsule and, for smaller doses, a liquid form).

However, for more than six years I have, by various means, routinely started Prozac at 1 mg to 5 mg per day to ease initial adjustment. Prozac's stimulating or energizing effects are generally desirable, especially as depression often robs energy, but as excessive dosage is reached, stimulation can become annoying agitation. Thus, it's especially important to start with a low dose in patients sensitive to stimulation. For example, about half of those suffering panic disorder would have an extremely unpleasant experience taking a 20 mg capsule of Prozac at the beginning of treatment.

The time of day at which one takes Prozac may matter. Prozac at mealtime can lessen nausea. However, studies have not found that insomnia improves with dosage timing. Still, individuals can experiment with timing if they have trouble sleeping. Agitation can be minimized with Valium-like medications, but I find the nonaddictive BuSpar generally far preferable. Often, 30 mg per day of this anxiety medication quickly reduces such agitation. Further, BuSpar may intensify the antidepressant effects of Prozac for some; and is generally very well tolerated. BuSpar can also reduce more unusual Prozac side effects such as excessive nighttime sweating, overly vivid dreams, and, as discussed below, sexual dysfunction.

REDUCING SEXUAL SIDE EFFECTS

When people discontinue Prozac without telling their doctor why, it's often because of sexual dysfunction. This is most unfortunate, because promising methods exist for overcoming this side effect.

Dosage reduction is the first thing to try. Many people need no more than 5 mg of Prozac to get good antidepressant relief. Some patients skip a day's medication when they want sexual relations, and this sometimes helps. Watch out for return of your underlying symptoms, however. Some patients report results by adding yohimbine, the only medication identified in the *Physician's Desk Reference* as arousing desire ("may have activity as an aphrodisiac"). A couple of published studies have found no problem with the combination. However, the *PDR* recommends against use of yohimbine with antidepressants, so your doctor may resist prescribing it.

Anecdotal reports support the addition of amantadine and cyproheptadine to combat sexual dysfunction; however, some studies say that cyproheptadine may undermine Prozac's therapeutic effects. Not yet published reports suggest that Wellbutrin, another antidepressant, in doses of 50 mg to 100 mg per day, can help. I recently published in the journal *Depression* one of the largest patient series in the literature on treating this problem, noting that BuSpar helped 70 percent of my patients who experienced sexual side effects.

Rarely will a person have to discontinue Prozac because of such side effects if his or her doctor tries the various techniques discussed. However, sometimes the "fit" just isn't quite right with Prozac and one should try another antidepressant. Wellbutrin and Serzone rarely have sexual side effects. These two medications are discussed in chapter 15.

ABUSE AND ADDICTION

Some have claimed that Prozac is basically a stimulant, with the problems of abuse associated with amphetamines. The argument goes that since taking Prozac reduces self-administration of amphetamines in animal studies, Prozac must be a substitution for the amphetamine and thus actually *be* a stimulant itself. But the administration of Prozac also reduces animals' use of alcohol, fundamentally a depressant, so by the same reasoning Prozac is a depressant. Indeed, since Prozac also reduces an animal's interest in food . . . you see the problem with this kind of reasoning.

In actual drug discrimination studies (the usual method for settling questions like these), both animals and people have no trouble distinguishing Prozac from amphetamines. One does, however, see occasional amphetaminelike reactions, but these last only a few days at the beginning of Prozac treatment. Prozac's actions are complex, as indeed are those of the serotonin system, but the bottom line remains that with more than 15 million people having taken Prozac, neither abuse nor addiction has been a problem. Of course, some people will abuse anything—aspirin, Prozac, even vitamins—but nearly everyone takes the lowest effective dose of Prozac, because taking more only means more side effects and more money.

Further, we see no problems of physical addiction. Withdrawing from Prozac, even after extended use, poses no difficulty. However, gradual tapering off is recommended to avoid abrupt return of any symptoms, especially irritability.

A NOTE ON ALCOHOL AND PROZAC

No doubt millions of people drink while taking Prozac. Combining Prozac and alcohol generally does not magnify the effects of alcohol, another advantage over older agents. Nonetheless, the interaction between alcohol and the serotonin system is a complex one. For depression in general, alcohol is best avoided. One study found recovery significantly slower from depression in those who drank alcohol. In my practice, I have found that for some, an evening of alcohol and Prozac turns ugly. One or 2 percent of my Prozac patients suffer serious mood crashes after drinking. The alcohol alone certainly may have caused this—in all cases, the amount consumed was more than moderate. However, these patients saw the effect as qualitatively different from previous alcohol-induced states, mainly because of more prominent suicidal ideation. I always hesitate to impose absolute lifestyle restrictions of uncertain necessity, so I'll simply note that all these patients vigorously and spontaneously resolved henceforth to avoid the combination.

IF PROZAC IS PRESCRIBED

Getting the Dose Right

The early availability of Prozac only in 20 mg capsules helped counter a well-documented practice by nonpsychiatric physicians of routinely prescribing antidepressants in doses too low to work. It was often said that if a doctor was half-sure someone was depressed, half the effective dosage was prescribed. Physician caution stems no doubt from earlier generations of antidepressants that had worrisome toxicity problems.

However, it turns out that with Prozac, a lower dose works comparably to the standard dosage. A study of people with major depression compared a 5 mg dosage with the standard 20 mg, as well as higher doses, and found no real variation in results. Researchers did uncover a slight trend toward higher percentage of full cures with 20 mg. By contrast, the lower dosage boasted fewer side effects.

As mentioned, I almost always have my Prozac patients begin with a fraction of a capsule, generally 1 mg to 5 mg, then over several days suggest an increase to 20 mg—assuming they've had no problems with side effects along the way. If there are any difficulties, we back off the dosage and stay for a longer period at the lower dosage. Usually, the dosage can eventually be raised to 20 mg. I consider 20 mg the standard because its effectiveness is most widely established, and many symptoms do respond best to higher dosage, including those related to overall stress tolerance. However, I have no hesitation in working with lower doses when toleration of side effects is an issue. Fortunately, most people who seem to need more also tolerate more.

Be it 5 mg or 60 mg, the ideal dose varies by individual. Some Harvard researchers studied a group of patients who had failed to respond to eight weeks of Prozac at the standard 20 mg per day. They compared adding a low dose of tricyclic antidepressant to the regimen versus adding a low dose of lithium to it versus simply doubling the Prozac dose. To practically everyone's surprise, doubling the Prozac proved the most effective of the three approaches.

Prozac doses also vary according to the type of condition treated. Winter depression, for instance, usually requires a higher dose than normal depression. My practice, which is composed largely of those afflicted with winter depression, has given me the opportunity to assess carefully optimal dosage for SAD. I have found that between 40 mg and 80 mg per day brings excellent response. At lower doses people get only limited relief. With Prozac costing over two dollars a capsule, most people do not take more than they absolutely need, and yet year after year my patients maintain these doses. Consistent with this, in the only placebo-controlled trial of Prozac and winter depression, investigators reported that a 20 mg dosage showed only marginal benefits.

I speculate that the high Prozac doses required for winter depression mean that serotonin deficiency plays a more central role than it does in nonseasonal depression. This also may be the case with conditions where stress intolerance or irritability dominate, including borderline personality disorder and PMS; all these problems also seem to respond better and better as one raises the dose, usually requiring more than 20 mg for optimal relief.

One condition requiring low doses is panic disorder. As mentioned earlier, the stimulation of Prozac can aggravate those who are prone to panic. In my experience, treatment should start at about 1 mg per day. Ultimately, my patients can generally work up, over a week or more, to 5 or 10 mg, with a final dosage reaching 10 mg to 20 mg per day. As emphasized, I now start almost everyone at these lower levels to avoid the occasional reaction of extreme panic or agitation. This reaction may represent an undiagnosed case of panic disorder, as the condition is quite common, occurring in several percent of the population.

One trial of individuals with unusual sensitivity to Prozac's side effects actually found that they tended to respond better than others after an appropriately low dosage was employed. Ultimately, the vast majority of people can tolerate Prozac with a properly adjusted dose, so start low to avoid problems that could completely upset treatment.

How Soon Will Prozac Work?

One of the great frustrations in any antidepressant therapy is waiting for the results to appear. Typically, Prozac response for depression takes two to four weeks, although careful evaluation often reveals mild improvement in the first week.

Response may, however, come as late as six to eight weeks. Patience may be rewarded, but a recent study showed the lack of at least a 20 percent improvement after four weeks of treatment strongly predicted ultimate failure. Further I believe that asking a patient to wait six or eight weeks before trying another medication is generally asking too much of someone seriously depressed.

With the conditions mentioned earlier where stress and irritability play major roles, Prozac offers more rapid relief. I often see benefits the first day of treatment and certainly after a week. Yet sometimes these patients claim no improvement until, upon questioning, they realize to their surprise that some daily habit—say, pounding the steering wheel in anger—did not occur during the past week.

How Long Should You Take Prozac?

As you may have guessed, the answer is: "It depends." For someone with depression, the standard recommendation is to continue treatment for six to twelve months past the point of feeling well again. Studies have found a high relapse rate in those who stop taking the medication any sooner than that.

For people who have had two or three previous episodes of major depression, psychiatrists now often recommend indefinite treatment to foil the high odds of recurrence. After three episodes of depression, recurrence runs about 90 percent, and it is much easier and healthier to prevent depression than to try to treat it once it's been established. Further, about 20 percent of depressions prove extremely difficult to treat, making it very important that the patient never begin such an episode.

In eating and panic disorders, as well as with obsessive compulsiveness, once on medication a person can learn a new pattern of behavior that does not require sustained medication. A gradual tapering off allows assessment of just how solid the recovery is and whether the medication should be continued. Because these conditions can be episodic, one might take the approach of discontinuing medication until symptoms recur, a strategy more risky in the case of depression.

When discontinuing medication, I always have patients taper off over a week or more. A week after stopping, half the Prozac still remains in the bloodstream. Dispite this long "half life" within one to five days of discontinuing dosage abruptly, I find that many people's symptoms return, especially, as noted, irritability. This short-lived "rebound" irritability may be worse than at the start of treatment. I have developed a healthy respect for the serotonin system and the importance of avoiding rapid or extreme alterations.

The approaches in part II of this book, "Natural Prozac," can reduce one's need for Prozac or in some cases even eliminate it. You may recall the case of Steven, who required 60 mg per day of Prozac, but with "natural Prozac," primarily the nutritional approaches, he no longer needed it at all. Adjustments of this sort must be done only in careful collaboration with your treating physician, however.

USING OTHER ANTIDEPRESSANTS WITH PROZAC

A major trend in psychopharmacology today is the use of medications in combination. This mirrors trends elsewhere in medicine, for example in cancer therapy, where combining several agents at lower dosage causes both better response and reduced side effects. For the same reasons, I often prescribe Prozac in combination with another medication. I have used Prozac, and similar medications, with BuSpar in well over one hundred patients; the combination has proved extremely helpful. Other findings bear this out. For example, one study of 24 patients with depression found that seventeen of them improved with the addition of BuSpar when Prozac failed to be effective.

If BuSpar fails, a small amount of an older antidepressant like Norpramin might work without causing significant side effects. However, I must emphasize that Prozac can greatly amplify blood levels of tricyclic antidepressants—typically several fold—so this must be closely monitored. Adding Desyrel, lithium, and various other agents has also proved quite helpful for some patients.

A FINAL THOUGHT: PROZAC AND $$$

Recent studies at health maintenance organizations shed light on the true cost of antidepressant therapy. Records revealed that Prozac treatment actually cost *less* than medication with "cheaper" generic tricyclic antidepressants. The Prozac pill did cost considerably more, but the patients taking Prozac required fewer lab tests, doctor visits, hospitalizations, and other services. With all factors accounted for, Prozac was a bargain.

The same applies to social costs. Another study found that over an eight-week period, Prozac patients lost two to five fewer workdays than did those taking the older antidepressants. Obviously, Prozac also means a lower personal cost to the individuals and to those around them.

• •

SUMMING UP

Prozac boasts relative ease of use and relieves many, many conditions. Older antidepressants leave some of these conditions untouched, although Prozac is no better than these antidepressants at relieving most depression. However, older agents cause many more side effects. Thus, the growing consensus among experts and the overwhelming vote of the marketplace is that Prozac-like medications are the first-line treatment for depression.

Yet, getting this first-line treatment may require some assertiveness if your doctor prefers older antidepressants. It may prove even more challenging if your health plan does not cover Prozac or other new agents. For Prozac is by no means the only representative of the new order. Chapter 15 offers a look at some of Prozac's impressive competitors.

CHAPTER 15

NEW MEDICATIONS: IMPORTANT ADVANCES

Nothing endures but change.

—HERACLITUS

Modern psychopharmacology was born during the postwar baby boom. By the end of the 1950s a true revolution had occurred, and psychiatrists had all the major classes of drugs that they would use for nearly a quarter century. Amazingly, while other areas of medicine were continually deluged with remarkable new pharmaceuticals, over this same period there were no significant advances in psychiatric medications. Minor refinements were made on existing drugs, and great progress was made in diagnosis and application of existing treatment, but not until the 1980s did a second revolution root.

This chapter looks at the medications of this second revolution, which serve as the main pharmaceutical alternatives to Prozac. Many will find one or a combination of agents far better than Prozac. While this recent revolution began before Prozac, the advance elements of the revolution received little fanfare.

BUSPAR: MOST UNDERRATED

BuSpar (buspirone) was introduced in 1986, possibly ahead of its time. I have placed this with the new medications because, although it came out slightly before Prozac, its potential is still largely unrecognized. Doctors and patients alike had trouble understanding the effects of this medication. Many still do not even believe that it works. BuSpar does work, however. People don't get the usual side effects or abrupt changes to tell them it's working—they just gradually get better. In principle, that should be ideal—a medication that does its job quietly. But when most people take something for anxiety, they want relief immediately, even if that means sedation or other side effects.

Perhaps BuSpar should have been introduced as an antidepressant instead of an antianxiety agent. As we have seen, what is helpful for depression is generally helpful for anxiety. In at least five controlled studies, BuSpar has been found effective against depression. However, at present no studies have directly compared BuSpar with other antidepressants. My clinical experience certainly confirms BuSpar's antidepressant efficacy. As an antidepressant, no one would have thought twice about its slow onset of action, since depression is generally slow to respond to all treatments. Its lack of significant side effects and unparalleled safety would have put it head and shoulders above the competition. But even as an antianxiety agent it is still far above the field—but widely unrecognized.

Evidence from at least nine controlled studies indicates that BuSpar relieves chronic anxiety as effectively as benzodiazepines such as Valium. However, those who take Valium generally realize that the Valium caused their improvement. After all, they felt it working from the first dose. People who take BuSpar often report that while they feel better, they doubt that the medication had anything to do with it.

Aside from failing to get credit for its work, BuSpar has been somewhat inconvenient to administer. The standard recommendation was to take BuSpar three times a day, a schedule people found hard to maintain, especially because they felt no immediate effect. When they missed a dose—as people always do—they typically didn't notice any difference. In contrast, with Xanax (alprazolam)—the leading anxiety medication—people can often tell you, without a clock, exactly when their next dose should be.

A recent study indicates that BuSpar works just as well when given only twice a day. I have found this true among my patients and routinely use this easier dosing schedule.

When you compare BuSpar with benzodiazepines like Valium or Xanax for treating chronic anxiety, all of the advantages lie with BuSpar except speed of action and cost, as generic benzodiazepines are much cheaper. BuSpar is nonsedating and non-addictive, while benzodiazepine habituation often causes serious withdrawal problems. BuSpar typically does not cause memory, concentration, or psychomotor impairment, nor does it exaggerate alcohol's effects—all of which can occur with benzodiazepines. Further, although benzodiazepines alone are relatively safe in overdose, they can fatally suppress breathing when mixed with other drugs, including alcohol. BuSpar is among the safest drugs known. People have taken more than fifty times the initial daily dose for extended periods without significant problems. Surely it is reassuring to use medication that has such low toxicity.

The most remarkable advantage of BuSpar is its long-term effects. In patients who had received either Tranxene (a benzodiazepine) or BuSpar for six months, investigators found that forty months later, only one-quarter of the BuSpar-treated patients had moderate to severe anxiety, while half of the patients treated with Tranxene still suffered. Remarkably, at this forty-month follow-up, not one of the BuSpar patients was currently taking any anxiety medication; about two-thirds of the Tranxene patients were.

BuSpar, like Prozac, is quite versatile. It has helped some people with aggression, especially those suffering dementias or such developmental disorders as autism. Preliminary evidence also shows possible efficacy for obsessive compulsive disorder; premenstrual syndrome; social phobia; substance abuse (alcohol and cigarettes); and tardive dyskinesia, a debilitating movement disorder caused by antipsychotic drugs.

BuSpar can strengthen the antidepressant effect of Prozac. Dr. Fredrick Jacobsen, a researcher at the National Institute of Mental Health, first reported this finding for both seasonal and nonseasonal depression. In another study, twenty-five patients who responded poorly to Prozac were supplemented with BuSpar; seventeen responded well. There is every reason to believe that

BuSpar will help boost the effect of other antidepressants as well.

The combination of two safe medications such as Prozac and BuSpar appears considerably safer than a single relatively toxic antidepressant. I have given this combination to well over a hundred patients and found that not only did therapeutic effects generally increase, but Prozac side effects actually decreased! Exceptional cases always exist, however. Some patients who find Prozac helpful in diminishing their irritability grow irritable once again when BuSpar is added. This is somewhat surprising, since BuSpar on its own seems a promising treatment for irritability.

Again, understand that BuSpar may take up to four weeks to match the anxiety relief offered by, say, Xanax, but since most patients with anxiety disorders have been suffering for some time, slow onset should *not* be of much concern, given BuSpar's many advantages. BuSpar should also be kept in mind as a safe and distinctly different antidepressant that can work on its own or as an adjunct to other treatment.

VARIATIONS ON PROZAC: THE SSRIS

Two antidepressants, Zoloft (sertraline) and Paxil (paroxetine), whose actions are very similar to those of Prozac, have come on the market in recent years. These medications belong to the class known as "selective serotonin re-uptake inhibitors," or SSRIs. Recently, a fourth SSRI, Luvox (fluvoxamine), has appeared, but so far the FDA has approved it only for treating obsessive compulsive disorder. This is primarily a question of marketing. In Europe, Luvox has long been marketed as an antidepressant.

Zoloft

Zoloft was the first SSRI to join ranks with Prozac. At first, it sounded to me like something out of *Star Trek*. Oddly enough, the name was probably one of the drug's main drawing points initially, although it might just as well have been called Not Prozac. At the time of Zoloft's arrival, Prozac was generating a considerable amount of bad publicity, making many doctors and patients uncomfortable about using it. This holds true today, although to a somewhat lesser degree.

If one SSRI causes side effects, will you do better on another? Quite possibly. Despite the fact that SSRIs are virtually inter-changeable in various studies over groups of people, this often is not the case for a given individual. In a Zoloft study of nearly one hundred patients intolerant of Prozac, more than three-quarters of the participants had no significant side effects, completed a full eight-week course of Zoloft, and elected to continue the drug.

This study matches my experience in switching patients from Prozac to Zoloft because of side effects. Notably, however, many requested a return to Prozac because they felt it worked better. Dosage may be at issue; some suggest that 100 mg or 150 mg of Zoloft, not the recommended starting dosage of 50 mg, is actually the equivalent of Prozac's standard 20 mg dose. It should be emphasized that generally there is no important difference in either efficacy or overall rate of side effects for the SSRIs, though for a given individual it can be like night and day. Obviously, these medications are not quite as similar as our limited understanding of their mechanisms leads us to believe.

We do, however, know of some differences between these medications. Zoloft leaves the body more rapidly than Prozac. Blood levels drop by one half in about a day, compared to about a week for Prozac. This can be a problem if one tends to miss occa-sional doses, but an advantage if one needs to stop a medication rapidly—for instance, because of a drug interaction, or when planning to switch to an incompatible medication such as an MAOI. Drug interaction problems appear less likely with Zoloft. Although SSRIs appear to share the same wide spectrum of effec-tiveness, Zoloft is the first medication to be shown effective in a controlled study for treating winter depression. Notably, the study allowed use of maximal dosage (200 mg per day).

Paxil

Paxil also appears to have certain advantages over Prozac. It may be preferable in the treatment of bipolar depression (manic-depression). Dr. Gary Sachs and colleagues at Harvard have found a relatively low rate of induction of mania with Paxil.

A study comparing Paxil with Prozac in depressed elderly patients found both drugs similarly effective, but a significant difference existed between the two in early treatment. At three weeks, those taking Paxil felt less depressed than those on Prozac and also showed greater improvement in cognitive function. Although the advantage of rapid onset has been claimed for many medications and subsequently failed to hold up, a comparison study with the tricyclic imipramine also showed faster action for Paxil, achieving superiority by the second week. This advantage was maintained over the six-week study.

Paxil seems to have a superior effect also in treating anxiety symptoms. A pooled analysis of worldwide data suggested that Paxil has a greater effect on anxiety and agitation associated with depression when compared to other medications. Here again, studies have shown somewhat faster action, although more work is needed to truly establish an advantage. Like Zoloft, Paxil leaves the body more rapidly than Prozac. While generally a desirable feature, a rapid change in blood levels when ending treatment may contribute to withdrawal symptoms including dizziness, insomnia, nausea, and confusion. These symptoms appear more of a concern for Paxil than for other SSRIs. Patients should taper off gradually—which is good advice for all psychotropic medications.

The manufacturer of Paxil states that a quarter of users will report sedation effects—double the number for Prozac or Zoloft. Surprisingly, however, lethargic patients often do well with Paxil and find it energizing. At any rate, the sedation side effect frequently disappears with a lower dosage or the passage of time.

Luvox: The Unofficial Antidepressant

In the United States Luvox is FDA approved only for the treatment of obsessive compulsive disorder. Obtaining FDA approval is a slow process, and the manufacturer is awaiting approval for depression. However, Luvox is well established internationally as an effective antidepressant. Though it only recently became available in the United States, it has been in use abroad longer than Prozac. It may never see wide acceptance in the United States as an antidepressant, but there is reason to believe it may be the best available SSRI.

Similar to studies of Prozac, early work with Luvox used excessively high doses. At these levels it produced considerable nausea. It still carries this reputation, but a recent study by Dr. Charles Nemeroff and others at Emory University reported Luvox fully as effective as Prozac in treating depression with fewer side effects overall and specifically less nausea. This and other recent studies have limited dosage from 50 mg to a maximum of 150 mg per day. Unlike Prozac, Luvox is very unlikely to cause agitation, and it appears to cause by far the least sexual dysfunction of the SSRIs—one study found three- to fourfold higher rates with Zoloft. Sexual dysfunction is such a common problem with *all* the others that this alone is a compelling reason to favor Luvox. Dry mouth and constipation are also notably uncommon. It is cleared from the body faster than any of the other SSRIs.

It is occasionally sedating and for this reason bedtime dosage is usually recommended, though insomnia can also be a problem. Some of the sedation may relate to its effect on raising morning melatonin levels. A study showed that this does not occur if the dosage is given in the morning. The ability to raise melatonin levels may be a very important side benefit as long as the elevation is restricted to the night. This is possible by proper timing of the dosage. Afternoon or early evening dosage may prove to be best for many people in terms of melatonin effects. In contrast, as noted, Prozac has either been found to leave melatonin levels unchanged, or, in one study of winter depression, to significantly depress levels. If all of these melatonin findings are confirmed to be true, this could mean that long-term usage of Luvox may be considerably healthier than Prozac. Data are not available on melatonin effects of Zoloft and Paxil. Given the unofficial status of Luvox as an antidepressant in the United States, and the resulting prohibition from marketing it for the treatment of depression, Luvox will likely continue to be a fairly well kept secret for some time—and one worth knowing.

WELLBUTRIN: ONE OF A KIND

Wellbutrin (bupropion) is a bit of an enigma. No one really knows how it works. While this can be said to some degree for all antidepressants, in this case we are particularly in the dark. The best guess is that Wellbutrin boosts norepinephrine function, as do the tricyclics. What it doesn't do is act on serotonin, so it is free of all the side effects and likewise devoid of all the advantages associated with serotonin. For example, Wellbutrin is about the only antidepressant believed ineffective in panic disorder. It tends to be more energizing than most antidepressants, which can be good or bad depending on the individual. Wellbutrin causes few of the sexual side effects common with the SSRIs. Discontinuation due to side effects appears markedly lower with Wellbutrin than with any other antidepressant currently marketed in the United States.

Wellbutrin is favored by many for use in bipolar depression because of possibly fewer problems concerning introduction of mania. Wellbutrin additionally has one special advantage: It may be effective in attention deficit/hyperactivity disorder (ADHD). Several preliminary studies have reported good results. This is especially welcome news for the many adults who have been diagnosed with this condition. Doctors are often reluctant to prescribe amphetamines or other stimulants, which are the usual treatments on children, to their adult patients.

Wellbutrin's main drawback is association with seizures. The tricyclics share this liability, but Wellbutrin appears worse than most. Still, seizures are reported in less than 1/2 of 1 percent of those on Wellbutrin. The rate, however, goes up dramatically with dosage: at 600 mg per day, the seizure rate is 10 times greater than at 300 mg. For this reason, dosage should be limited to a maximum of 450 mg per day, leaving Wellbutrin with one of the narrowest ranges of safe dosage among psychotropic medications. Further, dosage must be spread out three times daily, not to exceed 150 mg each time.

Because of its unique mechanism of action, Wellbutrin can be extremely useful alone or as an adjunct, but because of seizure concerns it has generally not been regarded as the antidepressant to try first. This should change with the introduction of the sustained-release formulation which is due out soon. Seizure rate does not appear to be elevated and is in line with the minimal levels of other newer antidepressants. Overall, Wellbutrin has a very favorable side effect profile with particularly low rates of sedation and sexual dysfunction.

EFFEXOR: "PROZAC-PLUS"

I think of Effexor (venlafaxine) as a stronger Prozac—somewhat more effective especially in resistant cases, and with somewhat more troublesome side effects. Effexor matches Prozac's strong action on serotonin, but it also has a second potent action, boosting norepinephrine in much the same way as tricyclic antidepressants. Fortunately, Effexor recreates the tricyclics' combined action without the panoply of serious tricyclic side effects. The main side effect relative to the SSRIs is more nausea and greater sleep disturbance, plus occasional blood pressure elevations. Blood pressure increases appear largely limited to the higher dose levels.

Five placebo-controlled comparisons of Effexor with the standard tricyclic antidepressant imipramine showed advantages of earlier onset of action and better control of certain symptoms. Effexor can apparently diminish depression within a week or so, at least if started at a high enough dose. Strikingly, nearly half of those who fail to respond to other drugs respond well to Effexor. Effexor's efficacy is thus similar to that of electroshock therapy (EST) in treatment-resistant depression, and it would certainly be preferable for most people. Effexor has even helped people who failed to respond to ECT, and it has the advantage of a much lower rate of relapse than ECT. Further, preliminary data show that Effexor may even be better at preventing relapse than other medications, although more study is needed for confirmation.

Effexor, in contrast to the SSRIs, appears to get more effective as dosage increases. Thus, aggressive dosing may be of great help to some patients. It also seems less inclined to interact with other medications, in contrast to the SSRIs and tricyclics. Further, it does not seem to intensify the effects of Valium, lithium, or alcohol. Effexor must be taken either two or three times per day owing to its short half-life. It may be important to monitor blood pressure, as significant increases can occur due to Effexor, although generally only at high dosage. When stopping treatment, dosages should be tapered off over a two-week period to avoid withdrawal symptoms.

In my experience, at times Effexor seems simply to work better than the SSRIs, generating more complete relief doing basically the same thing but doing it better. As with all medications, individual differences are key, and the same medication will not fit everyone. Although Effexor may sometimes cause sedation, it is often energizing and may be particularly well suited to treating depressions characterized by marked lethargy as opposed to agitation.

SERZONE: POSSIBLY THE LAST NEW ANTIDEPRESSANT OF THE MILLENNIUM

Serzone is the most recently approved antidepressant in the United States. It has the clear potential ultimately to prove to be the best initial choice for many depressed individuals, especially those experiencing anxiety, agitation, or insomnia. If you set out to design a better Prozac, you would aim at eliminating three main side effects: agitation, insomnia, and sexual dysfunction. It appears on this score that Serzone is pretty well three for three.

Serzone's proven advantages *at this point* lie largely in what the medication doesn't do. Preliminary evidence shows that Serzone does not incite the agitation that sometimes results from SSRIs. Serzone has not caused much sexual dysfunction as have other serotoninergic drugs, including Effexor. Finally, very little insomnia results; in fact, sleep generally improves rapidly and some people will experience daytime sedation. One study found that 80 percent of the Serzone patients improved considerably, compared to a mere 50 percent for imipramine (a standard tricyclic) and 30 percent for the placebo. Serzone probably proved more effective because patients stayed on the medication due to the lack of side effects.

Side effects with Serzone were relatively few and typically mild in the 2,200 patients reviewed in the manufacturer's premarketing trials. Overdose experience is very limited at this time, but two cases, involving more than a week's worth of medication taken in a single dose, showed no life-threatening toxicity. Significantly, we have as yet no reports of priapism, as we do for its predecessor, Desyrel.

The rate at which people quit a study because of adverse effects is one of the better ways to judge a medication; in a large-scale study recently published in the *British Journal of Psychiatry*, this dropout rate was half that of the tricyclic imipramine and was indistinguishable from a placebo. Theoretically, Serzone produces so few side effects because while making more serotonin available in the nerve synapses, which is what Prozac does, Serzone's action is milder, and it blocks the serotonin-2A receptor—associated with certain negative effects of serotonin. Possibly the mere blocking of this receptor produces antidepressant effects.

This second mode of action may confer special effectiveness on Serzone for certain populations. For instance, we know that medications capable of blocking serotonin-2A receptors improve irritability, aggression, and even psychosis. Further, this receptor is apparently overactive in many who are suicidal, so Serzone, like the related Desyrel, may prove more effective in reducing suicide risk. As discussed in appendix II, Desyrel is superior to Prozac in terms of reports of suicidal ideation.

Serzone offers a distinct cost advantage over the other new agents. It is priced significantly lower at the initial dosage levels, and the price is the same for tablets from 100 mg to 250 mg. Someone requiring high doses of either Prozac or Serzone (i.e., 80 mg and 500 mg respectively) would get more than a four-fold savings with Serzone. Given what we have discussed about the true costs associated with medications like Prozac relative to the generic tricyclics preferred by many HMOs, this may even mean that Serzone will find relatively quick acceptance by cost-conscious formulary committees.

MORE ON BRAD'S CASE

Although Prozac was able to reduce the terrible rashes that Brad was getting when overheated (see chapter 3), it produced some bizarre side effects including a feeling he could only describe as "spacy." He was not able to work in this condition. In changing over to Serzone after only a few days' interlude, he again had a similar reaction, but this gradually subsided and may have been related to the Prozac still in his system. Serzone proved to be helpful in stabilizing his mood swings, improving his sleep, and reducing his overwhelming feelings of stress and anxiety. Additionally, it did an even better job than Prozac in eliminating his heat-related rashes. Best of all, it accomplished all of this without creating problems of its own.

My initial clinical impressions of Serzone are very favorable. I have seen signs of broad effectiveness in a variety of conditions, similar to that seen for Prozac. The lack of sexual side effects is especially welcome for patients transferring from the SSRIs. The occasional person may still have difficulty. Although it must be taken twice a day because of its relatively short half-life, Serzone is in all other ways a very easy medication to use. A note of caution: Given the complexity of the serotonin system, it is possible that some people—like Brad, *possibly*—may experience difficult transitions between Serzone and other medications that affect serotonin. Many clinicians have reported difficulty transitioning some patients from Prozac specifically. *Further clinical experience will help clarify this issue.*

Serzone may one day end the beleaguered reign of Prozac and the other SSRIs as the first-line treatment for depression (and many other conditions). It appears most advantageous where anxiety and depression coexist. However, it will take years to gather broad acceptance. Time will tell if Serzone fully lives up to its considerable potential.

● ●

SUMMING UP

This generation of medications represents enormous progress in treatment. Each of these medications boasts certain advantages relative to the others. I believe in general one of these will be a better initial choice for treatment than Prozac. However, Prozac is ideal for some, and if it is working well for you and well tolerated there is little reason to consider a change. Yet, as safe, effective, and well tolerated as they may be for most, millions of Americans will still find them wanting and will look forward to the next generation. I hope that our next revolution will not be so long in coming. Chapter 16 looks to the future for some eagerly awaited medications already in use abroad, and at others still in development. We'll also look at some alternative directions from which the next advances may arise.

CHAPTER 16

A LOOK AHEAD

*To say that a particular psychiatric condition is incurable
or irreversible is to say more about the state of our
ignorance than about the state of the patient.*

—MILTON ROKEACH

TO MARKET, TO MARKET

According to a select panel of the American College of
Neuropsychopharmacology, over a dozen psychiatric medications
used abroad would offer important additions to treatment in the
United States. Most of these medications will never arrive in our
pharmacies, however, because getting government approval costs
so much, not to mention taking so long that many of the patents
would nearly have expired.

However, some new medications will appear. Since the 1970s,
drug company investment has doubled every five years. In 1994,
pharmaceutical companies spent more than $2 billion researching
nervous system diseases—including psychiatric disorders, which
makes this the second largest category of research (with heart disease being first). The research is bearing fruit. Today, pharmaceutical companies are developing more than forty new medications
for psychiatric disorders, and about half of these new drugs have
reached the final phase of human testing. For most such medications, the journey from discovery to market has taken some twelve
years.

The cost of bringing a new drug, say an antidepressant, to market is huge—roughly $150 to $250 million. In the early 1960s, the process cost about $500,000 and took only about two years. Even after adjusting for inflation, you can see how regulatory requirements and other factors have increased both costs and development time. After a company has finished all testing and turned in its results to the FDA, the review process itself takes about two and a half years.

We might speed the approval process without compromise of current safety levels by taking advantage of testing work already done in responsible countries. A medication approved in Norway, for example, and used there for some time provides more data on safety and efficacy than the FDA generally has when it allows a new medication onto the U.S. market. But the FDA tends to discount foreign studies. I hope this changes soon, as more and more research is being standardized internationally.

Many new medications will continue the trend toward a single specific mode of action we first saw with Prozac. In Prozac, researchers successfully developed a medication that both selectively and potently boosts serotonin function. Currently, a host of medications under development go even further in selectivity, stimulating only certain serotonin receptor subtypes. Indeed, a few available medications already incorporate some of this selectivity, including BuSpar, Desyrel, and Serzone. Others in development seek to combine different and complementary actions in a single agent.

One type of medication deserves singling out. The reversible inhibitors of monoamine oxidase A, or RIMAs, have been available in Europe and Canada for some time. These are the "kinder, gentler" MAOIs. I hope we will see them in the United States soon, but recent reports are discouraging in this regard. Unlike the currently available MAOIs, with their potentially fatal interactions (see appendix II), RIMAs seem to get fully comparable effects with few dietary restrictions. RIMAs are especially attractive because as we age, our levels of monoamine oxidase enzyme climb steadily, robbing our brains of several important neurotransmitters, including serotonin. In one study, MAO levels were found to more than double between the ages of twenty and eighty. By inhibiting this enzyme with RIMAs (or any other MAO inhibitor), we are helping to counter this important degenerative consequence of aging. We can see that living past the age 'of thirty, as few Stone Agers did, is in a sense yet another modern drain on serotonin. In this instance though, few complain.

The best-studied RIMA is moclobemide, known as Manerix in Canada. It possibly matches the effectiveness of other antidepressants, and amazingly the medication caused no more side effects than a placebo in an analysis of about two thousand patients. Some RIMAs have been coadministered with medications like Prozac, and apparently this increases effectiveness though the combination may produce symptoms of serotonin excess in some and is currently not recommended. Right now, at least ten RIMAs are under development.

Great interest has recently developed around dehydroxy-epiandosterone (DHEA). This compound is a building block of various steroids and appears to decline with age. Treatment with DHEA may prove helpful in a number of degenerative conditions. A preliminary study by Dr. Owen Wolkowitz and colleagues at the University of California, San Francisco, found significant benefit in treating depression. DHEA is available by prescription from certain pharmacies, but is not FDA approved for treating depression. (See appendix III: Resources: Pharmacies.)

Another important natural deficiency that is being explored is a neurohormone called phenylethylamine (PEA). Early findings by Dr. Hector Sabelli and colleagues in Chicago suggest about 60 percent of depressed patients may be responsive to treatment incorporating PEA. Intriguingly, about 60 percent of depressed patients are found in laboratory tests to have signs of reduced PEA. Therefore, it is possible that a significant portion of depressed patients are suffering from a true deficiency state that could be corrected easily.

Another class of medications act on the body's own opiate system. It has long been observed that some patients appear to get relief from their depression only by taking opiates. Needless to say they have had a difficult time convincing the medical establishment of their plight. Any need for opiates is likely to be seen as either abuse or addiction. Fortunately, medications are being developed that stimulate certain opiate receptors and appear to help relieve depression while avoiding any associated high. One such medication already available in the United States as a pain reliever is buprenorphine. It is also showing promise in treating addiction.

Psychopharmacology ignited in the late 1950s, producing medications such as Elavil and Valium. Then the pharmaceutical companies turned to refining these products, aiming simply for a better Elavil or Valium. As noted, while most other areas of medicine advanced rapidly, a quarter of a century would pass before we got medications like Prozac, Effexor, and Serzone—truly distinctive agents constituting significant improvements in treatment.

Why was progress so slow? Truly novel medications are much likelier to fail during development than a conservative upgrade of a well-known model. Indeed, historically new medications were rarely sought out but rather discovered by accident when an unexpected effect was observed and then pursued. Unless things change to allow for more innovation, we may have to rely on medications that are only slightly better than what already exists.

With medical knowledge exploding as we approach the millennium, however, we will probably do better than that, at least if regulatory disincentives don't short-circuit the process. Soon, possibly before the end of the twentieth century, we will have completely mapped the human genome, greatly aiding identification of most genetic diseases, understanding of their mechanisms, and development of highly specific therapies. Much work is now directed at developing gene therapy—the insertion of compensatory or "designer" genes to correct a problem at its source. The only question is: How long must we wait?

DOING BETTER WITH THE DRUGS WE HAVE

Important advances in treatment do not always depend on new medications. Once a medication comes to market, doctors may prescribe it for new illnesses without specific regulatory approval. Prozac continues to find new applications. Medications developed as anticonvulsants are now important for treating bipolar (manic-depressive) patients, and their use is broadening. For example, the well-tolerated anticonvulsant Depakote (tegretol) holds considerable promise for Prozac-type applications such as depression, irritability, and even panic.

When currently available medications cannot help patients, physicians often use medication combinations to good effect. This often happens when treating bipolar patients. Prescribing "polypharmacy" often means going without guidance from medical literature, relying instead on general principles and clinical experience. Many stand to benefit from such combination therapies. The new antidepressants, while not revolutionary, pinpoint various subtypes of serotonin receptors. This will allow precise manipulation of the serotonin system as our understanding of its intricacy grows. Leading figures at the NIMH similarly advocate more use of combination therapy, so-called rational polypharmacy.

Patient and practitioner must balance the risks of untreated illness against the unknowns of treatment, combination or otherwise. With bipolar patients, who suffer a truly dangerous and debilitating illness, it often makes sense to go ahead. Indeed, ending any significant depression may be worth some risk. After all, over 10 percent of their depressed patients ultimately take their own lives.

Keep in mind that the risk of death from common surgeries is usually quoted as one in a hundred. Yet we would hardly propose banning surgery. By not allowing new medications on the market, we deprive patients of choice. The combination therapies that patients might otherwise need can be riskier than the banned medications. We must understand that everything has risk—even seeing. Compared to the sighted, blind women have half the risk of breast cancer.

THE SPECIAL BIND OF ALTERNATIVE MEDICINE

It is an old maxim of mine that when you have excluded the impossible, whatever remains, however improbable, must be the truth.

—Sir Arthur Conan Doyle

Certainly, manufacturers will shepherd some medications through the regulatory process because of the tremendous profit potential. On one hand, many natural therapeutics or alternative medicine approaches would be doomed if the FDA regulated them as pharmaceuticals. However, quality control regulation has benefits. Every few years we read horror stories about generic preparations. We cannot assume that everything in a health food store is always as claimed either. When people use nutritional supplements as medical treatment, they had better be getting what they pay for in unadulterated form. We saw the dangers of contamination played out in extreme form with the L-tryptophan tragedy. What we don't need, however, are prohibitively expensive requirements for demonstrating efficacy to a federal bureaucracy.

Alternative therapies are tremendously understudied, and will likely continue to be, because companies cannot patent them. Unable to profit significantly from the product, the companies will not perform the costly research. Another barrier to study has been skepticism about the legitimacy of "alternative" therapy research. This is changing. Even the austere and prestigious British journal *Lancet* has recently published articles on various alternative treatments, including a positive study in the controversial area of homeopathy.

A trickle of publicly funded alternative therapy studies has begun. Recently, Congress granted the National Institute of Mental Health $150 million to study promising alternative treatments. While a good start, and one that will greatly increase the stature of the field if investigations prove efficacy, the funding is hardly the cost of developing a single antidepressant for market. I hope that the private sector will see the potential for advancing health care and provide financial support. For, given the delays inherent in developing new pharmaceuticals, some of the greatest advances in the near future may well come from alternative sources.

BETTER DETECTION

Advances in diagnosis will constitute much of the progress as we await new treatments. For most psychiatric illnesses, failure stems not from unavailability of an effective treatment but from failure to seek treatment, from misdiagnosis, or from inappropriate treatment. We might help remedy this by using medical screening tests to identify patients in need of treatment. Good tests might also help indicate the best treatment.

A good screening test would be of great help for patients often do not know that they have a problem, or, if they do, they are loath to get treatment for something that isn't "real." Recently, depression screening tests (consisting of a set of questions) have been developed for primary care settings, but whether physicians will take the time to use them, and whether insurers will cover the cost, remains in question. If a laboratory test can be developed, this would further encourage people to recognize the legitimacy of their illness and take steps to get well. It might also make it more difficult for insurers to deny coverage for treatment of "subjective" conditions.

Current tests have had limited success. The most famous, or perhaps notorious, was the dexamethasone suppression test, or DST, widely used in the early 1980s for diagnosing depression, and widely diagnosing as "depressed" people who actually had other psychiatric disorders. This prominent failure undoubtedly cooled enthusiasm for new tests.

Brain imaging is one of the most important developments in testing. Various procedures such as positron emission tomography (PET scans) allow us actually to see the brain at work. PET scans can reveal functional deficits in the brain. A depressed person observing obvious differences between his brain and the brain of someone who is not depressed gets a better grasp of the physical reality of his illness. Unfortunately, at present, PET scans are quite expensive and generally restricted to research applications.

Personally, I am convinced that the most promising path in testing for depression, as I stated in chapter 11, lies in measuring saliva for the so-called bad prostaglandins. Prostaglandin measures have readily distinguished depression using not only saliva but blood and spinal fluid. I hope that further work will allow clinical application soon.

Moving beyond depression, someday soon we may be able to

meaningfully measure brain serotonin. None of the tests currently used in research settings seems to work well. The approach I am pursuing, based on the Serotonin Theory of Stress presented in chapter 3, is to determine a person's ability to keep his or her body temperature down when subjected to heat. This method, in a study published in *Biological Psychiatry,* revealed cooling deficits in those who have winter depression. Notably, however, the investigators, assuming serotonin to have the opposite effect, did not interpret this finding as being related to serotonin.

• •

SUMMING UP

A number of promising treatments for stress and mood disorders are on the horizon. However, new medications may not arrive before the millennium. Fortunately, progress will also come from other sources. Improvements in screening and diagnosis will be important. Significant advances will likely continue in the development of new applications of existing medications, combination therapies, and various nontraditional approaches. Encouragingly, there appears to be some increasing convergence of traditional and nontraditional perspectives.

Many individuals who have struggled with serious mental illness worry particularly about what might happen to children they have or might have. I believe strongly that for most people, good treatment exists now, although therapies will have significant shortcomings for many. But if we maintain appropriate priority for developing new methods of screening, diagnosis, and treatment, psychiatric care should become a relatively minor concern for future generations. Of course, I believe that the best course is to promote serotonin function through healthy living, however challenging that may be.

We always underestimate the future.
—CHARLES KETTERING

EPILOGUE

Beyond Prozac has indeed gone considerably beyond Prozac. We have looked at ways to better use Prozac and various other medications and considered numerous approaches that for many will produce results superior to those of medication. Yet, virtually everything discussed falls within the "serotonin story," the power behind Prozac and the real story of this book.

Scientists often quote an old East Indian parable about five blind men describing an elephant: One grabs the tail and reports that the elephant is much like a snake; another feels his side and concludes that the elephant is rather like a wall. Each touches a different part and comes up with an accurate—but decidedly incomplete—description of the elephant. Serotonin is only one vantage point from which to grasp an understanding of the brain and behavior. But just as there are better and worse places to grab an elephant (certainly worse places), there are better and worse handles on our psyches. Serotonin appears one of the best.

Still, as we have seen, the serotonin system is only part of the picture, interacting with many other important influences on the brain. Following the thread of serotonin has led us to two exciting biological frontiers: prostaglandins and melatonin, which is serotonin's key metabolite. I certainly do not want to leave the impression that the serotonin system, important as it is, acts alone.

Neither do I want to leave the impression that biological treatments are the only effective approaches. If only to preserve reasonable scope and focus, I did not describe the myriad psychological therapies and stress-reduction techniques that often work quite well.

Early on I developed great respect for the therapeutic potential of psychotherapy. During medical school I had the opportunity to study and collaborate with two renowned psychotherapists, Drs. Irvin Yalom and David Spiegel. I was fortunate to be involved with a study of group therapy in terminal breast cancer patients. This was the first controlled study to show that a purely psychological treatment could improve mortality, impressively doubling patient survival times.

Psychological treatments clearly produce biological effects on the brain. The best example of this may be the work of Dr. Jeffrey Schwartz, who, along with others at the University of California at Los Angeles Medical Center, has recently shown that, similar to Prozac, a form of cognitive-behavioral therapy can correct abnormalities in brain metabolic rates of patients with obsessive compulsive behavior.

I have found that psychological therapy can readily be integrated with the biological treatments discussed in the preceding pages, often producing better results than either approach alone.

Whether or not serotonin is Agent Blue, the prime cause of our current epidemic of stress-related illnesses, we may never know. However, that modern life undermines serotonin, and that Prozac—which acts almost solely to boost serotonin—is effective with almost every major form of mental or stress-related disorder, strongly suggests that we have the culprit.

The Serotonin Theory of Stress described in chapter 3, which shows how serotonin might accomplish much of its stress-protection function, makes for a very neat package—perhaps too neat. Time will tell. Meanwhile, regardless of the ultimate fate of any given theory, we have a collection of both natural and medicinal approaches that boost serotonin and have proven their worth in treating many serious conditions.

A final word about the stigma of mental illness: The material presented in this book—especially the remarkable data concerning the pervasiveness of serious mental illness and the universality of various stress-related conditions—shows just how absurd such stigma really is. I hope that the view of depression and other mental illness provided here will help make these problems less threatening and engender a well-found optimism about treatment.

I find it sad when people with some form of mental illness think of their genes, and therefore themselves, as inherently defective. As we have seen, leading genetic researchers have recently concluded that genes rank *behind* stress in causing depression. An evolutionary perspective may be of additional help here. If after a day of holiday feasting you found that you couldn't get into your favorite jeans, you would not say that they were "bad jeans." You would recognize that the problem was simply one of poor fit and that the jeans were relatively blameless. The same is true for our chromosomal genes. They evolved over millions of years to "fit" a specific world. The genes associated with mental illness, in all its many variations, are not bad either; they just don't fit as well as they used to, because the world has gotten out of shape.

I hope this book provides for you some key antidotes to modern living, a sort of blueprint for getting yourself, your lifestyle, and your personal environment back to their natural form.

APPENDIX I

OVERHEATED BEHAVIOR AND SEROTONIN

What men call gallantry, and gods adultery,
Is much more common where the climate's sultry.
—Byron   Don Juan

Now we will look in detail at the information Dr. Avery and I uncovered regarding serotonin, heat, and behavior. As discussed in chapter 3, serotonin typically inhibits behaviors such as sexual activity, alcohol consumption, and aggression. However, this inhibition generally melts away in the heat.

AGGRESSION AND VIOLENCE

One might explain hot weather violence by blaming it on our increased drinking of alcohol in the heat. However, it is hard to find statistics on types of aggression in which alcohol likely played no role, although one study did analyze murders and alcohol sales and found no correlation. But it occurred to us to look more closely at the probably alcohol-free type of aggression displayed by major league pitchers when they intentionally hit batters with the ball. Indeed, we found that hot weather data revealed a "striking" increase in these unfortunate incidents—even after eliminating other factors such as poor control.

Despite all this, we realized that heat might not actually cause the violence but merely be linked to some mysterious third element, the true cause. Only controlled experimentation could eliminate this possibility. In experimental settings, hostile feelings, as opposed to actions, do rise with the temperature. Obviously, it is hard to study violence in the lab, if only for ethical reasons. One attempt involved putting people in a room heated to over 90 degrees Fahrenheit and then confronting subjects in a provocative way. The study turned in mixed results, possibly because subjects could easily guess the experimenters' intent. Another study, outside the lab, involved experimenters waiting at traffic signals for 15 seconds after the light turned green. The resulting horn honking increased directly with the rise in temperature—especially by those driving cars that appeared to have no air-conditioning.

IMPULSIVITY

Since no one has studied human impulsivity in the laboratory, we must look outside, to the real world. One of the problems with this, however, is distinguishing aggressive behavior from purely impulsive behavior. Investigators have established serotonin's connection with impulsivity by studying groups characterized by highly impulsive behavior without aggression. Arsonists, for example, show extremely impulsive behavior in setting fires, but a low level of direct interpersonal aggression. Unfortunately, the FBI does not currently publish data specifically on arson, so we turned our attention to other types of property crime. Although property crimes do not rise as sharply in response to heat as do crimes of violence, we found a clear relationship when looking at large enough sets of data.

Believing that accidents reflected at least some degree of impulsive behavior, we looked at various related statistics. Our finding: Higher temperatures lead not only to more traffic accidents and workplace accidents but to violent accidental deaths. Alarmingly, pilot errors increased markedly in the heat. Finally, we looked at drug overdoses, which showed a similar pattern of peaking in the heat of late July. While some overdoses might have been suicide attempts, research on suicide shows that only *violent* suicides show a seasonal pattern. Thus, the drug overdoses probably have a significant impulsivity component.

Next we examined data on crimes that match each other in violence but vary in the degree of impulsivity. While numerous studies have found that impulsive violence, such as assault and rape, rises in hot weather, some studies have failed to find this true for murder. Investigators explain this by suggesting that murder is more often premeditated rather than impulsive.

SUICIDE

More than sixty studies worldwide on the seasonal patterns of suicide overwhelmingly establish a later spring peak in incidence, generally in May. While the weather is certainly warming up in the spring, if heat is the key, why doesn't the peak occur in midsummer? One possibility is that for some people, rising spring temperatures are more demanding on the body's cooling machinery than sustained higher temperatures. After all, the heat of summer occurs when the body has had considerable time to acclimate.

Another possible explanation concerns the singularity of a suicide event. If in fact one's biological tendency toward suicide increased progressivly as it warmed up, reaching a maximum in midsummer, clearly some people would nevertheless commit suicide before this peak time of vulnerability. The fact that they acted in May, for example, does not say that their own biological tendency peaked then, for they might have been even more suicidal in July, but they were suicidal enough in May to carry out the act.

The situation is quite different with assaults, which do peak in the hottest months. Perpetrators can increase their rate of assaults throughout the summer, rather than contribute only the single instance (of their first assault) to the assault statistics—as occurs in the case of suicide. Simply put, you can only commit suicide once.

Seasonal patterns are always somewhat difficult to interpret because numerous other variables besides heat, both social and biological, change with the seasons. Finally, other types of evidence support a connection between suicide and heat. A sixteen-year national study in Belgium showed a highly significant correlation between violent suicide and temperature. The deaths also increased with humidity but declined with greater sunshine. Humidity makes it harder for the body to lose heat, but if light boosts serotonin this may help counteract the effect of heat. In nature, greater heat is usually accompanied by greater light, providing a sort of balance that indoor living has deprived us of.

Finally, some studies have contrasted regional suicide rates. While the results are complex because of regional social factors, one U.S. study found a strong association between suicide and elevated temperatures, even after social variables were controlled for. Yet more difficult to interpret are differences in suicide rates between countries. In a study of forty-one nations, suicide was higher in those with the lowest temperatures. As we have already discussed, however, heat stress may have much to do with rising temperatures. Countries of northern Europe, which generally have high suicide rates and low average temperatures, nevertheless experience the greatest temperature fluctuations and are found to have the most pronounced seasonal patterns of suicide—with the highest rates occurring when temperatures rise in spring.

ALCOHOL USE

Holidays aside, people drink more alcohol in hot weather and in the hot regions of the country. However, when Dr. Avery and I first looked at patterns nationwide, this seemed untrue, because warmer states had lower total yearly alcohol consumption. It occurred to us that this might be misleading because of higher rates of abstention in the South. Since abstention was most likely related to religious and social factors, we sought to determine the rate of alcohol consumption for all nonabstaining adults on a state-by-state basis. The analysis showed, as predicted, that higher temperatures were associated with higher alcohol consumption. This same pattern in relation to temperature has been observed in Europe without needing to control for abstention rates.

We also found that for the state of Washington, monthly figures for all alcohol sold in the state over the last ten years increased with the temperature—except, of course, for the end of the year, during the holiday period. We also looked at the yearly rate of alcohol-related automobile accidents in the entire United States and found that this, too, increased in relation to yearly average temperature. While these findings are consistent with our theory, one might object that increased drinking could be blamed on hot weather thirst. Further studies are needed to look at rates of consumption for other beverages. However, our Washington State figures show similar patterns for both beer and hard liquor, which suggests that thirst is not the key factor.

SEXUAL ACTIVITY

Do people become more amorous in the heat—or at least more sexual? We reviewed a number of statistics and studies related to sexual activity, including seasonal conception rates, gonorrhea, miscellaneous sex crimes (exclusive of rape, which is considered more a crime of aggression), and reports of first sexual intercourse. Conception rates have grown less and less seasonal with increasing industrialization, probably due to less exposure to the natural environment. Nevertheless, data on conceptions across many cultures exhibit a late spring or summer peak, according to Dr. Jurgen Ashoff, a leading European researcher. The striking consistency of this pattern and its variation with latitude strongly implicates a biological mechanism. The rate of sexual activity within a population is closely related to the rate of gonorrhea, since gonorrhea has a brief incubation period. As long as U.S. records have been kept—dating back to the early twentieth century—gonorrhea has always peaked in summer, typically either July or August.

Similarly, preliminary studies of various sex crimes such as indecent exposure show a late summer peak. We note that an extensive survey of people's first experience of sexual intercourse showed that summer led the field. Obviously, few people would likely credit air temperature for this, and clearly there are other reasons for this pattern that have nothing to do with heat or serotonin—summer vacation, for example. But the sex-heat connection is nevertheless consistent with many other behaviors we have studied, and certainly it had some intuitive appeal. Hot cities have more highly sexual images, notably L.A., New Orleans, and Miami. Ultimately, higher air temperature will lead to higher brain temperature. Our language is replete with images linking heat with sex. We speak of being in heat, of being hot and bothered—indeed, the very word *hot* can mean sexy. Folk wisdom even suggests that a cold shower may be helpful if one is sexually overheated. However, cold shower effects have not been subjected to scientific scrutiny.

PAIN AND SEIZURES

With pain, we can show a direct relationship to heat. If you heat your skin, you will increase the experience of pain in response to trauma. Similarly, a painful wound will hurt less if cooled with ice, even if swelling is not an issue. What has not been shown yet is whether this can be specifically tied to serotonin and whether this takes place as a response to hotter air temperatures. We have some evidence that certain conditions, arthritis for example, hurt more in the summer (note, however, that arthritis as a whole is not worse in summer).

Seizures, another phenomenon related to low serotonin, definitely increase in response to heat. Any brain if heated sufficiently will undergo a seizure. Some people, especially children, have seizures in response to fever, and others consistently have seizures when given a hot bath or shower. Many people who have seizure problems also have low serotonin function. This suggests that these people cannot effectively cool their brain due to the serotonin deficiency.

EATING PATTERNS

Of the ten behaviors expected to increase with low serotonin, the only one that doesn't increase in the heat is eating. As might be expected, the seasonal patterns of eating are complex. People generally eat more in winter, and there are good reasons for this, unrelated to serotonin. For example, we need more calories to generate heat in cold weather. It is also important to generate a layer of fat for insulation and storage in a season that historically is one of relative scarcity. Thus, for these and other, more biochemical reasons seasonal or temperature-related patterns of eating seem a poor indicator of serotonin function. Depression, which is linked with low serotonin function, is often characterized by loss of appetite, so once again we see that the picture of high serotonin depressing appetite is murky. Looking at conditions that represent extremes of eating behavior, mainly anorexia and bulimia, we see similar complexity. Both of these conditions have extremely variable periods of highest incidence, sometimes showing both summer and winter peaks. Additionally, there are complex physiological reasons to explain why eating may have a different relationship to serotonin than the other behaviors.

CONCLUSION

Our extensive investigation showed that all of these behaviors and more, such as sleep and circadian rhythm disturbances, clearly alter with heat. In all of these behaviors, with the exception of the complex patterns associated with eating, we can explain the direction of behavioral change by assuming that serotonin function falls as heat rises. This kind of consistency across highly diverse behaviors is rarely seen in the psychological or psychiatric literature. It strongly suggests that this new model relating heat and serotonin is possibly a fundamental natural relationship and certainly a powerful and useful explanatory tool that warrants considerable attention in the future.

The charts below summarize some of the key evidence that

Dr. Avery and I uncovered supporting serotonin's primary role in heat loss.

States Associated with High Serotonin

Mental Stress or Anxiety	Increased sweating
Exercise	Increased sweating
Digestion of a meal	Increased heat loss including sweating

States Associated with Low Serotonin

REM sleep	Virtual absence of sweating temperature
Premenstrual Phase (likely low serotonin)	Decreased sweating and increased body temperature
Winter depression (likely low serotonin)	Decreased heat tolerance
Some nonseasonal depression	Increased body temperature

Interventions That Enhance Serotonin

Serotoninergic antidepressants	Increased sweating more than with nonserotoninergic antidepressants; decreased brain temperature in preclinical studies
Alcohol	Generally increased heat loss
Serotonin antagonists (blockers)	Decrease in excessive sweating

What we see in the above is again a remarkably consistent picture that greatly threatens the old paradigm of serotonin relating primarily to heat-gain mechanisms.

AIR-CONDITIONING

Perhaps the only aspect of modern living that favors serotonin levels is air-conditioning. It truly makes us less irritable and more productive. In the United States, air-conditioning literally transformed the South, probably the single most important factor in that region's economic growth in the twentieth century. We see the same thing mirrored now throughout the world. Although because of air ion effects, gains in production as well as lessened irritability and aggression may be partly offset by a lowered sense of well-being caused by our modern buildings' constantly recycled air.

APPENDIX II

ESTABLISHED TREATMENT: THE OLD GUARD

There are some remedies worse than the disease.
—Publilius Syrus

It is important to know about these treatments because they are still widely prescribed, and you may want to discuss the options if your doctor prescribes one of them. Unfortunately, in many treatment settings these medications are virtually the only initial choices allowed, because of assumed cost savings, despite the fact that most experts now agree the newer agents should be the first-line treatment for depression. Nonetheless, it should be emphasized that for some individuals, members of the old guard will prove invaluable.

THE TRICYCLICS

Most tricyclic antidepressants have the same action as Prozac on serotonin, but much weaker. Generally they have a similar boosting action on another neurotransmitter, norepinephrine (noradrenaline). While these actions tend to be helpful, unfortunately the tricyclics also have a host of other effects on various systems that usually are anything but helpful, causing numerous and sometimes dangerous side effects.

Generic Names	**Brand Names**
amitriptyline	Elavil, Endep
clomipramine	Anafranil
desipramine	Norpramin, Pertofrane
doxepin	Sinequan, Adapin
imipramine	Tofranil, Janimine, Sk-Pramine
nortriptyline	Pamelor, Aventyl
protriptyline	Vivactil
trimipramine	Surmontil

Tricyclic descriptions generally apply as well to a related group of antide-pressants: tetracyclics, amoxapine (Asendin), and maprotiline (Ludiomil).

The Tricyclics' Strengths

Most studies have found all antidepressants about equally helpful in treating depression as a whole. Given this, since Prozac is demonstrably better in treating certain types of depression, such as rejection-sensitive dysphoria, it is certainly possible that it is less effective in others. One such case might be severe depression requiring hospitalization. Yet, most data seem to show compara-ble efficacy regardless of the severity of depression. This is cur-rently a hotly debated point. Recent studies, including one by Britain's Stuart Montgomery, found Prozac-like drugs actually superior to tricyclics in treating severe depression.

Some claim that with blood level monitoring for optimum tricyclic dosage, the usual depression improvement rate of 70 percent can be boosted to 80 percent. However, adding a sup-plemental treatment such as BuSpar to a failed SSRI generally converts about half of the nonresponders to responders, and is usually less toxic than the tricyclic alone. Combined treatment response rate thus is about 85 percent, beating even the tri-cyclic's ideal results.

I say ideal because outside the setting of a carefully monitored study, folks often fail to take all their medication. It matters little if tricyclics work better than newer antidepressants at optimal doses when in the real world people routinely take less than the optimal dose. And the evidence indicates that they do take less than the prescribed amount because of tricyclic side effects such as drowsiness, dry mouth, constipation, and so on.

Possibly tricyclics are better at maintaining treatment response. Mainly because they have been around longer, there is more evidence that they are effective in the long-term prevention of recurrent depression. However, studies are ongoing for Prozac-like drugs, and it appears that they too are effective, and in the case of Effexor, possibly more effective. In this context, the new medications have the pronounced advantage of being easier to tolerate and therefore more likely to be taken properly and consistently. This is all the more important when a drug is taken long term. Again, this possible advantage may only be seen when tricyclics are taken in optimal fashion, which is frequently not the case in real-world usage.

Tricyclic Toxicity and Other Drawbacks

Taking five times the usual daily dose of a tricyclic can cause serious toxicity, including fatal heart block. About 7 percent of patients are slow metabolizers of tricyclics and thus can suffer toxic concentrations even at conventional doses. Of course, most people do not know if they are slow metabolizers.

Aside from overdose, tricyclics can be toxic at normal blood levels. Central nervous system toxicity was observed in 6 percent of patients hospitalized for medical problems. In patients developing such toxicity, hospitalization was extended for an average of seven days.

Another cardiac danger is arrhythmias. Sadly, this may even occur in children. Recently, five children who were taking desipramine were felled by sudden cardiac death, most of them while exercising. Other tricyclics may have this tragic effect as well.

In older people such risks are greatly magnified, making these medications worrisome in geriatric populations. Another problem tricyclics pose for older people is increased risk of falls due to the side effects of sedation and orthostatic blood-pressure changes (low blood pressure upon rising). Breaking a hip can be a tremendous hardship in old age, so preventing falls is a priority.

Despite some suicide issues concerning Prozac, discussed in chapter 14, *minimizing* the risk of suicide is one of the best reasons for choosing Prozac over older antidepressants, especially tricyclics. Reviews of antidepressants revealed that not only were the tricyclics much more lethal than newer medications when taken in overdose, but more attempts were made. The tricyclic associated with the highest rate of "successful" suicide was desipramine. This surprised many because the drug had reputedly caused fewer side effects and was widely prescribed. British figures reveal that the rate of suicide *by overdose* per million prescriptions was more than twenty times higher in those receiving tricyclics relative to drugs like Prozac.

Side effects plague tricyclic users. People who stop medication after long-term use are often amazed at how much better they feel physically and mentally. Standard effective doses can induce a mental "fog." Being very depressed at the beginning of medication, patients often don't notice this effect, and because improvement is gradual, they become used to the fog or possibly they believe it to be a remnant of lingering depression. But after halting the tricyclic, the difference may hit them profoundly. At that point they are loath to return to these medications. Dry mouth, constipation, and sedation are some of the daily problems that tricyclics cause, but the side effect that frequently causes people to stop tricyclics is weight gain.

The bottom line: Tricyclics are not first-line treatment for depression. But you wouldn't think so if you were being treated at most of the Health Maintenance Organizations (HMOs) that I have checked.

The Cost of Prozac versus Tricyclics—Illusory Savings

Health care businesses and individuals alike make treatment decisions based in part on costs. At first glance, tricyclics, at about ten cents a dose, would seem to be the most cost-effective treatment, compared to Prozac at about $2.50 a dose. But appearances can be deceiving.

Because blood levels can vary by more than ten fold in

patients taking the same dose of a tricyclic, frequent professional evaluation is necessary to avoid side effects and toxicity. An electrocardiogram is often recommended before starting a tricyclic, particularly in those over forty or those at risk for heart disease. All this adds considerably to treatment cost.

Another common recommendation is to measure blood levels of the tricyclic at least once during treatment. Following the recent deaths of children taking a tricyclic, recommendations for this age group were modified to include both cardiac and blood-level monitoring whenever the dosage is increased, as well as periodically throughout treatment. Not all practitioners follow this advice, and with tests costing up to $100, the cost/benefit ratio is arguable. Obviously, to the extent that recommended testing is done, new antidepressants seem less burdensome.

This sort of testing is unnecessary for the newer antidepressants. Blood levels are not believed to be useful in guiding treatment, and in any case for most there is relatively little risk associated with higher levels.

To evaluate cost properly, you must also evaluate effectiveness. A half-price treatment that doesn't work is no bargain. While tricyclics' performance is comparable to that of Prozac and similar medications in formal studies, they frequently fare much poorer in practice because, as I mentioned before, people often drop their dosage in attempts to shake side effects. In one retrospective study of more than two thousand depressed outpatients, less than one-third actually took the recommended dosage.

Alarmingly, some managed-care organizations require that people first fail on one or more trials of old guard drugs before they can get the newer, more expensive ones. This saves no one money. One hospitalization for a suicide attempt, or one broken hip or heart problem, wipes out the small savings accrued by many patients forced to take the cheaper medication. Tricyclic antidepressants are the number one cause of emergency room visits for overdose toxicity. Patients end up in cardiac care units at a cost of between $50,000 and $100,000 for a few days' observation.

The field has been rather slow to anoint new generation medications as the first-line treatment for depression, but it clearly seems now the majority opinion. Of course, because of individual differences, certain people will need tricyclics either alone or in combination with other agents.

A NOTE ON MAOIS

Monoamine oxidase inhibitors (MAOIs) such as Nardil (phenelzine) and Parnate (tranylcypromine) have been tremendously underutilized in psychiatry. Patients and practitioners fear the so-called cheese reaction—a potentially fatal reaction to consuming foods that, like cheese, contain high amounts of the amino acid tyramine. Ironically, statistics show that overall, MAOIs are actually safer than tricyclics.

Interestingly, MAOIs share with Prozac a special efficacy in certain populations. But this was never widely exploited due to safety concerns. These are not first-choice drugs. Keep in mind, however, that MAOIs have often caused miraculous relief when other drugs have failed. The new forms of MAOIs (see chapter 16) now used in Europe and Canada are much safer and easier to use, but are not expected to be approved for marketing in the United States anytime in the foreseeable future.

BENZODIAZEPINES (VALIUM, XANAX, AND OTHERS)

In 1994, one in seven Americans took a benzodiazepine, a family of more than a dozen medications. Total U.S. use: some eight tons annually. Actually, benzodiazepines occur in the brain, with or without the addition of medication. We do not know if the brain manufactures these natural benzodiazepines or if they come from our diet. The highest concentrations are found in the brain's limbic structures and seem to play a role in the process of memory— or rather, in forgetting, which should not come as a surprise given the sedating nature of these medications.

An animal experiment illustrates the difference between Valium and Prozac. Giving an animal a choice between getting one food pellet now or waiting 30 seconds to get several pellets, animals are faced with a dilemma. After getting Valium, animals tend to choose immediate gratification; after getting Prozac, they usually wait for the better deal. Prozac promotes a sort of "patience," while Valium—perhaps because it actually diminishes serotonin function—makes the animals more impulsive (less inhibited). This latter effect reminds one of alcohol, a drug with which Valium shares other characteristics.

Despite its drawbacks, Valium remains a tremendous improvement over barbiturates and other drugs in use before the 1960s. Those caused heavy sedation and were toxic, even deadly, at doses little higher than were required to get the anxiety-reducing benefits. Certainly, barbiturates threatened more severe addiction problems.

For most, Valium poses little danger of addiction. In 1990, the American Psychiatric Association issued a task force report on benzodiazepine dependence, toxicity, and abuse. The conclusion was that of one in seven Americans who take a benzodiazepine, 66 percent do so for less than one month and 80 percent for less than four months. Only about 15 percent are long-term daily users—some several million Americans who, it turns out, usually get their medication from physicians other than psychiatrists. Long-term users generally appear to need medication, and true addiction appears extremely rare. Most people who abuse Valium do so simply as part of a pattern of abusing many drugs.

Xanax is perhaps another story. Unlike other benzodiazepines, though this point is controversial, this drug appears to pose a greater risk of addiction—or at least severe withdrawal. People stopping Xanax must do so very carefully, and it is often quite difficult. Withdrawal symptoms tend to be pronounced and, for some patients, make discontinuation a real struggle. Nonetheless, more than eighty published studies demonstrate Xanax as both safe and effective compared to other drugs for treating anxiety and panic. While Xanax is perhaps somewhat effective with depression, severe depression responded better to standard antidepressants.

Benzodiazepines tend to decrease psychological response to stress and thus offer promise for the prevention and treatment of heart disease, which, as we have discussed, is often stress-related. A 1986 study found that using Xanax caused a 70 percent reduction in the duration of silent ischemia, or insufficient circulation to the heart. The drug also helped relieve symptoms of angina.

Benzodiazepines are good for immediate effect. For example, if you suffer claustrophobia and must get a CAT scan of your head, you'll need something that works quickly. In chronic conditions, benzodiazepines are best used when other measures fail or as transitional tools to help ease people into a more appropriate medication that may cause initial agitation or insomnia.

In some cases, long-term Valium use does appear to be the best treatment. I find it unfortunate that this is so stigmatized. Many view this as shameful, and even some pharmacists and regulatory bodies frown upon this sometimes necessary treatment.

Taking Care with Benzodiazepines

Aside from addiction issues, benzodiazepine users must consider impaired motor performance. The greatest danger may come, as the label says, when "operating heavy machinery." Statistics on benzodiazepine use and traffic accidents are scary, but they may not be entirely to blame: Possibly the patient's underlying anxiety contributes to the poor driving—and who knows what the driver might be like unmedicated! Nonetheless, this is an excellent reason to avoid benzodiazepines if effective alternatives exist.

With Xanax, skipping the commonly prescribed dose for a day or two can pose a risk of seizures. I tell patients to think of Xanax like the American Express Card—don't leave home without it. Poor packing for a weekend trip can lead to unfortunate results.

A few reports have surfaced of Xanax, like Prozac, causing disinhibited behavior. However, given the huge number of people taking the medication, this is likely not significant. According to a 1993 report, controlled studies found no increase in problematic behavior in those taking Xanax compared to those on other medications. Still, from what we saw in preclinical studies with Valium about decreased "patience," this possibility cannot be completely discounted.

Alcoholics must take particular care with benzodiazepines. Alcohol and benzodiazeprines are cross-tolerant, meaning that their similarity of action allows a person to avoid withdrawal symptoms caused by stopping either substance. They may also stimulate a recovering alcoholic to return to drinking, or it may create a second addiction. Nonetheless, I would not flatly rule out using a benzodiazeprine in alcoholics. If, for example, the alcoholic has anxiety that caused the alcohol abuse initially, a benzodiazeprine may be appropriate. However, there are probably better treatments for such individuals.

Benzodiazeprines may also interfere with learning. Problems with memory may be experienced in the classroom, but they can also prevent desirable *unlearning*. For example, people who fear flying would likely "unlearn" their fear after a half-dozen coast-to-coast trips. But if they take benzodiazeprines or alcohol for the flight, they can block this process despite a hundred plane trips. Other medications for anxiety, such as various antidepressants or BuSpar (discussed in chapter 15), do not cause this problem.

A Closer Look at Xanax

Xanax is about ten times stronger than Valium, and is generally more worrisome. Yet, Xanax works well for anxiety or panic, and for certain individuals it is the only medication that does the job. People use a tremendous amount of Xanax—it had replaced Valium as the most prescribed psychiatric medication until Prozac came along.

If you use Xanax, realize that taking the drug, even over a period of years, does not mean that you are addicted, although, like those who use the drug for shorter periods, you may suffer withdrawal symptoms with any kind of abrupt cessation—and, yes, even with gradual cessation. Long-term use can meet real therapeutic need and not tempt a patient into increasing dosage over time. In fact, many with panic disorder tend to decrease dosage over time, and those who find that they can't, due to return of symptoms, generally wish that they could. Xanax does not tend to make people feel high, though a few do abuse the drug.

Some studies suggest that Xanax alleviates depression, but critics have countered that any improvement stems from anxiety reduction. Indeed, other evidence suggests that people who take Xanax or any other benzodiazepine are at greater risk of depression.

The bottom line? Xanax can be helpful as an adjunct to other treatments or as a replacement if other treatments fail; even then, however, this medication remains somewhat worrisome.

DESYREL: A REAL SLEEPER

Desyrel (trazadone), introduced in the United States in 1981, constituted the first major advance in psychotropics since the 1950s. It had a complex action involving both stimulation and blockade of serotonin receptors in the nervous system, and it generally left other systems alone, unlike its predecessors. Studies showed that Desyrel worked equally well in relieving depression, but was orders of magnitude safer in terms of overdose.

Despite many studies showing comparable effectiveness to the older agents, Desyrel got a reputation as being somewhat less effective and never gained real popularity. This reputation may have had to do partly with its side effect profile. Although lacking most of the serious problems of the tricyclics and MAOIs, Desyrel was as sedating as the most sedating of the older medications, and many had trouble taking it at full therapeutic doses. Another factor making it difficult to take is the inconvenient dosage recommendation, which is to take it with food three times daily. Poor compliance with recommended dosage may have led to real world results less impressive than those in studies.

Recently, Desyrel has grown popular as a sleeping pill, and it appears to retain its effectiveness in long-term use. Thus, its main liability has now evolved into a virtue. You can take Desyrel with other antidepressants that often cause insomnia (including the MAOIs, which cannot be administered safely with other antidepressants). It also may be useful as a supplement to other antidepressants to achieve better antidepressant response.

One other major problem came to light after marketing. Priapism. This is an abnormally persistent erection of the penis. This is no mere embarrassment or annoyance: Priapism can be a true medical emergency requiring the local injection of medication, or even surgery. Very rarely, impotence may result. Even though priapism is rare, after a full disclosure of side effect risks, men, not surprisingly, often choose another treatment. Desyrel poses no comparable risk to women.

The second revolution in psychiatric medications seemed off to a poor start and was to get worse. The next antidepressant, nomifensine maleate, looked promising as it helped many who were resistant to other treatments. However, it was withdrawn the very week it was released due to rare fatal reactions. Then, the antidepressant Wellbutrin was withheld just before scheduled release because of reports of seizures. As we have seen, Wellbutrin eventually entered the U.S. market, as the seizure problem was found to be relatively rare.

ELECTROCONVULSIVE THERAPY

ECT draws on the body's natural serotonin boost that accompanies a seizure. Although a seizure appears to have other important consequences for brain chemistry, bolstering brain serotonin has been documented repeatedly. As we might expect from the Serotonin Theory of Stress, following ECT there is an accompanying increase in heat loss (more blood flow to the skin). Again we may be seeing one of nature's elegant pieces of adaptive handiwork. As you may recall, serotonin seems to help stabilize the brain and opposes seizure activity, so self-treatment appears a built-in response to seizures.

ECT is not PC. To put it mildly, ECT has a major public relations problem. However, the problem has a historical basis, for electroconvulsive therapy as practiced initially was an unpleasant, dangerous treatment. But that treatment bears little relation to current practice. Modern anesthesia techniques make the procedure both safe and painless—safe enough even for pregnant women. It still stands as possibly the most effective treatment for depression, capable of helping even those who have failed to benefit from every other form of antidepressant therapy. ECT's primary therapeutic drawback is that the relapse rate is quite high relative to medication therapy.

The main concern patients have about ECT is memory loss. While memory during the period of treatment is certainly affected, we have little evidence of long-term memory loss and no evidence of any structural brain damage. The problem may be that memory complaints are so common in people generally that there will always be some who attribute their difficulties to the procedure. As François, duc de La Rochefoucauld, wryly observed, "Every man complains about his memory, but no one about his judgment." Celebrities are beginning to publicly discuss their favorable experiences with ECT. They do a great public service in helping to destigmatize this treatment and psychiatric treatment in general. Even if a rare individual does suffer memory loss, which is certainly possible, this must be viewed with an appreciation of the seriousness of major depression. In other medical contexts we readily accept much greater risk. Recall that the risk of death from most major surgery is at least 1 percent.

Unfortunately, because of the political climate, especially in states such as California, where I trained, few get ECT who could truly benefit. Increasingly, as statistics bear out, it is a treatment available only to the affluent. Fortunately, major advances in such medications as Effexor make it rare that one need resort to ECT, but when other treatments fail, it is nice to have a last resort.

APPENDIX III

RESOURCES

ADDITIONAL SOURCES OF INFORMATION

Depression and Related Affective Disorders Association (DRADA)
Johns Hopkins University School of Medicine
Meyer 3-181
600 N. Wolfe Street
Baltimore, MD 21287
(410) 955-4647

National Depressive and Manic-Depressive Association (NDMDA)
730 N. Franklin Street, Suite 501
Chicago, IL 60610
(800) 826-3632

National Foundation for Depressive Illness, Inc. (NFDI)
P.O. Box 2257
New York, NY 10116
(800) 248-4344

National Organization for Seasonal Affective Disorder (NOSAD)
P.O. Box 40133
Washington, DC 20016

Society for Light Research and Biological Rhythms
P.O. Box 478
Wilsonville, OR 97070

The National Alliance for the Mentally Ill (NAMI)
2101 Wilson Boulevard, Suite 302
Arlington, VA 22201
(800) 950-6264

The National Institute of Mental Health (NIMH)
The Depression/Awareness, Recognition, and Treatment Program
5600 Fishers Lane, Room 15-C-05
Rockville, MD 20857
(800) 421-4211

The National Mental Health Association (NMHA)
1021 Prince Street
Alexandria, VA 22314
(800) 969-6642

AIR IONIZERS

Sphere One Inc.
558 Highland Avenue
Upper Montclair, NJ 07043
(201) 746-9690

Bionic Products of America Inc.
466 Central Avenue, Suite 20
Northfield, IL 60093
(708) 441-6000

BRIGHT LIGHT UNITS

Apollo Light Systems Inc.
352 West 1060 South
Orem, UT 84058
(801) 226-2370

Hughes Lighting Technologies
Yacht Club Drive
Lake Hopatcong, NJ 07849
(201) 663-1214

The SunBox Company
19217 Orbit Drive
Gaithersburg, MD 20879
(800) 548-3968

DAWN SIMULATORS

Pi Square Inc. (Sun-up)
11036 1st South
Seattle, WA 98168
(206) 246-1101   (Seattle area)
(800) 786-3296

The SunBox Company
19217 Orbit Drive
Gaithersburg, MD 20879
(800) 548-3968

LIGHT VISORS

Bio-Bright, Inc.
7315 Wisconsin Avenue, #1300W
Bethesda, MD 20814-3202
(800) 621-5483

The SunBox Company
19217 Orbit Drive
Gaithersburg, MD 20879
(800) 548-3968

PHARMACIES

Sources of 5-Hydroxytryptophan and DHEA by prescription, call
Professionals and Patients for Customized Care (P2C2) to locate a compounding pharmacist in your area: (713) 933-8400.

REFERENCES

CHAPTER 1: IS NEARLY EVERYONE "PROZAC DEFICIENT"?

Batki, S. L., et al. Fluoxetine for cocaine dependence in methadone maintenance: quantitative plasma and urine cocaine/benzoylecgonine concentrations. *Journal of Clinical Psychopharmacology* 1993, 13 (4): 243–50.

Bolte, M., and D. Avery. Case of fluoxetine-induced remission of Raynaud's Phenomenon—a case report. *Angiology—The Journal of Vascular Diseases* 1992, January, MSC 284-1–3.

Broadhead, W. E., et al. Depression, disability days, and days lost from work in a prospective epidemiologic survey (see comments). *Journal of the American Medical Association* 1990, 264 (19): 2524–29.

Burke, K., et al. Comparing age at onset of major depression and other psychiatric disorders by birth cohorts in five US community populations. *Archives of General Psychiatry* 1991, 48: 789–95.

Coccaro, E. F., et al. Fluoxetine treatment of impulsive aggression in DSM-III-R personality disorder patients (letter). *Journal of Clinical Psychopharmacology* 1990, 10 (5): 373–75.

Cook, E. H., et al. Fluoxetine treatment of children and adults with autistic disorder and mental retardation. *Journal of the American Academy of Child & Adolescent Psychiatry* 1992, 31 (4): 739–45.

Dalack, G. W., and S. P. Roose. Perspectives on the relationship between cardiovascular disease and affective disorder. *Journal of Clinical Psychiatry* 1990, 51: 4–9.

Eaton, S., and M. Konner. Paleolithic nutrition: a consideration of its nature and current implications. *New England Journal of Medicine* 1985, 312 (5): 283–89.

Fava, M., et al. Anger attacks in unipolar depression, part 1: clinical correlates and response to fluoxetine treatment. *American Journal of Psychiatry* 1993, 150 (8): 1158–63.

Fombonne, E. Increased rates of depression: update of epidemiological findings and analytical problems. *Acta Psychiatrica Scandinavica* 1994, 90: 145–56.

Forster, P., and J. King. Fluoxetine for premature ejaculation (letter). *American Journal of Psychiatry* 1994, 151 (10): 1523.

Gatto, E., et al. Fluoxetine in Tourette's syndrome (letter). *American Journal of Psychiatry* 1994, 151 (6): 946–47.

Glassman, A. H. Cigarette smoking: implications for psychiatric illness. *American Journal of Psychiatry* 1993, 150 (4): 546–53.

Greenberg, P. E., et al. The economic burden of depression in 1990. *Journal of Clinical Psychiatry* 1993, 54 (11): 405–18.

———. Depression: a neglected major illness (see comments). *Journal of Clinical Psychiatry* 1993, 54 (11): 419–24.

Irwin, M., et al. Reduction of immune function in life stress and depression. *Biological Psychiatry* 1990, 27 (1): 22–30.

Kafka, M. P., and R. Prentky. Fluoxetine treatment of nonparaphilic sexual addictions and paraphilias in men. *Journal of Clinical Psychiatry* 1992, 53 (10): 351–58.

Katz, R. J., and M. Rosenthal. Adverse interaction of cyproheptadine with serotonergic antidepressants (letter). *Journal of Clinical Psychiatry* 1994, 55 (7): 314–15.

Keller, M. B., and D. L. Hanks. The natural history and heterogeneity of depressive disorders: Implications for rational antidepressant therapy. *Journal of Clinical Psychiatry* 1994, 55 (9, suppl A): 25–31.

Kendler, K. S., et al. Major depression and generalized anxiety disorder. *Archives of General Psychiatry* 1992, 49: 716–22.

Kessler, R. C., et al. Lifetime and 12-month prevalence of DSM-III-R psychiatric disorders in the United States. Results from the National Comorbidity Survey. *Archives of General Psychiatry* 1994, 51: 8–19.

Mandoki, M. W. Fluoxetine in the treatment of borderline personality disorder (abstract). *Biological Psychiatry* 1993, 33: 117A

Markovitz, P. J., et al. Fluoxetine in the treatment of borderline and schizotypal personality disorders. *American Journal of Psychiatry* 1991, 148 (8): 1064–67.

McElroy, S. L., et al. Compulsive buying: a report of 20 cases. *Journal of Clinical Psychiatry* 1994, 55 (6): 242–48.

Menkes, D. B, et al. Acute tryptophan depletion aggravates premenstrual syndrome. *Journal of Affective Disorders* 1994, 32: 37–44.

———. Fluoxetine's spectrum of action in premenstrual syndrome. *International Clinical Psychopharmacology* 1993, 8: 95–102.

Mesaros, J. D. Fluoxetine for primary enuresis. *Journal of the American Academy of Child and Adolescent Psychiatry* 1993, 32 (4): 877–78.

Nagy, L. M., et al. Open perspective trial of fluoxetine for posttraumatic stress disorder. *Journal of Clinical Psychopharmacology* 1993, 13 (2): 107–13.

Norden, M. J. Fluoxetine in borderline personality disorder. *Progress in Neuro-Psychopharmacology & Biological Psychiatry* 1989, 13: 885–93.

Ornstein, R. *The Evolution of Consciousness*. New York: Prentice Hall Press, 1991.

Pearlstein, T. B., and A. B. Stone. Long-term fluoxetine treatment of late luteal phase dysphoric disorder. *Journal of Clinical Psychiatry* 1994, 55 (8): 332–35.

Polson, R. G., et al. Fluoxetine in the treatment of amphetamine dependence. *Human Psychopharmacology Clinical & Experimental* 1993, 8 (1): 55–58.

Post, F. Creativity and psychopathology. *British Journal of Psychiatry* 1994, July 165 (2):22–34.

Regier, D. A., et al. The de facto U.S. mental and addictive disorders service system: epidemiologic catchment area prospective 1-year prevalence rates of disorders and services. *Archives of General Psychiatry* 1993, 50: 85–94.

Ricketts, R. W., et al. Fluoxetine treatment of severe self-injury in young adults with mental retardation. *Journal of the American Academy of Child and Adolescent Psychiatry* 1993, 32 (4): 865–69.

Rosenthal, J., et al. A preliminary study of serotonergic antidepressants in treatment of dysthymia. *Progress in Neuro-Psychopharmacology & Biological Psychiatry* 1992, 16 (6): 933–41.

Salzman, C., et al. Effect of fluoxetine on anger in symptomatic volunteers with borderline personality disorder. *Journal of Clinical Psychopharmacology* 1995, 15 (1): 23–29.

Silvestri, R., et al. Serotonergic agents in the treatment of Gilles de la Tourette's syndrome. *Acta Neurologica* (Napoli) 1994, 16 (1–2): 58–63.

Smith, D. M., and S. S. Levitte. Association of fluoxetine and return of sexual potency in three elderly men. *Journal of Clinical Psychiatry* 1993, 54 (8): 317–19.

Stein, D. J., et al. Serotonergic medications for sexual obsessions, sexual addictions, and paraphilias. *Journal of Clinical Psychiatry* 1992, 53 (8): 267–71.

———. Serotonin reuptake blockers for the treatment of obsessional jealousy. *Journal of Clinical Psychiatry* 1994, 55 (1): 30–33.

Stone, A. B., et al. Fluoxetine in the treatment of late luteal phase dysphoric disorder. *Journal of Clinical Psychiatry* 1991, 52 (7): 290–93.

Unseld, E., et al. Occurrence of "natural" diazepam in human brain. *Biochemical Pharmacology* 1990, 39: 210–12.

Van Ameringen, M., et al. Fluoxetine efficacy in social phobia. *Journal of Clinical Psychiatry* 1993, 54 (1): 27–32.

van der Kolk, B. A., et al. Fluoxetine in posttraumatic stress disorder. *Journal of Clinical Psychiatry* 1994, 55 (12): 517–22.

Wells, K. B., and M. A. Burnam. Caring for depression in America: lessons learned from early findings of the medical outcomes study. *Psychiatric Medicine* 1991, 9 (4): 503–19.

Wells, K. B., et al. Use of minor tranquilizers and antidepressant medications by depressed outpatients: results from the medical outcomes study. *American Journal of Psychiatry* 1994, 151 (5): 694–700.

————. The functioning and well-being of depressed patients. Results from the Medical Outcomes Studies (see comments). *Journal of the American Medical Association* 1989, 262 (7): 914–19.

————. How the medical comorbidity of depressed patients differs across health care settings: results from the medical outcomes study. *American Journal of Psychiatry* 1991, 148 (12): 1688–96.

Winchel, R. M., et al. Clinical characteristics of trichotillomania and its response to fluoxetine. *Journal of Clinical Psychiatry* 1992, 53 (9): 304–8.

CHAPTER 2: SEROTONIN: VIRTUAL MORALITY AND THE BRAIN'S SURROGATE PARENT

Benkelfat, C., et al. Mood-lowering effect of tryptophan depletion. *Archives of General Psychiatry* 1994, 51: 687–97.

Brown, C. M., and J. Seggie. Effects of antidepressants on entrainment of circadian rhythms. *Progress in Neuro-psychopharmacology & Biological Psychiatry* 1988, 12 (2–3): 288–300.

Coccaro, E. F., et al. Self- and other-directed human aggression: the role of the central serotonergic system. *International Clinical Psychopharmacology* 1992, 6 (6 suppl): 70–83.

Csaba, G. Presence in and effects of pineal indoleamines at very low level of phylogeny. *Experientia* 1993, 49 (8): 627–34.

Delgado, P. L., et al. Serotonin function and the mechanism of antidepressant action. *Archives of General Psychiatry* 1990, 47: 411–18.

Fausteman, W. O., et al. An association between low levels of 5-HIAA and HVA in cerebrospinal fluid and early mortality in a diagnostically mixed psychiatric sample. *British Journal of Psychiatry* 1993, 163: 519–21.

Hellstrand, K., and S. Hermodsson. Enhancement of human natural killer cell cytotoxicity by serotonin: role of non-T/CD16+NK cells, accessory monocytes, and 5-HT1A receptors. *Cell Immunology* 1990, 127 (1): 199–214.

Kawai, K., et al. Effect of long-term feeding with tryptophan-free diet on the circadian rhythm in rats. *Yakubutsu Seishin Kodo* 1992, 12 (2): 75–84.

Lejoyeux, M., et al. Prospective evaluation of the serotonin syndrome in depressed inpatients treated with clomipramine. *Acta Psychiatrica Scandinavica* 1993, 88: 369–71.

MacMurray, R. G., et al. Neuroendocrine responses of type A individuals to exercise. *Behavioral Medicine* 1989, 15 (2): 84–92.

Mehlman, P. T., et al. Low CSF 5-HIAA concentration and severe aggression and impaired impulse control in nonhuman primates. *American Journal of Psychiatry* 1994, 151 (10): 1485–91.

Naesh, O., et al. Platelet activation in mental stress. *Clinical Physiology* 1993, 13 (3): 299–307.

Roy, A., et al. Acting out hostility in normal volunteers: negative correlation with levels of 5-HIAA in cerebrospinal fluid. *Psychiatry Research* 1988, 24 (2): 187–94.

Sommerfelt, L., and R. Ursin. The 5-HT2 antagonist ritanserin decreases sleep in cats. *Sleep* 1993, 16 (1): 15–22.

Sternbach, H. The serotonin syndrome. *American Journal of Psychiatry* 1991, 148 (6): 705–13.

Virkkunen, M., and S. Narvanen. Plasma insulin, tryptophan and serotonin levels during the glucose tolerance test among habitually violent and impulsive offenders. *Neuropsychobiology* 1987, 17: 19–23.

Virkkunen, M., et al. Relationship of psychobiological variables to recidivism in violent offenders and impulsive fire setters. A follow-up study (published erratum appears in *Archives of General Psychiatry* 1989, 46 [10]: 913). *Archives of General Psychiatry* 1989, 46 (7): 600–3.

———. CSF biochemistries, glucose metabolism, and diurnal activity rhythms in alcoholics, violent offenders, fire setters, and healthy volunteers. *Archives of General Psychiatry* 1994, 51: 20–27.

CHAPTER 3: STRESS—THE BRAIN IN HEAT

Adell, A., et al. Chronic administration of clomipramine prevents the increase in serotonin and noradrenaline induced by chronic stress. *Psychopharmacology* (Berlin) 1989, 99 (1): 22–26.

Arbisi, P. A., et al. Heat-loss response to a thermal challenge in seasonal affective disorder. *Psychiatry Research* 1994, 52: 199–214.

Brodan, V., et al. The effect of stress on circadian rhythms. *Czech Medicine* 1982, 5 (1): 1–8.

Cabanac, R., and E. Briese. Handling elevates the colonic temperature of mice. *Physiological Behavior* 1992, 51 (1): 95–98.

Chaouloff, F., et al. Peripheral and central consequences of immobilization stress in genetically obese Zucker rats. *American Journal of Physiology* 1989, 256 (2 Pt 2): R435–R442.

Clement, H. W., et al. Stress-induced changes of extracellular 5-hydroxyindoleacetic acid concentrations followed in the nucleus raphe dorsalis and the frontal cortex of the rat. *Brain Research* 1993, 614 (1–2): 117–24.

Cohn, E. G. Weather and crime. *British Journal of Criminology* 1990, 30 (1): 51–64.

Cunningham, C. L., et al. Ambient temperature effects on taste aversion conditioned by ethanol: contribution of ethanol-induced hypothermia. *Alcoholism: Clinical & Experimental Research* 1992, 16 (6): 1117–24.

Dunn, A. J. Changes in plasma and brain tryptophan and brain serotonin and 5-hydroxyindoleacetic acid after footshock stress. *Life Sciences* 1988, 42 (19): 1847–53.

Dunn, A. J., and J. Welch. Stress and endotoxin-induced increases in brain tryptophan and serotonin metabolism depend on sympathetic nervous system activity. *Journal of Neurochemistry* 1991, 57 (5): 1615–22.

Gao, B., et al. Fluoxetine decreases brain temperature and REM sleep in Syrian hamsters. *Psychopharmacology* (Berlin) 1992, 106 (3): 321–29.

Goldberg, M. E., et al. Influence of chlorpromazine on brain serotonin turnover and body temperature in isolated aggressive mice. *Neuropharmacology* 1973, 12 (3): 249–60.

Hata, T., et al. Changes in CNS levels of serotonin and its metabolite in SART-stressed (repeatedly cold-stressed) rats. *Japanese Journal of Pharmacology* 1991, 56 (1): 101–4.

Helin, P., et al. Human urinary biogenic amines and some physiological responses during situation stress. *International Journal of Psychophysiology* 1988, 6 (2): 125–32.

Higley, J. D., et al. CSF monoamine metabolite concentrations vary according to age, rearing, and sex, and are influenced by the stressor of social separation in rhesus monkeys. *Psychopharmacology* (Berlin) 1991, 103 (4): 551–56.

Houdouin, F., et al. Detection of the release of 5-hydroxyindole compounds in the hypothalamus and the n. raphe dorsalis throughout the sleep-waking cycle and during stressful situations in the rat: a polygraphic and voltametric approach. *Experimental Brain Research* 1991, 85 (1): 153–62.

Jacobs, B. L. The relationship between 5-HT neuronal discharge and motor activity: 5-HT research in the Jacobs Laboratory. *Serotonin Notes* 1994, 1 (1): 1–4.

Keating, S. M., et al. Sexual assault patterns. *Journal of the Forensic Sciences Society* 1990, 30 (2): 71–88.

Kendler, K. S., et al. The prediction of major depression in women: toward an integrated etiologic model. *American Journal of Psychiatry* 1993, 150 (8): 1139–48.

Lelliott, P., et al. Onset of panic disorder with agoraphobia: toward an integrated model (see comments). *Archives of General Psychiatry* 1989, 46 (11): 1000–4.

Long, N. C., et al. Stress-induced rise of body temperature in rats is the same in warm and cool environments. *Physiological Behavior* 1990, 47 (4): 773–75.

Marazziti, D., et al. Psychological stress and body temperature changes in humans. *Physiological Behavior* 1992, 52 (2): 393–95.

Mitchell, S. N., and P. J. Thomas. Effect of restraint stress and anxiolytics on 5-HT turnover in rat brain. *Pharmacology* 1988, 37 (2): 105–13.

Naesh, O., et al. Platelet activation in mental stress. *Clinical Physiology* 1993, 13 (3): 299–307.

Norden, M. J. Is there an effective drug treatment for borderline personality disorder. *Harvard Medical School Mental Health Letter*, No. 6: 8, 1989.

Norden, M. J., and D. Avery. Heat and violence correlate independent of season. (Abstract) *New Research APA*, Annual meeting, San Francisco, 1993.

Sarrias, M. J., et al. Seasonal changes of plasma serotonin and related parameters: correlation with environmental measures. *Biological Psychiatry* 1989, 26, 695–706.

Severino, S. K., et al. High nocturnal body temperature in premenstrual syndrome and late luteal phase dysphoric disorder (see comments). *American Journal of Psychiatry* 1991, 148 (10): 1329–35.

Shimizu, N., et al. In vivo measurement of hypothalamic serotonin release by intracerebral microdialysis: significant enhancement by immobilization stress in rats. *Brain Research Bulletin* 1992, 28 (5): 727–34.

Simmonds, M. A. Effect of environmental temperature on the turnover of 5-HT in various areas of rat brain. *Journal of Physiology* (London) 1970, 211: 93–108.

Swann, A. C., et al. Stress, depression, and mania: relationship between perceived role of stressful events and clinical and biochemical characteristics. *Acta Psychiatrica Scandinavica* 1990, 81 (4): 389–97.

Tempel, G. E., and L. H. Parks. Brain norepinephrine and serotonin in the golden hamster during heat and cold acclimation and hypothermia. *Comparative Biochemical Physiology* 1982, 73C: 377–81.

Wehr, T. A., et al. Contrasts between symptoms of summer depression and winter depression. *Journal of Affective Disorders* 1991, 23 (4): 173–83.

Weststrate, J. A., et al. The effect of psychological stress on diet-induced thermogenesis and resting metabolic rate. *European Journal of Clinical Nutrition* 1990, 44 (4): 269–75.

Wolfersdorf, M., and R. Straub. Electrodermal reactivity in male and female depressive patients who later died by suicide. *Acta Psychiatrica Scandinavica* 1994, 89 (4): 279–84.

Zethof, T. J., et al. Stress-induced hyperthermia in mice: a methodological study. *Physiological Behavior* 1994, 55 (1): 109–15.

CHAPTER 4: LIGHT THERAPY: THE END OF THE MODERN DARK AGE

Avery, D. H., et al. Dawn simulation compared with a dim red signal in the treatment of winter depression. *Biological Psychiatry* 1994, 36 (3): 180–88.

———. Gradual versus rapid dawn simulation treatment of winter depression. *Journal of Clinical Psychiatry* 1992, 53 (10): 359–63.

———. Dawn simulation treatment of winter depression: a controlled study. *American Journal of Psychiatry* 1993, 150 (1): 113–17.

Bell, J., and P. H. Garthwaite. The psychological effects of service in British Antarctica: a study using the General Health Questionnaire. *British Journal of Psychiatry* 1987, 150: 213–18.

Blehar, M. C., and A. J. Lewy. Seasonal mood disorders: consensus and controversy. *Psychopharmacology Bulletin* 1990, 26 (4): 465–504.

Cohen, R. M., et al. Preliminary data on the metabolic brain pattern of patients with winter seasonal affective disorder. *Archives of General Psychiatry* 1992, 49: 545–52.

Czeisler, C. A., et al. Bright light induction of strong (type O) resetting of the human circadian pacemaker. *Science* 1989, 244 (16): 1328–32.

Czeisler, C. A., et al. Entrainment of human circadian rhythms by light-dark cycles: a reassessment. *Photochemistry and Photobiology* 1981, 34: 239–47.

Danesi, M. A. Electroencephalographic manifestations of grand mal epilepsy in Africans: observation of relative rarity of interictal abnormalities. *Epilepsia* 1988, 29 (4): 446–50.

George, F. R., and A. C. Collins. Ethanol's behavioral effects may be partly due to increases in brain prostaglandin production. *Alcoholism: Clinical & Experimental Research* 1985, 9 (2): 143–46.

Isobe, Y., et al. Diurnal variation of thermal resistance in rats. *Canadian Journal of Physiological Pharmacology* 1980, 58 (10): 1174–79.

Jacobsen, F. M., et al. Morning versus midday phototherapy of seasonal affective disorder. *American Journal of Psychiatry* 1987, 144 (10): 1301–5.

Kavanua, J. L., and C. R. Peters. Twilight zeitgebers, weather, and activity of nocturnal primates. *Folia Primatol* 1976, 26: 67–79.

Krauchi, K., et al. High intake of sweets late in the day predicts a rapid and persistent response to light therapy in winter depression. *Psychiatry Research* 1993, 46: 107–17.

Laakso, M., et al. Twenty-four-hour patterns of pineal melatonin and pituitary and plasma prolactin in male rats under "natural" and artificial lighting conditions. *Neuroendocrinology* 1988, 48: 308–13.

Lam, R. W. Light therapy for seasonal bulimia (letter). *American Journal of Psychiatry* 1989, 146: 1640–41.

———. Morning light therapy for winter depression: Predictors of response. *Acta Psychiatrica Scandinavica* 1994, 97–101.

Lam, R. W., et al. Ultraviolet versus non-ultraviolet light therapy for seasonal affective disorder. *Journal of Clinical Psychiatry* 1991, 52 (5): 213–16.

———. A controlled study of light therapy for bulimia nervosa. *American Journal of Psychiatry* 1994, 151 (5): 744–50.

Levitt, A. J., et al. Bright light augmentation in antidepressant nonresponders. *Journal of Clinical Psychiatry* 1991, 52 (8): 336–37.

Lewy, A. J., et al. Light suppresses melatonin secretion in humans. *Science* 1980, 210 (4475): 1267–69.

Livermore, Jr., A. H., and J. R. Stevens. Light transducer for the biological clock: a function for rapid eye movements. *Journal of Neural Transmission* 1988, 72: 37–42.

McGrath, R. E., et al. The effect of L-tryptophan on seasonal affective disorder. *Journal of Clinical Psychiatry* 1990, 51 (4): 162–63.

Meijer, J. H., et al. Luminance coding in a circadian pacemaker: the suprachiasmatic nucleus of the rat and the hamster. *Brain Research* 1986, 382: 109–18.

Norden, M. J., and D. H. Avery. A controlled study of dawn simulation in subsyndromal winter depression. *Acta Psychiatrica Scandinavica* 1993, 88 (1): 67–71.

Oren, D. A., et al. Treatment of seasonal affective disorder with green light and red light. *American Journal of Psychiatry* 1991, 148 (4): 509.

O'Rourke, D. A., et al. Serotonin implicated in etiology of seasonal affective disorder. *Psychopharmacology Bulletin* 1987, 23 (3): 358–59.

Parry, B. L., et al. Light therapy of late luteal phase dysphoric disorder: an extended study. *American Journal of Psychiatry* 1993, 150 (9): 1417–19.

Rao, M. L., et al. Blood serotonin, serum melatonin and light therapy in healthy subjects in patients with nonseasonal depression. *Acta Psychiatrica Scandinavica* 1992, 86 (2): 127–32.

Rosenthal, N. E., et al. No mood-altering effects found after treatment of normal subjects with bright light in the morning. *Psychiatry Research* 1987, 22 (1): 1–9.

———. Effects of light treatment on core body temperature in seasonal affective disorder. *Biological Psychiatry* 1990, 27 (1): 39–50.

Rosenthal, N. E. Light Therapy: theory and practice. *Primary Psychiatry* 1994, September/October: 31–33.

Satlin, A., et al. Bright light treatment of behavioral and sleep disturbances in patients with Alzheimer's disease. *American Journal of Psychiatry* 1992, 149 (8): 1028–32.

Savides, T. J., et al. Natural light exposure of young adults. *Physiology and Behavior* 1986, 38: 571–74.

Terman, M., et al. Daylight deprivation and replenishment: a psychobiological problem with a naturalistic solution. International Daylighting Conference 1986.

———. Dawn and dusk simulation as a therapeutic intervention. *Biological Psychiatry* 1989, 25: 966–70.

Terman, M., Schlager, D. S. Twilight therapeutics, winter depression, melatonin, and sleep. In *Sleep and Biological Rhythms,* J. Montplaisir and R. Godbout, editors. (New York: Oxford University Press), pp. 113–28.

Terman, M., et al. Light therapy for seasonal affective disorder. A review of efficacy. *Neuropsychopharmacology* 1989, 2 (1): 1–22.

Wehr, T. A., et al. Eye versus skin phototherapy of seasonal affective disorder. *American Journal of Psychiatry* 1987, 144 (6): 753–57.

Wirz-Justice, A., et al. Dose relationships of morning bright white light in seasonal affective disorder (SAD). *Experientia* 1987, 43 (5): 574–76.

————. Light therapy in seasonal affective disorder is independent of time of day or circadian phase. *Archives of General Psychiatry* 1993, 50 (12): 929–37.

CHAPTER 5: MELATONIN: THE NATURAL HEIR TO SEROTONIN

Anton-Tay, F., et al. Brain serotonin concentration: elevation following intraperitoneal administration of melatonin. *Science* 1968, 162: 277–78.

Attanasio, A., et al. Ontogeny of circadian rhythmicity for melatonin, serotonin, and N-acetylserotonin in humans. *Journal of Pineal Research* 1986, 3 (3): 251–56.

Aubert, M. L., et al. Delayed sexual maturation induced by daily melatonin administration eliminates the LH response to naloxone despite normal responsiveness to GnRH in juvenile male rats. *Neuroendocrinology* 1988, 48 (1): 72–80.

Barni, S., et al. A study of the pineal hormone melatonin as a second line therapy in metastatic colorectal cancer resistant to fluorouracil plus folates. *Tumori* 1990, 76 (1): 58–60.

Beck, F. J., et al. Melatonin, cortisol and ACTH in patients with major depressive disorder and healthy humans with special reference to the outcome of the dexamethasone suppression test. *Psychoneuroendocrinology* 1985, 10 (2): 173–86.

Brismar, K, et al. Melatonin secretion related to side-effects of beta-blockers from the central nervous system. *Acta Psychiatrica Scandinavica* 1988, 223 (6): 525–30.

Brown, R. P., et al. Depressed mood and reality disturbance correlate with decreased nocturnal melatonin in depressed patients. *Acta Psychiatrica Scandinavica* 1987, 76 (3): 272–75.

Bubenik, G. A., Dhanvantari S. Influence of serotonin and melatonin on some parameters of gastrointestinal activity. *Journal of Pineal Research* 1989, 7 (4): 333–44.

————. The effect of food deprivation on brain and gastrointestinal tissue levels of tryptophan, serotonin, 5-hydroxyindoleacetic acid, and melatonin. *Journal of Pineal Research* 1992, 12 (1): 7–16.

Cagnacci, A., et al. Melatonin: a major regulator of the circadian rhythm of core temperature in humans. *Journal of Clinical Endocrinology and Metabolism* 1992, 75 (2): 447–52.

Caroleo, M. C., et al. Melatonin as immunomodulator in immunodeficient mice. *Immunopharmacology* 1992, 23 (2): 81–89.

Catapano, F., et al. Melatonin and cortisol secretion in patients with primary obsessive compulsive disorder. *Psychiatry Research* 1992, 44 (3): 217–25.

Chazot, G., et al. Rapid antidepressant activity of destyr gamma endorphin: correlation with urinary melatonin. *Biological Psychiatry* 1985, 20 (9): 1026–30.

Chuang, J. J., et al. Melatonin decreases brain serotonin release, arterial pressure and heart rate in rats. *Pharmacology* 1993, 47 (2): 91–97.

Claustrat, B., et al. Melatonin and jet lag: confirmatory result using a simplified protocol (see comments). *Biological Psychiatry* 1992, 32 (8): 705–11.

Dahlitz, M., et al. Delayed sleep phase syndrome response to melatonin. *Lancet* 1991, 337 (8750): 1121–24.

den Boer, J. A., and H. G. Westenberg. Behavioral, neuroendocrine, and biochemical effects of 5-hydroxytryptophan administration in panic disorder. *Psychiatry Research* 1990, 31 (3): 267–78.

Dogliotti, L., et al. Melatonin and human cancer. *Journal of Steroid Biochemistry and Molecular Biology* 1990, 37 (6): 983–87.

Dollins, A. B., et al. Effect of inducing nocturnal serum melatonin concentrations in daytime on sleep, mood, body temperature, and performance. *Proceedings of the National Academy of Science USA* 1994, 91: 1824–28.

Dowdall, M., and C. De Montigny. Effect of atmospheric ions on hippocampal pyramidal neuron responsiveness to serotonin. *Brain Research* 1985, 342 (1): 103–9.

Duffy, J. D., and P. F. Malloy. Efficacy of buspirone in the treatment of posttraumatic stress disorder.: an open trial. *Annals of Clinical Psychiatry* 1994, 6 (1): 33–37.

Ekman, A. C., et al. Ethanol inhibits melatonin secretion in healthy volunteers in a dose-dependent randomized double blind cross-over study. *Journal of Clinical Endocrinology and Metabolism* 1993, 77 (3): 780–83.

Folkard, S., et al. Can melatonin improve shift workers' tolerance of the night shift? Some preliminary findings. *Chronobiology International* 1993, 10 (5): 315–20.

Gazzah, N., et al. Effect of an n-3 fatty acid–deficient diet on the adenosine-dependent melatonin release in cultured rat pineal. *Journal of Neurochemistry* 1993, 61 (3): 1057–63.

Gonzalez, R., et al. Melatonin therapy of advanced human malignant melanoma. *Melanoma Research* 1991, 1 (4): 237–43.

Hardeland, R., et al. The significance of the metabolism of the neurohormone melatonin: antioxidative protection and formation of bioactive substances. *Neuroscience and Biobehavioral Reviews* 1993, 17: 347–57.

Hawkins, L. H. The influence of air ions, temperature and humidity on subjective well-being and comfort. *Journal of Environmental Psychology* 1981, 1 (4): 279–92.

Hill, S. M., et al. The growth inhibitory action of melatonin on human breast cancer cells is linked to the estrogen response system. *Cancer Letter* 1992, 64 (3): 249–56.

Huether, G., et al. Effects of indirectly acting 5-HT receptor agonists on circulating melatonin levels in rats. *European Journal of Pharmacology* 1993, 238: 249–54.

James, S. P., et al. Melatonin administration in insomnia. *Neuropsychopharmacology* 1990, 3 (1): 19–23.

Jan, J. E., et al. The treatment of sleep disorders with melatonin. *Developmental Medicine and Child Neurology* 1994, 36 (2): 97–107.

Ja'skowski, J., and A. My'sliwski. Effect of air ions on healing of wounds of rat skin. *Experimental Pathology* 1986, 29 (2): 113–17.

Kennedy, G. H., et al. Melatonin and cortisol "switches" during mania, depression, and euthymia in a drug free bipolar patient. *Journal Nervous Mental Disorders* 1988, 177 (5): 300–3.

Kerenyi, N. A., et al. Why the incidence of cancer is increasing: the role of "light pollution." *Medical Hypotheses* 1990, 33 (2): 75–78.

Kloeden, P. E., et al. Does a centralized clock for ageing exist? *Gerontology* 1990, 36: 314–22.

———. Timekeeping in genetically programmed aging. *Experimental Gerontology* 1993, 28: 109–18.

Lewy, A. J., et al. Melatonin shifts human circadian rhythms according to a phase response curve. *Chronobiology International* 1992, 9 (5): 380–92.

Liburdy, R. P., et al. ELF magnetic fields, breast cancer, and melatonin: 60 Hz fields block melatonin's oncostatic action on ER+breast cancer cell proliferation. *Journal of Pineal Research* 1993, 14 (2): 89–97.

Lissoni, P., et al. Clinical study of melatonin in untreatable advanced cancer patients. *Tumori* 1987, 73 (5): 475–80.

———. Immunotherapy with subcutaneous low-dose interleukin-2 and the pineal indole melatonin as a new effective therapy in advanced cancers of the digestive tract. *British Journal of Cancer* 1993, 67 (6): 1404–7.

————. Clinical results with the pineal hormone melatonin in advanced cancer resistant to standard antitumor therapies. *Oncology* 1991, 48 (6): 448–50.

————. Biological and clinical results of a neuroimmunotherapy with interleukin-2 and the pineal hormone melatonin as a first line treatment in advanced non-small cell lung cancer. *British Journal of Cancer* 1992, 66 (1): 155–58.

————. Randomized study with the pineal hormone melatonin versus supportive care alone in advanced nonsmall cell lung cancer resistant to a first-line chemotherapy containing cisplatin. *Oncology* 1992, 49 (5): 336–39.

————. Neuroimmunotherapy of advanced solid neoplasms with single evening subcutaneous injection of low-dose interleukin-2 and melatonin: preliminary results. *European Journal of Cancer* 1993, 29A (2): 185–89.

————. A randomized study with the pineal hormone melatonin versus supportive care alone in patients with brain metastases due to solid neoplasms. *Cancer* 1994, 73 (3): 699–701.

————. A randomized study with subcutaneous low-dose interleukin 2 alone vs interleukin 2 plus the pineal neurohormone melatonin in advanced solid neoplasms other than renal cancer and melanoma. *British Journal of Cancer* 1994, 69 (1): 196–99.

MacFarlane, J. G., et al. The effects of exogenous melatonin on the total sleep time and daytime alertness of chronic insomniacs: a preliminary study. *Biological Psychiatry* 1991, 30 (4): 371–76.

Martinuzzo, M., et al. Melatonin effect on arachidonic acid metabolism to cyclooxygenase derivatives in human platelets. *Journal of Pineal Research* 1991, 11 (3–4): 111–15.

Maurizi, C. P. The therapeutic potential for tryptophan and melatonin: Possible roles in depression, sleep, Alzheimer's disease and abnormal aging. *Medical Hypotheses* 1990, 31: 233–42.

McIntyre, I. M., et al. Plasma melatonin levels in affective states. *International Journal of Clinical Pharmacological Research* 1989, 9 (2): 158–64.

Mills, M. H., and T. A. Faunce. Melatonin supplementation from early morning auto-urine drinking. *Medical Hypotheses* 1991, 36: 195–99.

Morton, L. L., and Kershner, J. R. Negative air ionization improves memory and attention in learning-disabled and mentally retarded children. *Journal of Abnormal Child Psychology* 1984, 12 (2): 353–65.

Murphy, D. L., et al. Human plasma melatonin is elevated during treatment with the monoamine oxidase inhibitors clorgyline and tranylcypromine but not deprenyl. *Psychiatry Research* 1986, 17 (2): 119–27.

Nair, N. P., et al. Plasma melatonin—an index of brain aging in humans? *Biological Psychiatry* 1986, 21 (2): 141–50.

Nickelsen, T., et al. Influence of subchronic intake of melatonin at various times of the day on fatigue and hormonal levels: a placebo-controlled, double-blind trial. *Journal of Pineal Research* 1989, 6 (4): 325–34.

Niles, L. Melatonin interaction with the benzodiazepine-GABA receptor complex in the CNS. *Kynurenine and Serotonin Pathways* 1991: 267–77.

Persinger, M. A. Increased geomagnetic activity and the occurrence of bereavement hallucinations: evidence for melatonin-mediated microseizuring in the temporal lobe? *Neuroscience Letters* 1988, 88 (3): 271–74.

———. Average diurnal changes in melatonin levels are associated with hourly incidence of bereavement apparitions: support for the hypothesis of temporal (limbic) lobe microseizuring. *Perceptual and Motor Skills* 1993, 76: 444–46.

Petrie, K., et al. Effect of melatonin on jet lag after long haul flights. *British Medical Journal* 1989, 298 (6675): 705–7.

———. A double-blind trial of melatonin as a treatment for jet lag in international cabin crew. *Biological Psychiatry* 1993, 33 (7): 526–30.

Pierpaoli, W., and W. Regelson. Pineal control of aging: effect of melatonin and pineal grafting on aging mice. *Proceedings of National Academy of Sciences USA* 1994, 91: 787–91.

Pierpaoli, W., and G. J. M. Maestroni. Melatonin: a principal neuroimmunoregulatory and anti-stress hormone: its anti-aging effects. *Immunology Letters* 1987, 16: 355–62.

Pierpaoli, W., et al. Aging-postponing effects of circadian melatonin: experimental evidence, significance and possible mechanisms. *International Journal of Neuroscience* 1990, 51: 339–340.

Pierrefiche, G., et al. Antioxidant activity of melatonin in mice. *Research Communications in Chemical Pathology and Pharmacology* 1993, 80 (2): 211–23.

Pioli, C., et al. Melatonin increases antigen presentation and amplifies specific and non specific signals for t-cell proliferation. *International Journal of Immunopharmacology* 1993, 15 (4): 463–68.

Poeggeler, B. Melatonin and the light-dark zeitgeber in vertebrates, invertebrates and unicellular organisms. *Experientia* 1993, 49: 611–13.

Poeggeler, B., et al. Melatonin, hydroxyl radical-mediated oxidative damage, and aging: a hypothesis. *Journal of Pineal Research* 1993, 14 (4): 151–68.

Reilly, T., and I. C. Stevenson. An investigation of the effects of negative air ions on responses to submaximal exercise at different times of day. *Journal of Human Ergology* (Tokyo) 1993, 22 (1): 1–.

Reiter, R. J. Alterations of the circadian melatonin rhythm by the electro-magnetic spectrum: a study in environmental toxicology. *Regulatory Toxicology and Pharmacology* 1992, 15 (3): 226–44.

———. Melatonin synthesis: multiplicity of regulation. *Kynurenine and Serotonin Pathways* 1991: 149–58.

Rosenthal, N. E., et al. Atenolol in seasonal affective disorder: a test of the melatonin hypothesis. *American Journal of Psychiatry* 1988, 145 (1): 52–56.

Rozencwaig, R., et al. The role of melatonin and serotonin in aging. *Medical Hypotheses* 1987, 23: 337–52.

Rubin, R. T., et al. Neuroendocrine aspects of primary endogenous depression. *Archives of General Psychiatry* 1992, 49: 558–67.

Sack, R. L., et al. Melatonin administration to blind people: phase advances and entrainment. *Journal of Biological Rhythms* 1991, 6 (3): 249–61.

Samel, A., et al. Influence of melatonin treatment on human circadian rhythmicity before and after a simulated 9-hr time shift. *Journal of Biological Rhythms* 1991, 6 (3): 235–48.

Sandyk, R. Possible role of pineal melatonin in the mechanisms of aging. *International Journal of Neuroscience* 1990, 52 (1–2): 85–92.

Sandyk, R., and R. Pardeshi. The relationship between ECT nonrespon-siveness and calcification of the pineal gland in bipolar patients. *International Journal of Neuroscience* 1990, 54 (3–4): 301–6.

Schlager, D. S. Early-morning administration of short-acting beta block-ers for treatment of winter depression. *American Journal of Psychiatry* 1994, 151 (9): 1383–85.

Schmid, H. A. Decreased melatonin biosynthesis, calcium flux, pineal gland calcification and aging: A hypothetical framework. *Gerontology* 1993, 39: 189–99.

Silman, R. E. Melatonin: a contraceptive for the nineties. *European Journal of Obstetrics and Gynecological Reproduction Biology* 1993, 49 (1–2): 3–9.

Souetre, E., et al. Abnormal melatonin response to 5-Methoxypsoralen in Dementia. *American Journal of Psychiatry* 1989, 146 (8): 1037–40.

————. 5-Methoxypsoralen as a specific stimulating agent of melatonin secretion in humans. *Journal of Clinical Endocrinology and Metabolism* 1990, 71 (3): 670–74.

Stevens, R. G., et al. Electric power, pineal function, and the risk of breast cancer. *FASEB Journal* 1992, 6: 853–60.

Stokkan, K. A., et al. Low temperature stimulates pineal activity in Syrian hamsters. *Journal of Pineal Research* 1991, 10 (1): 43–48.

Stoupel, E., and Shimshoni M. Hospital cardiovascular deaths and total distribution of deaths in 180 consecutive months with different cosmic physical activity: a correlative study (1974–88). *International Journal of Biometeorology* 1991, 35 (1): 6–9.

Strassman, R. J., et al. Elevated rectal temperature produced by all-night bright light is reversed by melatonin infusion in men. *Journal of Applied Physiology* 1991, 71 (6): 2178–82.

Trentini, G. P., et al. Melatonin treatment delays reproductive aging of female rat via the opiatergic system. *Neuroendocrinology* 1992, 56 (3): 364–70.

T'unyi, I., and O. Tesarov'a. Suicide and geomagnetic activity. *Soudní Lekarství* 1991, 36 (1–2): 1–11.

Valcavi, R., et al. Melatonin stimulates growth hormone secretion through pathways other than the growth hormone–releasing hormone. *Clinical Endocrinology* (Oxford) 1993, 39 (2): 193–99.

Voordouw, B. C., et al. Melatonin and melatonin-progestin combinations alter pituitary-ovarian function in women and can inhibit ovulation. *Journal of Clinical Endocrinology and Metabolism* 1992, 74 (1): 108–17.

Vriend, J., et al. Melatonin increases serum growth hormone and insulin-like growth factor I (IGF-I) levels in male Syrian hamsters via hypothalamic neurotransmitters. *Growth, Development and Aging* 1990, 54 (4): 165–71.

Wakabayashi, H., et al. Effects of diazepam administration on melatonin synthesis in the rat pineal gland in vivo. *Chemical Pharmacology Bulletin* (Tokyo) 1991, 39 (10): 2674–76.

————. Effect of psychotropic drugs on the contents of melatonin, serotonin, and N-acetylserotonin in rat pineal gland. *Japanese Journal of Pharmacology* 1989, 49 (2): 225–34.

Wehr, T. A. The durations of human melatonin secretion and sleep respond to changes in daylength (photoperiod). *Journal of Clinical Endocrinology and Metabolism* 1991, 73 (6): 1276–80.

Wetterberg, L., et al. Age, alcoholism and depression are associated with low levels of urinary melatonin. *Journal of Psychiatry and Neuroscience* 1992, 17 (5): 215–24.

Wilson, B. W. Chronic exposure to ELF fields may induce depression. *Bioelectromagnetics* 1988, 9 (2): 195–205.

Wirz-Justice, A., et al. Morning or night-time melatonin is ineffective in seasonal affective disorder. *Journal of Psychiatric Research* 1990, 24 (2): 129–37.

Ying, S., et al. Human malignant melanoma cells express high-affinity receptors for melatonin: antiproliferative effects of melatonin and 6-chloromelatonin. *European Journal of Pharmacology—Molecular Pharmacology Section* 1993, 246: 89–96.

Zimmermann, R. C., et al. Effects of acute tryptophan depletion on nocturnal melatonin secretion in humans. *Journal of Clinical Endocrinology and Metabolism* 1993, 76 (5): 1160–64.

CHAPTER 6: SLEEP AS IT WAS MEANT TO BE

Bootzin, R. R., and M. L. Perlis. Nonpharmacologic treatments of insomnia. *Journal of Clinical Psychiatry* 1992, 53 (6, suppl): 37–41.

Fahay, V. How sleep deprived are you (includes related quiz)? *Health* 1993, v7 (p5): 16 (1).

Kasper, S., et al. Serotonergically induced hormonal responses and the antidepressant effect of total sleep deprivation in patients with major depression. *Psychopharmacology Bulletin* 1988, 24(3): 450–53.

Kripke, D. F., et al. Short and long sleep and sleeping pills. Is increased mortality associated? *Archives of General Psychiatry* 1979, 36: 103–16.

Leibenluft, E., and T. A. Wehr. Is sleep deprivation useful in the treatment of depression? *American Journal of Psychiatry* 1992, 149 (2): 159–68.

Lugaresi, E., et al. Fatal familial insomnia and dysautonomia with selective degeneration of thalamic nuclei. *New England Journal of Medicine* 1986, 315: 997–1003.

Morin, C. M., et al. Nonpharmacological interventions for insomnia: A meta-analyis of treatment efficacy. *American Journal of Psychiatry* 1994, 151 (8): 1172–80.

Mrosovsky, N. Photic phase shifting in hamsters: More than meets the eye. *Light Treatment and Biological Rhythms* 1993, 5: 34–36.

National Commission on Sleep Disorders Research. *Wake up America: a national sleep alert.* Executive summary and executive report. January 1993.

Okawa, M., et al. Vitamin B12 treatment for sleep-wake rhythm disorders. *Sleep* 1990, 13 (1): 15–23.

Reinink, E., et al. Prediction of the antidepressant response to total sleep deprivation by diurnal variation of mood. *Psychiatry Research* 1990, 32: 113–24.

Rosekind, M. The epidemiology and occurrence of insomnia. *Journal of Clinical Psychiatry* 1992, 53 (6 suppl): 4–6.

Sandyk, R., et al. Magnetic fields mimic the behavioral effects of REM sleep deprivation in humans. *International Journal of Neuroscience* 1992, 65 (1–4): 61–68.

Scharf, M. B., et al. A multicenter, placebo-controlled study evaluating zolpidem in the treatment of chronic insomnia. *Journal of Clinical Psychiatry* 1994, 55 (5): 192–99.

Schmidt, K. P., et al. Locomotor activity accelerates the adjustment of temperature rhythms in shiftwork. In: Diez-Noguera, A., Cambras, T. (eds): *Chronobiology & Chronomedicine* (Frankfurt am Main: Verlag Peter Lang, 1992), p. 389.

Wehr, T. A. Manipulations of sleep and phototherapy: Nonpharmacological alternatives in the treatment of depression. *Clinical Neuropharmacology* 1990, 13 (1): S54–S65.

Weiss, E., et al. Changes in brain serotonin (5HT) and 5-hydroxy-indole 3-acetic acid (5HIAA) in REM sleep deprived rats. *Psychophysiology* 1968, 5 (2): 209.

Zarcone, V. P. Sleep hygiene, in M. H. Kryger, T. Roth and W. C. Dement (eds.), *Principles and Practice of Sleep Medicine* 1994, 2: 542–46.

CHAPTER 7: EXERCISE AND YOUR BRAIN: PUMPING NEURONS

Bailey, S. P., et al. Serotoninergic agonists and antagonists affect endurance performance in the rat. *International Journal of Sports Medicine* 1993, 14 (6): 330–33.

———. Neuroendocrine and substrate responses to altered brain 5-HT activity during prolonged exercise to fatigue. *Journal of Applied Physiology* 1993, 74 (6): 3006–12.

Brown, J. D., and M. Lawton. Stress and well-being in adolescence: the moderating role of physical exercise. *Journal of Human Stress* 1986, 12 (3): 125–31.

Buono, M. J., et al. Effects of ageing and physical training on the peripheral sweat production of the human eccrine sweat gland. *Age and Ageing* 1991, 20: 439–41.

Byrne, A., and D. G. Byrne. The effect of exercise on depression, anxiety and other mood states: a review. *Journal of Psychosomatic Research* 1993, 37 (6): 565–74.

Casper, R. C. Exercise and Mood. *World Review of Nutrition and Dietetics* (Basel) 1993, 71: 115–43.

Chaouloff, F. Physical exercise and brain monoamines: a review. *Acta Physiologica Scandinavica* 1989, 137: 1–13.

Dey, S. Physical exercise as a novel antidepressant agent: possible role of serotonin receptor subtypes. *Physiological Behavior* 1994, 55 (2): 323–29.

Dey, S., et al. Exercise training: significance of regional alterations in serotonin metabolism of rat brain in relation to antidepressant effect of exercise. *Physiological Behavior* 1992, 52 (6): 1095–99.

Dupler, T. L., and C. Cortes. Effects of whole-body resistive training regimen in the elderly. *Gerontology* 1993, 39 (6): 314–19.

Evans, W. J. Exercise, nutrition, and aging. *Journal of Nutrition* 1992, 122 (3): 790–801.

Fiatarone, M. A., et al. High-intensity strength training in nonagenarians. Effects on skeletal muscle. *Journal of the American Medical Association* 1990, 263 (22): 3029–34.

King, A. C., et al. Effects of differing intensities and formats of 12 months of exercise training on psychological outcomes in older adults (published erratum appears in *Health Psychology* 1993, 12 [5]: 405). *Health Psychology* 1993, 12 (4): 292–300.

Lobstein, D. D., et al. Beta-endorphin and components of depression as powerful discriminators between joggers and sedentary middle-aged men. *Journal of Psychosomatic Research* 1989, 33 (3): 293–305.

Norris, R., et al. The effects of physical activity and exercise training on psychological stress and well-being in an adolescent population. *Journal of Psychosomatic Research* 1992, 36 (1): 55–65.

Palmer, J., et al. Adult inpatient alcoholics: physical exercise as a treatment intervention. *Journal of Studies on Alcohol* 1988, 49 (5): 418–21.

Raglin, J. S. Exercise and mental health. *Sports Medicine* 1990, 9 (6): 323–29.

Rejeski, W. J., et al. Acute exercise: buffering psychosocial stress responses in women. *Health Psychology* 1992, 11 (6): 355–62.

Segura, R., and J. L. Ventura. Effect of L-tryptophan supplementation on exercise performance. *International Journal of Sports Medicine* 1988, 9 (5): 301–5.

Sharma, H. S., et al. Increased blood-brain barrier permeability following acute short-term swimming exercise in conscious normotensive young rats. *Neuroscience Research* 1991, 10 (3): 211–21.

Steege, J. F., and J. A. Blumenthal. The effects of aerobic exercise on premenstrual symptoms in middle-aged women: a preliminary study. *Journal of Psychosomatic Research* 1993, 37 (2): 127–33.

Stein, P. N., and R. W. Motta. Effects of aerobic and nonaerobic exercise on depression and self-concept. *Perceptual & Motor Skills* 1992, 74 (1): 79–89.

Taylor, C. B., et al. The relation of physical activity and exercise to mental health. *Public Health Reports* 1985, 100 (2): 195–202.

Tucker, L. A. Effect of a weight-training program on the self-concepts of college males. *Perceptual & Motor Skills* 1982, 54 (3, Pt. 2): 1055–61.

Weyerer, S., and B. Kupfer. Physical exercise and psychological health. *Sports Medicine* 1994, 17 (2): 108–16.

Wilson, W. M., and R. J. Maughan. Evidence for a possible role of 5-hydroxytryptamine in the genesis of fatigue in man: administration of paroxetine, a 5-HT re-uptake inhibitor, reduces the capacity to perform prolonged exercise. *Experimental Physiology* 1992, 77: 921–24.

CHAPTER 8: THE BODY ELECTRIC

Baron, R. A. Effects of negative ions on cognitive performance. *Journal of Applied Psychology* 1987, 72 (1): 131–37.

Bassett, C. A. Beneficial effects of electromagnetic fields. *Journal of Cellular Biochemistry* 1993, 51 (4): 387–93.

Becker, R. O. Electromagnetism and the revolution in medicine. *Acupuncture and Electrotherapy Research* 1987, 12 (1): 75–79.

Blackman, C. F., et al. Effect of ambient levels of power-line-frequency electric fields on a developing vertebrate. *Bioelectromagnetics* 1988, 9 (2): 129–40.

Briere, J., and A. Downes. Summer in the city: urban weather conditions and psychiatric emergency-room visits. *Journal of Abnormal Psychology* 1983, 92 (1): 77–80.

Buckalew, L. W., and A. Rizzuto. Subjective response to negative air ion exposure. *Aviation, Space, and Environmental Medicine* 1982, 53 (8): 822–23.

Centzkow, C. D. Electrical stimulation to heal dermal wounds. *Journal of Dermatologic Surgery and Oncology* 1993, 19 (8): 753–58.

Chan, A. An introduction to sequential electric acupuncture (SEA) in the treatment of stress related physical and mental disorders. *Acupuncture and Electrotherapy Research* 1992, 17 (4): 273–83.

Charry, J. M., and F. B. Hawkinshire. Effects of atmospheric electricity on some substrates of disordered social behavior. *Journal of Personality & Social Psychology* 1981, 41 (1): 185–97.

Cohn, E. G. The prediction of police calls for service: The influence of weather and temporal variables on rape and domestic violence. Special Issue: Crime and the environment. *Journal of Environmental Psychology* 1993, 13 (1): 71–83.

Cook, M. R., et al. A replication study of human exposure to 60 Hz fields: effects on neurobehavioral measures. *Bioelectromagnetics* 1992, 13 (4): 281–85.

Daniell, W., et al. Trial of a negative ion generator device in remediating problems related to indoor air quality. *Journal of Occupational Medicine* 1991, 33 (6): 681–87.

De Matteis, G., et al. Geomagnetic activity, humidity, temperature and headache: is there any correlation? *Headache* 1994, 34 (1): 41–43.

Dowdall, M., and C. DeMontigny. Effect of atmospheric ions on hippocampal pyramidal neuron responsiveness to serotonin. *Brain Research* 1985, 342 (1)-103–9.

Foster, M. G., and B. P. Sweeney. The mechanisms of acupuncture analgesia. *British Journal of Hospital Medicine,* 1987: 308–12.

Hawkins, L. H., and T. Barker. Air ions and human performance. *Ergonomics* 1978, 21 (4): 273–78.

Hodge, K. A., and M. A. Persinger. Quantitative increases in temporal lobe symptoms in human males are proportional to postnatal geomagnetic activity: verification by canonical correlation. *Neuroscience Letters* 1991, 125 (2): 205–8.

Jacobson, J. I. Exploring the potential of magnetorecrystallization of genes and associated structures with respect to nerve regeneration and cancer. *International Journal of Neuroscience* 1992, 64: 153–65.

———. Electromagnetism in medicine. *Indian Journal of Medical Sciences* 1992, 46 (11): 321–27.

Kasper, S., and T. A. Wehr. The role of sleep and wakefulness in the genesis of depression and mania. *L'Encephale* 1992, 18: 45–50.

Kay, R. W. Geomagnetic storms: Association with incidence of depression as measured by hospital admission. *British Journal of Psychiatry* 1994, 164: 403–9.

Kellogg, E. W., et al. Superoxide involvement in the bactericidal effects of negative air ions on Staphylococcus albus. *Nature* 1979, 281 (5730): 400–1.

Krueger, A. P., and E. J. Reed. Biological impact of small air ions. *Science* 1976, 193: 1209–13.

Kuritzky, A., et al. Geomagnetic activity and the severity of the migraine attack. *Headache* 1987, 27: 87–89.

Lewy, A. J., et al. Melatonin shifts human circadian rhythms according to a phase-response curve. *Chronobiology International* 1992, 9 (5): 380–92.

Mammi, C. I., et al. The electrical stimulation of tibial osteotomies. Double blind study. *Clinical Orthopedics* 1993, 288: 248–53.

McLellan, A., et al. Acupuncture treatment for drug abuse: a technical review. *Journal of Substance Abuse Treatment* 1993, 10: 569–76.

Misiaszek, J., et al. The calming effects of negative air ions on manic patients: A pilot study. *Biological Psychiatry* 1987, 22 (1): 107–10.

Perry, S., et al. Power frequency magnetic field, depressive illness and myocardial infarction. *Public Health* 1989, 103: 177–80.

Randall, W. An eleven year cycle in human births. *International Journal of Biometeorology* 1991, 35 (1): 33–38.

———. The solar wind and human birth rate: a possible relationship due to magnetic disturbances. *International Journal of Biometeorology* 1990, 34 (1): 42–48.

Randall, W., and W. S. Moos. The 11-year cycle in human births. *International Journal of Biometeorology* 1993, 37 (2): 72–77.

Raps, A., et al. Solar activity and admissions of psychiatric inpatients, relations and possible implications on seasonality. *Israel Journal of Psychiatry & Related Sciences* 1991, 28 (2): 50–59.

———. Geophysical variables and behavior: LXIX. Solar activity and admission of psychiatric patients. *Perceptual & Motor Skills* 1992, 74 (2): 449–50.

Reilly, T., and I. C. Stevenson. An investigation of the effects of negative air ions on responses to submaximal exercise at different times of day. *Journal of Human Ergology* (Tokyo) 1993, 22 (1): 1–9.

Reite, M., et al. Sleep inducing effect of low energy emission therapy. *Bioelectromagnetics* 1994, 15 (1): 67–75.

Reiter, R. J., and B. A. Richardson. Magnetic field effects pineal indoleamine metabolism and possible biological consequences. *FASEB Journal* 1992, 6 (6): 2283–87.

Sandyk, R., et al. Magnetic fields and seasonality of affective illness: implications for therapy. *International Journal of Neuroscience* 1991, 58: 261–67.

Shibib, K., et al. The geomagnetic field: a factor in cellular interactions? I. Magnetism and Schwann cell-axon interaction in the peripheral nerves of the newborn rat. *Neurology Research* 1987, 9 (4): 225–35.

Stefanovska, A., et al. Treatment of chronic wounds by means of electric and electromagnetic fields. Part 2. Values of FES parameters for pressure sore treatment. *Medical and Biological Engineering and Computing* 1993, 31 (3): 213–20.

Stevens, R. G., et al. Electric power, pineal function, and the risk of breast cancer. *FASEB Journal* 1992, 6: 853–60.

Stoupel, E., and M. Shimshoni. Hospital cardiovascular deaths and total distribution of deaths in 180 consecutive months with different cosmic physical activity: a correlative study (1974–1988). *International Journal of Biometeorology* 1991, 35 (1): 6–9.

Stoupel, E., et al. Admissions of patients with epileptic seizures (E) and dizziness (D) related to geomagnetic and solar activity levels: differences in female and male patients. *Medical Hypotheses* 1991, 36: 384–88.

Terman, M., and J. S. Terman. A controlled trial of light therapy and negative ions. *Society for Light Treatment and Biological Rhythms Abstracts* 1994, 6: 6.

Trock, D. H., et al. A double blind trial of the clinical effects of pulsed electromagnetic fields in osteoarthritis. *Journal of Rheumatology* 1993, 20 (3): 456–60.

Zis, A. P., et al. ECT induced PRL release: a 5-HT1A-mediated event? *Biological Psychiatry* 1992, 31 (4): 415–18.

CHAPTER 9: VITAMIN, MINERAL, AND AMINO ACID SUPPLEMENTS

Alino, J. J., et al. 5-hydroxytryptophan (5-HTP) and a MAOI (nialamide) in the treatment of depressions. A double-blind controlled study. *International Pharmacopsychiatry* 1976, 11 (1): 9–15.

Byerley, W. F., et al. 5-hydroxytryptophan: A review of its antidepressant efficacy and adverse effects. *Journal of Clinical Psychopharmacology* 1987, 7 (3): 127–137.

Campioni, A., and G. Russo-Perez. Treatment of delirium tremens with 5-hydroxytryptophan. *Italian Journal of Neurological Science* 1981, 2 (3): 307–8.

Cangiano, O., et al. Eating behavior and adherence to dietary prescriptions in obese adult subjects treated with 5-hydroxytryptophan. *American Journal of Clinical Nutrition* 1992, 56 (5): 863–67.

Caruso, I., et al. Double-blind study of 5-hydroxytryptophan versus placebo in the treatment of primary fibromyalgia syndrome. *Journal of International Medical Research* 1990, 18 (3): 201–9.

Castano, A., et al. Changes in the turnover of monoamines in prefrontal cortex of rats fed on vitamin E–deficient diet. *Journal of Neurochemistry* 1992, 58 (5): 1889–95.

————. Turnover of monoamines in hippocampus of rats fed on vitamin E–deficient diet. *Brain Research* 1993, 604 (1–2): 154–59.

Coci, F., et al. The effects of oral 5-hydroxytryptophan administration on feeding behavior in obese adult female subjects. *Journal of Neural Transmission* 1989, 76 (2): 109–17.

Dawson, E. B., et al. Relationship of lithium metabolism to mental hospital admission and homicide. *Diseases of the Nervous System* 1972, 33 (8): 546–56.

Dawson, E. B., et al. The mathematical relationship of drinking water, lithium and rainfall to mental hospital admission. *Diseases of the Nervous System* 1970, 31 (12): 811–20.

Fuller, R. W. Role of serotonin in therapy of depression and related disorders. *Journal of Clinical Psychiatry* 1991, 52: 52–57.

George, C. F., et al. The effect of L-tryptophan on daytime sleep latency in normals: correlation with blood levels. *Sleep* 1989, 12 (4): 345–53.

Ghadirian, A. M., et al. Folic acid deficiency and depression. *Psychosomatics* 1980, 21: 926–29.

Hill, Jr., R. H., et al. Contaminants in L-tryptophan associated with eosinophilia myalgia syndrome. *Archives of Environmental Contamination and Toxicology* 1993, 25 (1): 134–42.

Irwin, M. R., et al. L-5-hydroxytryptophan attenuates positive psychotic symptoms induced by D-amphetamine. *Psychiatry Research* 1987, 22 (4): 283–89.

Kahn, R. S., et al. Effect of a serotonin precursor and uptake inhibitor in anxiety disorders: a double-blind comparison of 5-hydroxytryptophan, clomipramine, and placebo. *International Clinical Psychopharmacology* 1987, 2 (1): 33–45.

Korner, E, et al. Sleep-inducing effect of L-tryptophan. *European Neurology* 1986, 25 (2): 75–81.

Mortola, J. F. A risk-benefit appraisal of drugs used in the management of premenstrual syndrome. *Drug Safety* 1994, 10 (2): 160–69.

Nolen, W. A., et al. Treatment strategy in depression. II. MAO inhibitors in depression resistant to cyclic antidepressants: two controlled crossover studies with tranylcypromine versus L-5-hydroxytryptophan and nomifensine. *Acta Psychiatrica Scandinavica* 1988, 78 (5): 676–83.

Pietz, J., et al. Treatment of infantile spasms with high-dosage vitamin B6. *Epilepsia* 1993, 43 (4): 757–63.

Puttini, P. S., and I. Caruso. Primary fibromyalgia syndrome and 5-hydroxy-L-tryptophan: a 90 day open study. *Journal of International Medical Research* 1992, 20 (2): 182–89.

Quadbeck, H., et al. Comparison of the antidepressant action of tryptophan, tryptophan/5-Hydroxytryptophan combination and nomifensine. *Neuropsychobiology* 1984, 11 (2): 111–15.

Reus, V. Rational Polypharmacy in the treatment of mood disorders. *Annals of Clinical Psychiatry* 1993, 5: 91–100.

Sandyk, R. L-tryptophan in neuropsychiatric disorder: a review. *International Journal of Neuroscience* 1992, 67 (1–4): 127–44.

Schrauzer, G. N., and K. P. Shrestha. Lithium in drinking water and the incidence of crimes, suicides, and arrests related to drug addictions. *Biological Trace Elements Research* 1990, 25 (2): 105–13.

Schrauzer, G. N., and E. de Vroey. Effects of nutritional lithium supplementation on mood. A placebo-controlled study with former drug users. *Biological Trace Elements Research* 1994, 40 (1): 89–101.

Spinweber, C. L. L-tryptophan administered to chronic sleep-onset insomniacs: late-appearing reduction of sleep latency. *Psychopharmacology* (Berlin) 1986, 90 (2): 151–55.

Titus, F., et al. 5-hydroxytryptophan versus methysergide in the prophylaxis of migraine. Randomized clinical trial. *European Neurology* 1986, 25 (5): 327–29.

Volavka, J., et al. Tryptophan treatment of aggressive psychiatric inpatients. *Biological Psychiatry* 1990, 28 (8): 728–32.

Young, S. N. Use of tryptophan in combination with other antidepressant treatments: a review. *Journal of Psychiatry and Neuroscience* 1991, 16 (5): 241–46.

Zarcone, Jr., V. P., and E. Hoddes. Effects of 5-hydroxytryptophan on fragmentation of REM sleep in alcoholics. *American Journal of Psychiatry* 1975, 132 (1): 74–76.

CHAPTER 10: CHOLESTEROL'S GOOD SIDE

Atrens, D. M. The questionable wisdom of a low-fat diet and cholesterol reduction. *Social Science and Medicine* 1994, 39 (3): 433–47.

Block, E. R., and D. Edwards. Effect of plasma membrane fluidity on serotonin transport by endothelial cells. *American Journal of Physiology* 1987, 253: 672–78.

Faustman, W. O., et al. An association between low levels of 5-HIAA and HVA in cerebrospinal fluid and early mortality in a diagnostically mixed psychiatric sample. *British Journal of Psychiatry* 1993, 163: 519–21.

Guicheney, P., et al. Platelet 5-HT content and uptake in essential hypertension: role of endogenous digitalis-like factors and plasma cholesterol. *Journal of Hypertension* 1988, 6: 873–79.

Hawton, K., et al. Low serum cholesterol and suicide. *British Journal of Psychiatry* 1993, 162: 818–25.

Krumholz, H. M., et al. Lack of association between cholesterol and coronary heart disease mortality and morbidity and all-cause mortality in persons older than 70 years (see comments). *Journal of the American Medical Association* 1994, 272 (17): 1335–40.

Modai, I., et al. Serum cholesterol levels and suicidal tendencies in psychiatric inpatients. *Journal of Clinical Psychiatry* 1994, 55 (6): 252–54.

Morgan, R. E., et al. Plasma cholesterol and depressive symptoms in older men. *Lancet* 1993, 341: 75–79.

Shestov, D. B., et al. Increased risk of coronary heart disease death in men with low total and low-density lipoprotein cholesterol in the Russian Lipid Research Clinics Prevalence Follow-up Study (see comments). *Circulation* 1993, 88 (3): 846–53.

Simes, R. J. Low cholesterol and risk of noncoronary mortality. *Australia/New Zealand Journal of Medicine* 1994, 24 (1): 113–19.

Sullivan, P. F., et al. Total cholesterol and suicidality in depression. *Biological Psychiatry* 1994, 36: 472–77.

CHAPTER 11: PROSTAGLANDIN POWER: THE UNEXPECTED ROLE OF FOOD

Abdulla, Y. H., and K. Hamadah. Effects of ADP on PGE formation in blood platelets from patients with depression, mania and schizophrenia. *British Journal of Psychiatry* 1975, 127: 591–95.

Baile, C. A., and F. H. Martin. Relationship between prostaglandin E1, polyphloretin phosphate and a and b adrenoceptor-bound feeding loci in the hypothalamus of sheep. *Pharmacology, Biochemistry & Behavior* 1973, 1 (5): 539–45.

Barcelli, V. O., et al. A diet containing n-3 and n-6 fatty acids favorably alters the renal phospholipids, eicosanoid synthesis and plasma lipids in nephrotic rats. *Lipids* 1988, 23 (11): 1059–63.

Bhattacharya, S. K., and A. K. Sanyal. Prostaglandin E1-induced potentiation of the anticonvulsant action of phenobarbitone in the rat. Role of brain monoamines. *Prostaglandins and Medicine* 1978, 1 (2): 159–64.

Bhattacharya, S. K., and P. J. R. Mohan Rao. Prostaglandin D2-induced catalepsy in rats: role of 5-hydroxytryptamine. *Journal of Pharmacy and Pharmacology* 1987, 39: 743–45.

Bhattacharya, S. K., and A. K. Sanyal. Inhibition of pentylenetetrazol-induced convulsions in rats by prostaglandin E-sub-1: role of brain monoamines. *Psychopharmacology* 1978, 56 (2): 235–37.

Bloom, E. T., and J. T. Babbitt. Prostaglandin E2, monocyte adherence and interleukin-1 in the regulation of human natural killer cell activity by monocytes. *Natural Immunity and Cell Growth Regulation* 1990, 9 (1): 36–48.

Brus, R., et al. Mediation of central prostaglandin effects by serotonergic neurons. *Psychopharmacology* 1979, 64 (1): 113–20.

Calabrese, J. R., et al. Depression, immunocompetence, and prostaglandins of the E series. *Psychiatry Research* 1986, 17 (1): 41–47.

Chaouloff, F., et al. Peripheral and central consequences of immobilization stress in genetically obese Zucker rats. *American Journal of Physiology* 1989: 256 (2 Pt.2): R435–42.

Debnath, P. K., et al. Prostaglandins: effect of prostaglandin E1 on brain, stomach and intestinal serotonin in rat. *Biochemical Pharmacology* 1978, 27 (1): 130–32.

Doggett, N. S., and K. Jawaharlal. Anorectic activity of prostaglandin precursors. *British Journal of Pharmacology* 1977, 60 (3): 417–23.

George, F. R., et al. Indomethacin antagonism of ethanol-induced sleep time: Sex and genotypic factors. *Psychopharmacology* 1985, 85 (2): 151–53.

Hollingsworth, E. B., and G. A. Patrick. Involvement of the serotonergic system in the prolongation of pentobarbital sleeping time produced by prostaglandin D-sub-2. *Pharmacology, Biochemistry & Behavior* 1985, 22 (3): 365–70.

Horrobin, D. F. Post-viral fatigue syndrome, viral infections in atopic eczema, and essential fatty acids. *Medical Hypotheses* 1990, 32: 211–17.

Kafka, M. S., et al. Alpha-sub-Z-adrenergic receptor function in patients with unipolar and bipolar affective disorders. *Journal of Affective Disorders* 1986, 10 (2): 163–69.

Kanof, P. D., et al. Prostaglandin receptor sensitivity in psychiatric disorders. *Archives of General Psychiatry* 1986: 43: 987–93.

Koshikawa, N., et al. Prostaglandins and premenstrual syndrome. *Prostaglandins Leukotrienes and Essential Fatty Acids* 1992, 45 (1): 33–36.

Laghrissi-Thode, F., et al. Comparative effects of sertraline and nortriptyline on body sway in elderly depressed patients. Presented in part at the 34th Annual Meeting of the New Clinical Drug Evaluation Unit of the National Institute of Mental Health, Marco Island, FL, May 31, 1994. (New Investigator Awardee Poster Session.)

MacMurray, J. P., and L. P. Bozzetti. Prostaglandin synthesis among alcoholic suicide attempters and nonattempters. *Neuropsychobiology* 1987, 17: 178–81.

Malygin, A. M., et al. Regulation of natural killer cell activity by transforming growth factor–beta and prostaglandin E2. *Scandinavian Journal of Immunology* 1993, 37 (1): 71–76.

Marazziti, D., et al. Psychological stress and body temperature changes in humans. *Physiology & Behavior* 1992, 52 (2): 393–95.

Morimoto, A., et al. The effect of prostaglandin E-sub-2 on the body temperature of restrained rats. *Physiology & Behavior* 1991, 50 (1): 249–53.

Nishino, S., et al. Salivary prostaglandin concentrations: possible state indicators for major depression. *American Journal of Psychiatry* 1989, 146 (3): 365–68.

Ohishi, K., et al. Increased level of salivary prostaglandins in patients with major depression. *Biological Psychiatry* 1988, 23 (4): 326–34.

Roy, A., and M. S. Kafka. Platelet adrenoceptors and prostaglandin responses in depressed patients. *Psychiatry Research* 1989, 30 (2): 181–89.

Saito, R, et al. The effect of neurotransmitters on cataleptic behavior induced by PGD2 in rats. *Pharmacology, Biochemistry & Behavior* 1987, 26 (3): 543–46.

Sanyal, A. K., et al. The antinociceptive effect of intracerebroventricularly administered prostaglandin E-sub-1 in the rat. *Psychopharmacology* 1979, 60 (2): 159–63.

Segarnick, D. J., et al. Prostanoid modulation (mediation?) of certain behavioral effects of ethanol. *Pharmacology, Biochemistry & Behavior* 1985, 23 (1): 71–75.

van Miert, A. S., and C. T. van Duin. Feed intake and rumen motility in dwarf goats. Effects of some alpha 2-adrenergic agonists, prostaglandins, and posterior pituitary hormones. *Veterinary Research Communications* 1991, 15 (1): 57–67.

Virkkunen, M. E., et al. Plasma phospholipid essential fatty acids and prostaglandins in alcoholic, habitually violent, and impulsive offenders. *Biological Psychiatry* 1987, 22: 1087–96.

Winokur, A., et al. Insulin resistance after oral glucose tolerance testing in patients with major depression. *American Journal of Psychiatry* 1988, 145 (3): 325–30.

CHAPTER 12: ESSENTIAL FATS

Anti, M., et al. Effect of omega-3 fatty acids on rectal mucosal cell proliferation in subjects at risk for colon cancer (see comments). *Gastroenterology* 1992, 103 (3): 883–91.

Arm, J. P., et al. The effects of dietary supplementation with fish oil lipids on the airways response to inhaled allergen in bronchial asthma. *American Review of Respiratory Diseases* 1989, 139 (6): 1395–1400.

Aslan, A., and G. Triadafilopoulos. Fish oil fatty acid supplementation in active ulcerative colitis: a double-blind, placebo-controlled, crossover study. *American Journal of Gastroenterology* 1992, 87 (4): 432–37.

Behan, P. O., et al. Effect of high doses of essential fatty acids on the postviral fatigue syndrome. *Acta Neurologica Scandinavica* 1990, 82: 209–16.

Belch, J. J., et al. Effects of altering dietary essential fatty acids on requirements for non-steroidal anti-inflammatory drugs in patients with rheumatoid arthritis: a double blind placebo controlled study. *Annals of Rheumatological Diseases* 1988, 47 (2): 96–104.

Berth-Jones, J., and R. A. O. Graham-Brown. Placebo-controlled trial of essential fatty acid supplementation in atopic dermatitis. *Lancet* 1993, v341 (8880): 1557–60.

Biagi, P. L., et al. A long-term study on the use of evening primrose oil (Efamol) in atopic children. *Drugs, Experimental and Clinical Research* 1988, 14 (4): 285–90.

Bilo, H. J. G., and R. O. B. Gans. Fish oil: a panacea? *Biomedical Pharmacotherapy* 1990, 44: 169–74.

Brzeski, M., et al. Evening primrose oil in patients with rheumatoid arthritis and side-effects of non-steroidal anti-inflammatory drugs. *British Journal of Rheumatology* 1991, 30 (5): 370–72.

Bordoni, A., et al. Evening primrose oil (Efamol) in the treatment of children with atopic eczema. *Drugs, Experimental and Clinical Research* 1988, 14 (4): 291–97.

Collins, A., et al. Essential fatty acids in the treatment of premenstrual syndrome. *Obstetrics and Gynecology* 1993, 81 (1): 93–98.

Corrigan, F. M., et al. Essential fatty acids in Alzheimer's disease. *Annals of the New York Academy of Science* 1991, 640: 250–52.

Cotterell, J. C., et al. Double blind, crossover trial of evening primrose oil in women with menstrually-related irritable bowel syndrome. In: Horrobin, D. F. (ed). *Omega-6 essential fatty acids: pathophysiology and roles in clinical medicine.* New York: Wiley-Liss 1990: 421–26.

Escobar, S. O., et al. Topical fish oil in psoriasis—a controlled and blind study. *Clinical Experimental Dermatology* 1992, 17 (3): 159–62.

Gapinski, J. P., et al. Preventing restenosis with fish oils following coronary angioplasty. A meta-analysis. *Archives of Internal Medicine* 1993, 153 (13): 1595–1601.

Gateley, C A., et al. Drug treatments for mastalgia: 17 years experience in the Cardiff Mastalgia Clinic. *Journal of the Royal Society of Medicine* 1992, 85 (1): 12–15.

Gazzah, N., et al. Effect of an n-3 fatty acid–deficient diet on the adenosine-dependent melatonin release in cultured rat pineal. *Journal of Neurochemistry* 1993, 61 (3): 1057–63.

Greenfield, S. M., et al. A randomized controlled study of evening primrose oil and fish oil in ulcerative colitis. *Alimentary Pharmacology and Therapeutics* 1993, 7 (2): 159–66.

Hawthorne, A. B., et al. Treatment of ulcerative colitis with fish oil supplementation: a perspective 12 month randomized controlled trial. *Gut* 1992, 33 (7): 922–28.

Horrobin, D. F., and M. S. Manku. Premenstrual syndrome and premenstrual breast pain (cyclical mastalgia): disorders of essential fatty acid (EFA) metabolism. *Prostaglandins Leukotrienes and Essential Fatty Acids* 1989, 37: 255–61.

Jantti, J., et al. Evening primrose oil and olive oil in treatment of rheumatoid arthritis. *Clinical Rheumatology* 1989, 8 (2): 238–44.

———. Evening primrose oil in rheumatoid arthritis: changes in serum lipids and fatty acids (see comments in *Annals of Rheumatological Diseases* 1989, 48 (11): 965–66). *Annals of Rheumatological Diseases* 1989, 48 (2): 124–27.

Kerscher, M. J., and H. C. Korting. Treatment of atopic eczema with evening primrose oils rationale and clinical results. *Clinical Investigations* 1992, 70 (2): 167–71.

Khoo, S. K., et al. Evening primrose oil and treatment of premenstrual syndrome (see comments). *Medical Journal of Australia* 1990, 153 (4): 189–92.

Lowell, J. A., et al. Dietary immunomodulation: beneficial effects on oncogenesis and tumor growth. *Critical Care Medicine* 1990, 18 (2 suppl): S145–48.

Margolin, G., et al. Blood pressure lowering in elderly subjects: a double-blind crossover study of omega-3 and omega-6 fatty acids. *American Journal of Clinical Nutrition* 1991, 53 (2): 562–72.

Moodley, J., and R. J. Norman. Attempts at dietary alteration of prostaglandin pathways in the management of pre-eclampsia. *Prostaglandins, Leukotrienes and Essential Fatty Acids* 1989, 37 (3): 145–47.

Morris, M. C., et al. Does fish oil lower blood pressure? A meta-analysis of controlled trials. *Circulation* 1993, 88 (2): 523–33.

Morse, P. F., et al. Meta-analysis of placebo-controlled studies of the efficacy of Epogam in the treatment of atopic eczema. Relationship between plasma essential fatty acid changes and clinical response. *British Journal of Dermatology* 1989, 121 (1): 75–90.

O'Brien, P. M. S., and H. Massil. Premenstrual syndrome: clinical studies on essential fatty acids. In Horrobin, D. F. (ed). *Omega-6 essential fatty acids: pathophysiology and roles in clinical medicine.* New York: Wiley-Liss 1990: 523–46.

Ockerman, P. A., et al. Evening primrose oil as a treatment of premenstrual syndrome. *Recent Advances in Clinical Nutrition* 1986, 2: 404–05.

Olsen, S. F., et al. Randomized controlled trial of effect of fish-oil supplementation on pregnancy duration. *Lancet* 1992, v339 (p8800): p1003 (5).

Sears, B. Essential fatty acids and dietary endocrinology: a hypothesis for cardiovascular treatment. *Journal of Advancement in Medicine* 1993, 6 (4): 211–24.

Soyland, E., et al. Effect of dietary supplementation with very long chain p-3 fatty acids in patients with psoriasis. *New England Journal of Medicine* 1993, v328 (p25): 1812 (5).

van der Merwe, C. F., et al. The effect of gamma-linolenic acid, and in vitro cytostatic substance contained in evening primrose oil on primary liver cancer. A double-blind placebo controlled trial. *Prostaglandins, Leukotrienes and Essential Fatty Acids* 1990, 40 (3): 199–202.

van der Tempel, H., et al. Effects of fish oil supplementation in rheumatoid arthritis (see comments). *Annals of Rheumatological Diseases* 1990, 49 (2): 76–80.

CHAPTER 13: THE NATURAL DIET OF HOMO SAPIENS—UPDATED

Eaton, S. B., and M. J. Konner. Paleolithic nutrition: a consideration of its nature and current implications. *New England Journal of Medicine* 1985, 312: 283–89.

Felig, P., and J. Wahren. Role of insulin and glucagon in the regulation of hepatic glucose production during exercise. *Diabetes* 1979, 28: 71–73.

Garg, A., et al. Effects of varying carbohydrate content of diet in patients with non-insulin dependent diabetes mellitus. *Journal of the American Medical Association* 1994, 271 (18): 1421–28.

Jenkins, D. J. A., et al. Glycemic index of food: a physiological basis for carbohydrate exchange. *American Journal of Clinical Nutrition* 1981, 34: 362–66.

Kuczmarski, R. J., et al. Increasing prevalence of overweight among U.S. adults. *Journal of the American Medical Association* 1994, 272: 205–11.

Laws, A., et al. Insulin resistance and hypertriglyceridemia in non-diabetic relatives of patients with non-insulin-dependent diabetes mellitus. *Journal of Clinical Endocrinology and Metabolism* 1989, 69: 343–47.

Masoro, E. J. Nutrition and aging—a current assessment. *Journal of Nutrition* 1985, 115: 842–48.

McCall, T. B., et al. Therapeutic potential of fish oil in the treatment of ulcerative colitis. *Alimentary Pharmacology and Therapeutics* 1989, 3 (5): 415–24.

Reaven, G. M. Role of insulin resistance in human disease. *Diabetes* 1988, 37: 1595–1607.

———. Role of insulin resistance in non-insulin dependent diabetes mellitus. *Progress in Endocrinology*. H. Imura et al. eds. Elsevier Science Publishers, New York, pp. 383–91.

Sears, B. Dietary endocrinology: a hypothesis for cardiovascular treatment. *Journal of Advances in Medicine* 1993, 6: 211.

Stokkan, K., et al. Food restriction retards aging of the pineal gland. *Brain Research* 1991, 545: 66–72.

Swisolcki, A. L., et al. Insulin resistance, glucose intolerance and hyperinsulinemia in patients with hypertension. *American Journal of Hypertension* 1989, 2: 419–23.

Tarnopolsky, M. A., et al. Influence of protein intake and training status on nitrogen balance and lean body mass. *Journal of Applied Physiology* 1988, 64 (1): 187–93.

Unger, R. H., and P. J. Lefebvre. *Glucagon: molecular physiology, clinical and therapeutic implications.* Pergamon Press, Oxford 1972.

Walford, R. L. Caloric restriction and aging. *Chemical Engineering News* 1986, 64: 3.

————. *The 120-Year Diet.* Simon & Schuster 1986, New York.

Weindruch, R., and R. L. Walford. *The Retardation of Aging and Disease by Dietary Restriction.* C. C. Thomas 1988, Springfield IL.

Westphal, S. A., et al. Metabolic response to glucose ingested with various amounts of protein. *American Journal of Clinical Nutrition* 1990, 52: 267–72.

CHAPTER 14: PROZAC: THE REFERENCE STANDARD

Aguglia, E., et al. Double-blind study of the efficacy and safety of sertraline versus fluoxetine in major depression. *International Clinical Psychopharmacology* 1993, 8 (3): 197–202.

Altamura, A. C., et al. The evidence for 20 mg a day of fluoxetine as the optimal dose in the treatment of depression. *British Journal of Psychiatry* 1988, 153 (3): 109–12.

Baldwin, D., et al. 5-HT reuptake inhibitors, tricyclic antidepressants and suicidal behavior. *International Clinical Psychopharmacology* 1991, 6 (3): 49–55.

Balogh, S., et al. Treatment of fluoxetine-induced anorgasmia with amantadine (letter). *Journal of Clinical Psychiatry* 1992, 53 (6): 212–13.

Balon, R., et al. Sexual dysfunction during antidepressant treatment. *Journal of Clinical Psychiatry* 1993, 54 (6): 209–12.

Batki, S. L., et al. Fluoxetine for cocaine dependence in methadone maintenance: quantitative plasma and urine cocaine/benzoylacgoninc concentrations. *Journal of Clinical Psychopharmacology.* 1993, 13 (4): 243–50.

Beasley, Jr., C. M., et al. Possible monoamine oxidase inhibitory-serotonin uptake inhibitor interactions: fluoxetine clinical data and preclinical finds. *Journal of Clinical Psychopharmacology* 1993, 13 (5): 312–20.

————. High-dose fluoxetine: efficacy and activating-sedating effects in agitated and retarded depression. *Journal of Clinical Psychopharmacology* 1991, 11 (3): 166–74.

————. Fluoxetine compared with imipramine in the treatment of inpatient depression. A multicenter trial. *Annals of Clinical Psychiatry* 1993, 5 (3): 199–207.

Beasley, Jr., C. M., and J. H. Potvin. Fluoxetine: activating and sedating effects. *International Clinical Psychopharmacology* 1993, 8: 271–75.

Beuzen, J. N., et al. Impact of fluoxetine on work loss in depression. *International Clinical Psychopharmacology* 1993, 8: 319–21.

Black, B., et al. Fluoxetine for the treatment of social phobia. *Journal of Clinical Psychopharmacology* 1992, 12 (4): 293–95.

Brewerton, T. D. Fluoxetine-induced suicidality, serotonin, and seasonality. *Biological Psychiatry* 1991, 30: 190–96.

Broadhead, W. E., et al. Depression, disability days, and days lost from work in a prospective epidemiologic survey (see comments). *Journal of the American Medical Association* 1990, 264 (19): 2524–28.

Cain, J. W. Poor response to fluoxetine: underlying depression, serotonergic overstimulation, or a "therapeutic window"? (see comments). *Journal of Clinical Psychiatry* 1992, 53 (8): 272–77.

Childs, P. A., et al. Effect of fluoxetine on melatonin in patients with seasonal affective disorder and matched controls. *British Journal of Psychiatry* 1995, 166: 196–98.

Chouinard, G. Fluoxetine and preoccupation with suicide (letter to the editor), *American Journal of Psychiatry* 1991, 148 (9): 1258–59.

Cohn, J. B., et al. A comparison of fluoxetine, imipramine and placebo in patients with bipolar depressive disorder. *International Clinical Psychopharmacology* 1989, 4: 313–22.

Cornelius, J. R., et al. Continuation pharmacotherapy of borderline personality disorder with haloperidol and phenelzine. *American Journal of Psychiatry* 1993, 150 (12): 1843–48.

Crundwell, J. K. Fluoxetine and suicidal ideation—a review of the literature. *International Journal of Neuroscience* 1993, 68 (1–2): 73–84.

Daamen, M. J., and W. A. Brown. Treatment of fluoxetine-induced anorgasmia with amantadine. *Journal of Clinical Psychiatry* 1992, 53 (6): 212–13.

Ellison, J. M. SSRI withdrawal buzz (letter). *Journal of Clinical Psychiatry* 1994, 55: 12.

Fava, M., et al. Lithium and tricyclic augmentation of fluoxetine treatment for resistant major depression: a double-blind, controlled study. *American Journal of Psychiatry* 1994, 151: 1372–74.

Fava, M., and J. F. Rosenbaum. Suicidality and fluoxetine: Is there a relationship? *Journal of Clinical Psychiatry* 1991, 52 (3): 108–11.

Fisher, S., et al. Postmarketing surveillance by patient self-monitoring: trazodone versus fluoxetine. *Journal of Clinical Psychopharmacology* 1993, 13 (4): 235–42.

Fux, M., et al. Emergence of depressive symptoms during treatment for panic disorder with specific 5-hydroxytryptophan reuptake inhibitors. *Acta Psychiatrica Scandinavica* 1993, 88 (4): 235–37.

George, M. S., and M. R. Trimble. A fluvoxamine-induced frontal lobe syndrome in a patient with comorbid Gilles de la Tourette's syndrome and obsessive compulsive disorder. *Journal of Clinical Psychiatry* 1992, 53 (10): 379.

Goldstein, D. J., et al. Analyses of suicidality in double-blind, placebo-controlled trials of pharmacotherapy for weight reduction. *Journal of Clinical Psychiatry* 1993, 54 (8): 309–16.

Gram, L. F. Fluoxetine. *New England Journal of Medicine* 1994, 331 (20): 1354–60.

Hamilton, M. S. , and L. A. Opler. Akathisia, suicidality, and fluoxetine. *Journal of Clinical Psychiatry* 1992, 53 (11): 401–06.

Heiligenstein, J. H., et al: Fluoxetine not associated with increased violence or aggression in controlled clinical trials. *Annals of Clinical Psychiatry* 1992, 4: 285–95.

———. Fluoxetine not associated with increased aggression in controlled clinical trials. *International Clinical Psychopharmacology* 1993, 8 (4): 277–80.

Hoehn-Saric, R., et al. Apathy and indifference in patients on fluvoxamine and fluoxetine. *Journal of Clinical Psychopharmacology* 1990, 10 (5): 343–45.

Hollander, E., and A. McCarley. Yohimbine treatment of sexual side effects induced by serotonin reuptake blockers. *Journal of Clinical Psychiatry* 1992, 53 (6): 207–9.

Hopwood, S. E., et al. The combination of fluoxetine and lithium in clinical practice. *International Clinical Psychopharmacology* 1993, 8: 325–27.

Jacobsen, F. M. Fluoxetine-induced sexual dysfunction and an open trial of yohimbine (see comments). *Journal of Clinical Psychiatry* 1992, 54 (4): 119–22.

———. Possible augmentation of antidepressant response by buspirone. *Journal of Clinical Psychiatry* 1991, 52 (5): 217–220.

Joffe, R. T., and D. R. Schuller. An open study of buspirone augmentation of serotonin reuptake inhibitors in refractory depression. *Journal of Clinical Psychiatry* 1993, 54 (7): 269–71.

Joffe, R. T., et al. A placebo-controlled comparison of lithium and tri-iodothyronine augmentation of tricyclic antidepressants in unipolar refractory depression. *Archives of General Psychiatry* 1993, 50: 387–93.

Kafka, M. P., and R. Prentky. Fluoxetine treatment of nonparaphilic sexual addictions and paraphilias in men. *Journal of Clinical Psychiatry* 1992, 53 (10): 351–58.

Lebegue, B. Sudden self-harm while taking fluoxetine. *American Journal of Psychiatry* 1992, 149 (8): 1113.

Louie, A. K., et al. Use of low-dose fluoxetine in major depression and panic disorder. *Journal of Clinical Psychiatry* 1993, 54 (11): 435–38.

Markowitz, P. I. Effect of fluoxetine on self-injurious behavior in the developmentally disabled: a preliminary study. *Journal of Clinical Psychopharmacology* 1992, 12 (1): 27–31.

Masica, D. N., et al. Trend in suicide rates since fluoxetine introduction. *American Journal of Public Health* 1992, 82 (9): 1295.

McDougle, C. J., et al. An open trial of fluoxetine in the treatment of posttraumatic stress disorder. *Journal of Clinical Psychopharmacology* 1991, 11 (5): 325–27.

Medina, J. H., et al. Naturally occurring benzodiazepines and benzodiazepine-like molecules in brain. *Behavioural Brain Research* 1993, 58: 1–8.

Menkes, D. B., et al. Fluoxetine's spectrum of action in premenstrual syndrome. *International Clinical Psychopharmacology* 1993, 8: 95–102.

Mesaros, J. D. Fluoxetine for primary enuresis. *Journal of the American Academy of Child and Adolescent Psychiatry* 1993, 32 (4): 877–78.

Messiha, F. S. Fluoxetine: A spectrum of clinical applications and postulates of underlying mechanisms. *Neuroscience and Biobehavioral Reviews* 1993, 17: 385–96.

———. Fluoxetine: adverse effects and drug-drug interactions. *Clinical Toxicology* 1993, 31 (4): 603–30.

Monteleone, P., et al. Lack of effect of short-term fluoxetine administration on nighttime plasma melatonin levels in healthy subjects. *Biological Psychiatry* 1994, 35 (2): 139–42.

Montgomery, S. A. Suicide prevention and serotoninergic drugs. *International Clinical Psychopharmacology* 1993, 8 (2 suppl): 83–85.

Montgomery, S. A., et al. Selective serotonin reuptake inhibitors: meta-analysis of discontinuation rates. *International Clinical Psychopharmacology* 1994, 9 (1): 47–53.

———. The prophylactic efficacy of fluoxetine in unipolar depression. *British Journal of Psychiatry* 1988, 153 (3): 69–76.

Morton, W. A., et al. Fluoxetine-associated side effects and suicidality (letter) (see comments). *Journal of Clinical Psychopharmacology* 1993, 13 (4): 292–95.

Nelson, J. C., et al. A preliminary, open study of the combination of fluoxetine and desipramine for rapid treatment of major depression. *Archives of General Psychiatry* 1991, 48: 303–7.

Nierenberg, A. A. The treatment of severe depression: is there an efficacy gap between SSRI and TCA antidepressant generations? *Journal of Clinical Psychiatry* 1994, 55 (9, suppl A): 55–59.

———. Treatment-resistant depression in the age of serotonin. *Psychiatric Annals* 1994, 24 (5): 217–19.

———. Trazodone for antidepressant-associated insomnia. *American Journal of Psychiatry* 1994, 151 (7): 1069–72.

Pastuszak, A., et al. Pregnancy outcome following first-trimester exposure to fluoxetine. *Journal of the American Medical Association* 1993, 269: 2246–48.

Phillips, K. A., and A. A. Nierenberg. The assessment and treatment of refractory depression. *Journal of Clinical Psychiatry* 1994, 55 (2, suppl): 20–26.

Pope, H. G., et al. Possible synergism between fluoxetine and lithium in refractory depression. *American Journal of Psychiatry* 1988, 145 (10): 1292–94.

Power, A. C., and P. J. Cowen. Fluoxetine and suicidal behavior. Some clinical and theoretical aspects of a controversy. *British Journal of Psychiatry* 1992, 161: 735–41.

Rosenthal, N. E., et al. Psychobiological effects of carbohydrate and protein-rich meals in patients with seasonal affective disorder and normal controls. *Biological Psychiatry* 1989, 25: 1029–40.

Rothschild, A. J., and C. A. Locke. Reexposure to fluoxetine after serious suicide attempts by three patients: the role of akathisia. *Journal of Clinical Psychiatry* 1991, 52 (12): 491–93.

Sclar, D. A., et al. Antidepressant pharmacotherapy: economic outcomes in a health maintenance organization. *Clinical Therapeutics* 1994, 16 (4): 715–30.

Shrivastava, R. K., et al. Amantadine in the treatment of sexual dysfunction associated with selective serotonin reuptake inhibitors. *Journal of Clinical Psychopharmacology* 1995, 15 (1): 83–84.

Smith, D. M., and S. S. Levitte. Association of fluoxetine and return of sexual potency in three elderly men. *Journal of Clinical Psychiatry* 1993, 54 (8): 317–19.

Stein, D. J., et al. Serotonergic medications for sexual obsessions, sexual addictions, and paraphilias. *Journal of Clinical Psychiatry* 1992, 53: 267–71.

Su, T. P., et al. Fluoxetine in the treatment of patients with premenstrual syndrome. *Biological Psychiatry* 1993, 33: 159A.

Teicher, M. H., et al. Emergence of intense suicidal preoccupation during fluoxetine treatment. *American Journal of Psychiatry* 1990, 147 (2): 207–10.

Tiffon, L., et al. Augmentation strategies with tricyclic or fluoxetine treatment in seven partially responsive panic disorder patients. *Journal of Clinical Psychiatry* 1994, 55 (2): 66–69.

Tinsley, J. A., et al. Fluoxetine abuse. Case report. *Mayo Clinic Proceedings* 1994, 69: 166–68.

Tollefson, G. D., and S. L. Holman. Analysis of the Hamilton Depression Rating Scale factors from a double-blind, placebo-controlled trial of fluoxetine in geriatric major depression. *International Clinical Psychopharmacology* 1993, 8 (4): 253–59.

———. Adverse drug reactions/interactions in maintenance therapy. *Journal of Clinical Psychiatry* 1993, 54 (suppl): 48–58, discussion 59–60.

———. Does pharmacotherapy induce paradoxical worsening in some patients? *Depression* 1993, 1: 105–7.

Usher, R. W., et al. Efficacy and safety of morning versus evening fluoxetine administration. *Journal of Clinical Psychiatry* 1991, 52 (3): 134–36.

van Ameringen, M., et al. Fluoxetine efficacy in social phobia. *Journal of Clinical Psychiatry* 1993, 54 (1): 27–32.

Wirshing, W. C., et al. Fluoxetine, akathisia, and suicidality: is there a causal connection? (letter to the editor), *Archives of General Psychiatry* 1992, 49: 580–81.

Wood, S., et al. Treatment of Premenstrual syndrome with fluoxetine: a double-blind, placebo-controlled, cross over study. *Obstetrics and Gynecology*, 1992, 80: 339–44.

CHAPTER 15: NEW MEDICATIONS:
IMPORTANT ADVANCES

APA Task Force. Major depressive disorder in adults. *American Journal of Psychiatry* 1993, 150 (4, suppl): 2–22.

Ayd, F. J. Dyskinesias and serotonin reuptake inhibitors. *International Drug Therapy Newsletter* 1993, 28: 21–22.

Baldwin, D., et al. 5-HT reuptake inhibitors, tricyclic antidepressants and suicidal behavior. *International Clinical Psychopharmacology* 1991, 6 (3): 49–55, discussion 55–56.

Burke, M. J., et al. Pharmacoeconomic considerations when evaluating treatment options for major depressive disorder. *Journal of Clinical Psychiatry* 1994, 55 (9 suppl A): 42–52.

Clerc, G. E., et al. A double-blind comparison of venlafaxine and fluoxetine in patients hospitalized for major depression and melancholia. *International Clinical Psychopharmacology* 1994, 9: 139–43.

De Wilde, J., et al. A double-blind, comparative, multicentre study comparing paroxetine with fluoxetine in depressed patients. *Acta Psychiatrica Scandinavica* 1993, 87: 141–45.

Eison, A. S., et al. Nefazodone: preclinical pharmacology of a new antidepressant. *Psychopharmacology Bulletin* 1990, 26 (3): 311–15.

Fabre, L. F. Buspirone in the management of major depression: a placebo-controlled comparison. *Journal of Clinical Psychiatry* 1990, 51: 55–61.

Feighner, J. P. The role of venlafaxine in rational antidepressant therapy. *Journal of Clinical Psychiatry* 1994, 55 (9, suppl A): 62–68.

Ferris, R. M., and B. R. Cooper. Mechanism of antidepressant activity of bupropion. *Journal of Clinical Psychiatry Monograph* 1993, 11 (1): 2–14.

Fontaine, R. Novel serotonergic mechanisms and clinical experience with nefazodone. *Clinical Neuropharmacology* 1993, 16 (3): S45–50.

————. A double-blind comparison of nefazodone, imipramine, and placebo in major depression. *Journal of Clinical Psychiatry* 1994, 55 (6): 234–41.

Gelenberg, A. J. Buspirone: Seven year update. *Journal of Clinical Psychiatry* 1994, 55 (5): 222–29.

Geretsegger, C., et al. Paroxetine in the elderly depressed patient: randomized comparison with fluoxetine of efficacy, cognitive and behavioural effects. *International Clinical Psychopharmacology* 1994, 9: 25–29.

Gregor, K. J., et al. Selective serotonin reuptake inhibitor dose titration in the naturalistic setting. *Clinical Therapeutics* 1994, 16 (2): 306–15.

Jacobsen, F. M. Possible augmentation of antidepressant response by buspirone. *Journal of Clinical Psychiatry* 1991, 52 (5): 217–20.

————. Low-dose trazodone as a hypnotic in patients treated with MAOIs and other psychotropics: a pilot study. *Journal of Clinical Psychiatry* 1990, 51 (7): 298–302.

Jick, H., et al. Comparison of frequencies of suicidal tendencies among patients receiving fluoxetine, lofepramine, mianserin, or trazodone. *Pharmacotherapy* 1992, 12 (6): 451–54.

Joffe, R. T., and D. R. Schuller. An open study of buspirone augmentation of serotonin reuptake inhibitors in refractory depression. *Journal of Clinical Psychiatry* 1993, 54 (7): 269–271.

Jonas, J. M., and M. S. Cohon. A comparison of the safety and efficacy of alprazolam versus other agents in the treatment of anxiety, panic, and depression: a review of the literature. *Journal of Clinical Psychiatry* 1993, 54: 25–35.

Laghrissi-Thode, F., et al. Comparative effects of sertraline and nortriptyline on body sway in elderly depressed patients. Presented in part at the 34th Annual Meeting of the New Clinical Drug Evaluation Unit of the National Institute of Mental Health, Marco Island, FL, May 31, 1994. (New Investigator Awardee Poster Session).

Markovitz, P. J., et al. Buspirone augmentation of fluoxetine in obsessive compulsive disorder. *American Journal of Psychiatry* 1990, 147 (6): 798–800.

Maruno, C. A., and L. L. Hart. Buspirone in obsessive-compulsive disorder. *Annals of Pharmacotherapy* 1992, 26 (10): 1248–51.

Nierenberg, A. A., et al. Trazodone for antidepressant-associated insomnia. *American Journal of Psychiatry* 1994, 151 (7): 1069–72.

———. Possible trazodone potentiation of fluoxetine: a case series. *Journal of Clinical Psychiatry* 1992, 53 (3): 83–85.

Pinner, E., and C. L. Rich. Effects of Trazodone on aggressive behavior in seven patients with organic mental disorders. *American Journal of Psychiatry* 1988, 145 (10): 1295–96.

Rickels, K., at al. Nefazodone and imipramine in major depression: A placebo-controlled trial. *British Journal of Psychiatry* 1994, 164, 802–5.

———. Buspirone in major depression: a controlled study. *Journal of Clinical Psychiatry* 1991, 52 (1): 34–38.

Schneier, F. R., et al. Buspirone in social phobia. *Journal of Clinical Psychopharmacology* 1993, 13: 251–56.

Schone, W., and M. Ludwig. A double-blind study of paroxetine compared with fluoxetine in geriatric patients with major depression. *Journal of Clinical Psychopharmacology* 1993, 13 (6 suppl 2): 34S-39S.

Ware Catesby, J., and J. T. Pittard. Increased deep sleep after trazodone use: A double-blind placebo-controlled study in healthy young adults. *Journal of Clinical Psychiatry* 1990, 51 (9, suppl): 18–22.

Wender, P. H., and F. W. Reimherr. Bupropion treatment of attention-deficit hyperactivity disorder in adults. *American Journal of Psychiatry* 1990, 147 (8): 1018–20.

CHAPTER 16: A LOOK AHEAD

Altamura, A. C., et al. The evidence for 20 mg a day of fluoxetine as the optimal dose in the treatment of depression. *British Journal of Psychiatry,* 1988, 153 (3): 109–12.

Baxter, L. R., et al. Caudate glucose metabolic rate changes with both drug and behavior therapy for obsessive-compulsive disorder. *Archives of General Psychiatry* 1992, 49: 681–89.

Beasley, Jr., C. M., and J. H. Potvin. Fluoxetine: activating and sedating effects. *International Clinical Psychopharmacology* 1993, 8: 271–75.

Buie, J. 46 new drugs for mental illness could reach market within 3 to 6 years. *Psychiatric Times,* July 1994, page 44.

Cain, J. W. Poor response to fluoxetine: underlying depression, serotonergic overstimulation, or a "therapeutic window"? *Journal of Clinical Psychiatry* 1992, 53: 272–77.

Cohen, R. M., et al. Preliminary data on the metabolic brain pattern of patients with winter seasonal affective disorder. *Archives of General Psychiatry* 1992, 49: 545–52.

Feighner, J. P., et al. A comparison of nefazodone, imipramine, and placebo in patients with moderate to severe depression. *Psychopharmacology Bulletin* 1989, 25 (2): 219–21.

George, M. S., et al. SPECT and PET imaging in mood disorders. *Journal of Clinical Psychiatry* 1993, 54 (11, suppl): 6–13.

Hopwood, S. E., et al: The combination of fluoxetine and lithium in clinical practice. *International Clinical Psychopharmacology* 1993, 8: 325–27.

Joffe, R. T., and D. Bakish. Combined SSRI-Moclobemide treatment of psychiatric illness. *Journal of Clinical Psychiatry* 1994, 55 (1): 24–25.

Louie, A. K., et al. Use of low-dose fluoxetine in major depression and panic disorder. *Journal of Clinical Psychiatry* 1993, 54: 435–38.

Maes, M., et al. Leukocytosis, monocytosis and neutrophilia: hallmarks of severe depression. *Journal of Psychiatric Research* 1992, 26 (2): 125–34.

————. Higher alpha 1-antitrypsin, haptoglobin, ceruloplasmin and lower retinol binding protein plasma levels during depression: further evidence for the existence of an inflammatory response during that illness. *Journal of Affective Disorders* 1992, 24 (3): 183–92.

Mendels, J. The acute and long-term treatment of major depression. *International Clinical Psychopharmacology* 1992, 7 (2, suppl): 21–29.

Nair, N. P. V., et al. Biochemistry and pharmacology of reversible inhibitiors of MAO-A agents: focus on moclobemide. *Journal Psychiatric Neuroscience* 1993, 18 (5): 214–24.

Nelson, J. C. Combined treatment strategies in psychiatry. *Journal of Clinical Psychiatry* 1993, 54 (9 suppl): 42–49.

Nordstrom, P., and M. Asberg. Suicide risk and serotonin. *International Clinical Psychopharmacology* 1992, 6 (6): 12–21.

Preskorn, S. H. Antidepressant drug selection: criteria and options. *Journal of Clinical Psychiatry* 1994, 55 (9, suppl A): 6–22.

Rickels, K., et al: Nefazodone and imipramine in major depression: A placebo-controlled trial. *British Journal of Psychiatry* 1994, 164: 802–5.

Rogers, W. H., et al. Outcomes for adult outpatients with depression under prepaid or fee-for-service financing. *Archives of General Psychiatry* 1993, 50 (7): 517–25.

Schwartz, J. M., et al. Neuroimaging and cognitive-biobehavioral self-treatment for obsessive compulsive disorder: practical and philosophical considerations, In Hand, I., and W. K. Goodman (eds), *Obsessive Compulsive Disorders: New Research Results.* Springer Verlag, Berlin 1992, 15BN 3-540-55618-4: 83–101.

Skene, D. J., et al. Comparison of the effects of acute fluvoxamine and desipramine administration on melatonin and cortisol production in humans. *British Journal of Clinical Pharmacology* 1994, 37 (2): 181–86.

Sussman, N. The potential benefits of serotonin receptor-specific agents. *Journal of Clinical Psychiatry* 1994, 55 (2, suppl): 45–51.

EPILOGUE

Durham, R. C., et al. Cognitive therapy, analytic psychotherapy and anxiety management training for generalised anxiety disorder. *British Journal of Psychiatry* 1994, 165: 315–23.

Frank, E., et al. Efficacy of interpersonal psychotherapy as a maintenance treatment of recurrent depression. *Archives of General Psychiatry* 1991, 48: 1053–59.

Spiegel, D., et al. Effect of psychological treatment of survival of patients with metastatic breast cancer (see comments). Comments in *Lancet* 1989, 2 (8673): 1209–10; *Lancet* 1989, 2 (8668): 888–91.

APPENDIX I

Arroyo, H. A., et al. A syndrome of hyperhidrosis, hypothermia, and bradycardia possibly due to central monoaminergic dysfunction. *Neurology* 1990, 40 (3 pt 1): 556–57.

Barker, A., et al. Seasonal and weather factors in parasuicide. *British Journal of Psychiatry* 1994, 165: 375–80.

Fossey, E., and C. M. Shapiro. Seasonality in psychiatry—a review. *Canadian Journal of Psychiatry* 1992, 37 (5): 299–308.

Breuer Hans-Willi, M., et al. Social, Toxicological and meteorological data on suicide attempts. *European Archives of Psychiatry and Neurological Sciences* 1986, 235: 367–70.

Froom, P., et al. Heat stress and helicopter pilot errors. *Journal of Occupational Medicine* 1993, 35 (7): 720–24.

Hribersek, E., et al: Influence of the day of the week and the weather on people using a telephone support system. *British Journal of Psychiatry* 1987, 150: 189–92.

Lemmens, P. H., and R. A. Knibbe. Seasonal variation in survey and sales estimates of alcohol consumption. *Journal of Studies on Alcohol* 1993, 54 (2): 157–63.

Lester, D. The climate of urban areas in the United States and their rates of personal violence (suicide and homicide). *Death Studies* 1991, 15: 611–16.

Libert, J. P., et al. Effect of continuous heat exposure on sleep stages in humans. *Sleep* 1988, 11 (2): 195–209.

Linkowski, P., et al. Effect of some climatic factors on violent and non-violent suicides in Belgium. *Journal of Affective Disorders* 1992, 25: 161–66.

Lowenfels, A. B., and P. S. Wynn. One less for the road. International trends in alcohol consumption and vehicular fatalities. *Annals of Epidemiology* 1992, 2 (3): 339–41.

Norden, M. J., and D. Avery, Heat and violence correlate independent of season. (Abstract), New Research APA, Annual meeting, San Francisco, 1993.

Ross, D. R., et al. The psychiatric uses of cold wet sheet packs. *American Journal of Psychiatry* 1988, 145 (2): 242–45.

Schnell, D., et al. A time series analysis of gonorrhea surveillance data. *Statistics in Medicine* 1989, 8 (3): 343–52.

Souetre, E., et al. Seasonality of suicides: environmental, sociological and biological covariations. *Journal of Affective Disorders* 1987, 13: 215–25.

Whitton, J. L., et al. Weather and infradian rhythms in self-reports of health, sleep and mood measures. *Journal of Psychosomatic Research* 1982, 26 (2): 231–35.

APPENDIX II

Barbee, J. G. Memory, benzodiazepines, and anxiety: integration of theoretical and clinical perspectives. *Journal of Clinical Psychiatry* 1993, 54: 86–97.

Burke, M. J., et al. Pharmacoeconomic considerations when evaluating treatment options for major depressive disorder. *Journal of Clinical Psychiatry* 1994, 55 (9, suppl A): 42–52.

Peet, M. Induction of mania with selective serotonin re-uptake inhibitors and tricyclic antidepressants. *British Journal of Psychiatry* 1994, 164: 549–50.

Pereira, J., and J. Rebello. Production problems at genetic drug firm lead to serious claims. *The Wall Street Journal* 1995, Thursday, February 2, 1995, page A1.

Richardson, J. S., et al. Verbal learning by major depressive disorder patients during treatment with fluoxetine or amitriptyline. *International Clinical Psychopharmacology* 1994, 9: 35–40.

Robinson, et al. Clinical effects of the 5-T1A partial agonists in depression: a composite analysis of buspirone in the treatment of depression. *Journal of Clinical Psychopharmacology* 1990, 10 (3 Suppl): 67S–76S.

Salzman, C. Benzodiazepine treatment of panic and agoraphobic symptoms: use, dependence, toxicity, abuse. *Journal of Psychiatric Research* 1993, 27 (1): 97–110.

Sellers, E. M., et al. Alprazolam and benzodiazepine dependence. *Journal of Clinical Psychiatry* 1993, 54 (10, suppl): 64–75.

Timbal, J., et al. Circadian variations in the sweating mechanism. *Journal of Applied Physiology* 1975, 39 (2): 226–30.

INDEX